Spain, Britain, and the
American Revolution
in Florida, 1763–1783

ALSO BY JAMES W. RAAB

*Confederate General Lloyd Tilghman:
A Biography* (McFarland, 2006)

*J. Patton Anderson, Confederate General:
A Biography* (McFarland, 2004)

Spain, Britain, and the American Revolution in Florida, 1763–1783

James W. Raab

McFarland & Company, Inc., Publishers
Jefferson, North Carolina, and London

LIBRARY OF CONGRESS CATALOGUING-IN-PUBLICATION DATA

Raab, James W.
  Spain, Britain and the American Revolution in Florida, 1763–1783 / James W. Raab.
    p.   cm.
  Includes bibliographical references and index.

  ISBN-13: 978-0-7864-3213-4
  softcover : 50# alkaline paper ∞

  1. Florida — History — English colony, 1763–1784.   2. Florida — History — Revolution, 1775–1783.   3. Florida — History — Revolution, 1775–1783 — Campaigns.   4. United States — History — Revolution, 1775–1783 — Campaigns.   5. Spain — Colonies — America.   6. Great Britain — Colonies — America.   7. Florida — Boundaries — Georgia.   8. Georgia — Boundaries — Florida.   I. Title.
  F314.R33   2008
  975.9'02 — dc22   2007034067

British Library cataloguing data are available

©2008 James W. Raab. All rights reserved

No part of this book may be reproduced or transmitted in any form or by any means, electronic or mechanical, including photocopying or recording, or by any information storage and retrieval system, without permission in writing from the publisher.

On the cover: Fort Matanzas today, part of the U.S. National Park system (courtesy Ken Barrett Jr.); background ©2008 clipart.com; borders Treaty of Paris (Library of Congress)

Manufactured in the United States of America

McFarland & Company, Inc., Publishers
  Box 611, Jefferson, North Carolina 28640
  www.mcfarlandpub.com

Table of Contents

Preface	1

PART I: SPANISH AND BRITISH PREREVOLUTIONARY PERIOD

Prologue: The "Garden of Eden"	3
1. Spanish Florida to 1763, the Treaty of Paris 1763, and the Changing of the Guard	7
2. The Floridas: East Florida Colony and West Florida Colony	21
3. Interim Governors and the King's Road	50
4. The Georgia-Florida Border Dispute, and the Beginning of the American Revolution	66
5. The Southern District Brigade and Headquarters, St. Augustine	82

PART II: FLORIDA IN THE AMERICAN REVOLUTION, 1776–1783

Prologue: Accept or Oppose the Idea of Independence?	93
6. The Fighting Begins in the South with the Invasion of East Florida	97
7. Battles for Georgia and South Carolina	113
8. Spain Seizes West Florida	129

9.	Boom Towns	147
10.	The Defining Peace Negotiation	162
11.	The Spaniards Return	173

Appendix   183
Notes   185
Bibliography   191
Index   193

Preface

This book is devoted to recording the events of the new Floridas as they were established by the Treaty of Paris in 1763 between Spain and England. Under the terms of the treaty, Spain relinquished its 200-year-old empire in Florida to regain its control of Havana and Cuba, proving the pen is mightier than the sword. Just like that, England had two new colonies in America, so named East Florida colony, number 14, and West Florida colony, number 15. As the countdown to the American Revolution unfolded, the two new British colonies were populated as fast as possible, but with loyalists steadfast to the Crown. Therefore the settlements in the two Floridas were dominated not by American patriots but by British loyalists.

A brief summary of Spanish history in America is provided as a reference point leading up to the 20 years' occupation by the Tories in the new Floridas. As the move to separation from England progressed, East Florida became a rallying point for loyalist forces, with plots, conspiracies, and open hostilities that would result in the invasion of Georgia and South Carolina, and the conquest of Savannah and Charleston. St. Augustine became the British headquarters in the South. From here the soldiers of the Crown fought in dozens of encounters with the patriots. And then, again by the pen, the victors went from being citizens of the Crown to refugees without a country. It's almost an unbelievable story, all the way to the end when Spain regains Florida.

There is of course no photographic record of the American Revolution. The events of the Revolutionary era have been totally shaped and conditioned by the work of a mixed group of writers and artists. The question of historical accuracy must always enter into the discussion. The immense image of *Washington Crossing the Delaware*, by Emanuel Leutze, was truly a work of his imagination, yet is still an image indelibly stamped on our pictorial consciousness of the Revolution.[1]

Regarding the historical information, my approach was to read as much on the American Revolution by as many authors as I could find, then combine the material with sources on Florida, producing an accurate and balanced portrait of the 20-year struggle. Extensive use of several reference volumes must be acknowledged. These include *History of East Florida: East Florida as a British Province, 1763–1784,* by Charles L. Mowat, and *Loyalists in East Florida, 1774–1785,* in two volumes, by Wilbur Henry Siebert. In addition, Mark M. Boatner III's *Encyclopedia of the American Revolution* was invaluable in providing background material of personalities and events. There is a storehouse of books on St. Augustine's history published by the Historic St. Augustine Preservation Board in its *El Escribano,* written by local scholars. I leaned heavily on some of their works and less heavily on others, but all sources were invaluable.

I am indebted to Beth Mansbridge, of Mansbridge Editing and Transcription, who was generous with her time and expertise in editing the manuscript; and to Jean Light Willis, artist, who provided the fine maps for the book.

PART I

Spanish and British Prerevolutionary Period

Prologue: The "Garden of Eden"

The Associated Press recently announced that a 500-year-old printed map of the New World was sold for a record one million dollars. German cartographer Martin Waldseemüller used accounts from explorers and adventurers such as Christopher Columbus and Amerigo Vespucci to draw his map of the New World in 1507. Vespucci claimed the land mass discovered by Columbus in 1492 was a new continent, not part of Asia as first believed. Therefore Waldseemüller labeled the new land "America" in honor of Amerigo Vespucci. The Waldseemüller Gores, as they are now referred to, are sometimes called America's birth certificate.[1]

After the discovery of the New World in 1492, a struggle ensued among the maritime powers of Europe over the rights to trade and to acquire territory there. The 17th-century combatants would be Spain, France, and England. These nations had been facing land shortages for agriculture, were overpopulated, and had shrinking treasuries. Sailing to, exploring, and trading on the North American continent would span the next 150 years.

The gold and silver of Mexico and Peru had enriched Spain for years, giving it the financial power to support fleets and armies that kept most of the world in fear and subjection. This all shifted when English seamen defeated the Spanish Armada in 1588, establishing England's position not only as a naval power but as a contender for part of the New World, which Spain had previously controlled.[2] England's prosperity would depend upon access to America, new sources of raw materials, and new markets with opportunities to curtail the power of Spain, the country which most Englishmen believed was the greatest threat to the liberties of free men.

Aware of the potentialities of American resources, shrewd merchants in London, Plymouth, and Bristol began investing very early in dubious voyages all in the name of profit. Even Queen Elizabeth herself took a cut from every buccaneer and privateer who brought back riches. Inspired by tales from the explorer and his seamen, pamphleteers of the day vastly sharpened the delusion of forthcoming wealth. And the notion that earthly paradise — one similar to the site of the scriptural Eden — might be found in some part of the New World heightened the imagination.

Englishmen concerned about the welfare of their economy began seeking sources of exotic commodities — colonies where Englishmen might produce wealth for themselves and the Crown. All through the 17th and 18th centuries, the official favor of the English government was lavished on southern colonies of the plantation type rather than commercial colonies of New England.[3] English businessmen and their investors were thinking of colonies as sources of trade and profit rather than as mines of gold and silver bullion. The bounty of nature would provide the commodities to make England prosperous; the unpeopled land across the seas would also furnish a place for the surplus population plaguing Europe, creating a market for English goods. This hope led in years to come to the settlement of the Carolinas and Georgia. Promoters earnestly tried to make Georgia the combination of Eden and Utopia that they had envisioned for settling poor persons from London, and opened the colony to oppressed folk not only from England but the Continent as well.[4]

The ink on the Treaty of Paris was hardly dry, in 1763, when early promotional literature again was filled with extravagant descriptions of nature's abundance in this new land south of Georgia. It was almost too good to be true, another chance to get in on the ground floor of two new British colonies. An additional new enchantment was added to this virgin land: the Floridas could produce many rare drugs, and gums, oils, wine, cedar wood, turpentine, rice, and indigo. The production of indigo, which had come into English trade, occupied a place of first importance in the imperial economy. Furthermore, all these products could be raised with unskilled African slaves, themselves an article of profitable commerce to the Royal African Company.[5] Florida, long neglected by the Spaniards, was truly the "Garden of Eden" that everyone had been seeking; they hoped not to find any lurking serpents.

1

Spanish Florida to 1763, the Treaty of Paris 1763, and the Changing of the Guard

By the 1500s the massive Spanish empire expanded beyond its European boundaries to include Africa, the Philippines, most of South America, the Caribbean Sea, and parts of North America. Naturally the roster of early explorers and adventurers in the early centuries is dotted with failure and disappointment, and not all of those who played a part in founding our nation were among the Founding Fathers. The Spanish were the leaders in world exploration; their goals were gold, silver, jewels, and wealth, and at any price. We all have heard of Juan Ponce de León who on April 2, 1513, came ashore in America in the vicinity of present-day St. Augustine. He proclaimed the sovereignty of his new-found land for the Spanish Crown, naming it Florida. Although authorized to colonize the land, he never did so; instead he said he had found the Fountain of Youth, which was better than gold or silver.

For the next 50 years other explorers set out to investigate the North American continent. King Charles IX of France approved French explorer Rene de Laudonniere's plan to colonize Florida. With a handful of settlers Laudonniere established a small settlement on St. Johns Bluff, a 70-foot-high point of land at the entrance of the St. Johns River from the Atlantic Ocean. When Spanish King Philip II was informed of French Protestants within his claimed Catholic territory, he assigned Captain Don Pedro Menéndez de Avilés, a callous military officer, to expel the French interlopers from Spanish soil, conquer local Indian tribes, and establish a colony under the Spanish flag.

A flotilla of ships with settlers, soldiers, and Negro slaves set sail from Spain, arriving off the coast of Florida on August 28, 1565. The captain named his colony Saint Augustine in commemoration of having sighted the coast of Florida on the feast day of Saint Augustine, an early Catholic Church father and author. On September 6, 1565, as Indians stood and watched, Pedro Menéndez de Avilés, who was announced by trumpets and cannon firing, stepped from his launch. A Catholic chaplain walked forward to greet him, carrying a cross and intoning the Te Deum laudamus, a hymn of praise. Avilés and company knelt, kissed the cross, then heard Mass in honor of the Nativity of Our Lady. He took possession of Florida in the name of His Most Catholic Majesty King Philip II of Spain, and laid the foundation for the town of St. Augustine, the first permanent European settlement in North America, 43 years before the first English settlement at Jamestown, Virginia. Captain Menéndez gathered 50 Spanish settlers and formed a militia to defend the newly founded settlement; this militia became the cornerstone for the future Florida National Guard.

The Spanish Crown would become Florida's largest slaveholder, with Negroes coming from other areas of the huge Spanish empire. They were employed cutting and gathering wood, stevedoring, and constructing of defense works. At first the slaves lived dispersed among the white population; later on they lived in huts, depending on where they were needed.[1]

Leaving his new outpost of St. Augustine, Menéndez sailed south to Cape Canaveral and then on to Havana, Cuba. The next spring, Captain Menéndez de Avilés returned to the east coast of Florida with additional settlers and soldiers. He traveled north of St. Augustine and founded a settlement at Santa Elena, in the vicinity of present-day Beaufort, Parris Island, South Carolina. Leaving settlers and soldiers at this fine harbor outpost, he sailed south, establishing an outpost at San Mateo, Cumberland Island, Georgia, then revisited St. Augustine. This second trip by Menéndez laid claim to all land south of present-day Beaufort, the land mass of present-day Georgia, to St. Augustine. It soon became a major point of contention between England and Spain as to who owned the territory. Jesuit missionaries began their work of teaching God's word and the conversion of Indians. At the court in Spain the king rewarded Menéndez with income, land, and honors, making him governor of Cuba and Florida. In addition, the king ordered him to design and command an armada for the defense of the Indies. Menéndez proceeded to build 12 great ships named for the 12 Apostles.[2]

Nevertheless, the conquests of Menéndez in his boundless Florida began to deteriorate over the next decade as assaults by the French and the local Indians took their toll. At Santa Elena, Parris Island, Spanish soldiers, militia, and colonists were massacred by the Indians, forcing the Jesuits to leave in 1571. With the farms and fort destroyed, the remainder found their way to St. Augustine, over 100 miles south of them. And the same disaster had happened here, as they found houses torn down, and the women and children sheltered in the wooden fort. The few able-bodied militia had been unable to protect their homes from Indian assaults. As a result, the Council of the Indies had begun taking steps to convert the Menéndez family's lord proprietorship to a regular Crown colony. Captain Menéndez never lived to see the results of these endeavors, for he died in 1574. His nephew Pedro Menéndez Marquez was named governor, and selected St. Augustine for his headquarters and seat of government, reducing the scope of conquest by abandoning the more distant claims of his uncle.[3]

At this time Spanish Franciscan missions began to appear, and the Gospel and the catechism of Christianity were taught to Indians, traders, trappers, and Negroes. Eventually, 25 mission churches stood in a line across the northern peninsula of Florida, from St. Augustine's Nombre de Dios to Mission San Luis at present-day Tallahassee. The Florida missionaries lived among the principal chiefdoms of the Timucua and Apalache nations, also teaching Europeans farming, cattle and hog raising, weaving, and reading and writing. The mission period extended from 1577 to 1706.[4]

The year 1586 saw the village of St. Augustine attacked by pirates. This time it was the sea dog himself, Sir Francis Drake. Traveling in 23 armed vessels, the 2,000 buccaneers made port in the vicinity of St. Augustine. One fleeing Spaniard fired at and killed one of Drake's cutthroats; in revenge for this act Drake burnt the entire village, destroying dwellings, and gardens, and seizing the meager treasury. After the dastardly deed they retired to their vessels with the loot, and set sail. This, and similar attacks by the Indians, aroused the Spanish authorities to provide funds for a wooden wall to be erected around the village, copying the centuries-old walled cities found in Europe.

For the next 100 years the town sustained itself in spite of scarcity of food, destructive fires, hurricanes, and Indian attacks, by the faith of its citizens, nine wooden forts built within this period, and of course the Spanish hierarchy. One day in 1668 the soldier at the Matanzas Inlet watchtower, south of town, signaled unknown ships approaching from the south. Fluttering in the breeze were black and white flags bearing the skull and bones, immediately showing the guard that they were pirates looking for St. Augustine.

Captained by Robert Searle, alias John Davis, these were Jamaicans who had just absconded with a Spanish frigate off Havana and were fleeing the scene of their crime. Within a day, 100 bandits landed at the St. Augustine wharf below the Spanish plaza. Quickly they seized the guardhouse, the counting house, and the royal warehouse containing sail canvas, candles, and halyard. They stripped the Franciscan convent, at the Catholic church they seized the gold chalices, and they then searched dwellings for utensils and other valuables. "There were only 120 Spanish soldiers present for defense, most of them fleeing the sword of the pirates, hiding outside the village. The cowards killed 60 persons in the streets, and carried off hostages."[5] Davis offered to free the hostages in exchange for fresh water, meats, and wood.

While the ransom was being gathered, the pirates charted the sandbars and inlets, and recorded landmarks for channel navigation. This indicated their intentions of returning to St. Augustine village with a larger force of plunderers to capture and hold hostage the complete area as a base of operations for raiding Spanish galleons off the coast of Florida as they traveled the Gulf Stream. By seizing the walled city which was located near the exit of the Bahamas Channel, Davis's forces would endanger the vital Spanish intercontinental lane. The fact that the village had been spared the torch lent credence to the idea that the pirates would return later. "Captain Davis released the wives and daughters of principal citizens, but refused to set free the Indians, free black or mestizo [mixed European and Indian ancestry] residents, saying that his license from the governor of Jamaica permitted him to sell as a slave anyone who was not a full-blooded Spaniard."[6]

When free of the interlopers, officials of the royal treasury sent a full report to Havana and Mexico City, with a recommendation that a large stone fortress for defense of the town should be constructed. In the interval friendly Indians from the north captured several Englishmen and brought them to St. Augustine as prisoners. These prisoners revealed that three vessels had carried English colonists to the old Spanish port of Santa Elena, and that a permanent English settlement was being established at Albemarle Point on the west bank of the Ashley River, becoming Charles Town (later Charleston), South Carolina, in 1670. This heralded the emergence of Anglo-Spanish rivalry over who owned the future Carolina and Georgia lands. Now, more than ever, the Spanish had to construct a fortress at St. Augustine.

Queen Mariana of Spain decreed that a permanent fortification should be constructed; Don Ignacio Daza, a military engineer, was sent from Havana, Cuba.[7] The plans proceeded methodically and the new castillo was designed according to the most advanced principles of military science. However, manpower to construct the fort was in short supply. The Spaniards went forth, drafting and capturing Indians from eastern Florida — most serving unwillingly. To fill the workers' ranks, convicts in Mexico found themselves sentenced to six years' labor on the fortification at St. Augustine.

The Castillo de San Marcos at St. Augustine. This Spanish fort was renamed Fort Saint Marks by the British. In the distance is the Atlantic Ocean, the breaking waves indicating the shallow and tricky entrance into the St. Augustine Inlet. To the right is Anastasia Island, location of the St. Augustine Lighthouse. Twenty miles south is Fort Matanzas at Matanzas Inlet. Both forts are part of the U.S. National Park system and may be visited. (Reproduced by permission from the St. Augustine Historical Society.)

At times there were 30 stonecutters employed in quarrying coquina rock from ten quarries on Anastasia Island across the river from the site. Coquina consists of tiny mollusk shells that are easily cemented together by their own lime. It took eight yokes of oxen to haul the cut coquina to the water's edge, where it was transported across the bay to the bulwark. The walls of the new garrison were three foot thick of coquina rock, 21 feet high, with two large towers, mounting 26 cannon. Out from the fort went strong earthworks and palm log palisades. With a bastion at each corner, and a deep fresh-water well inside, the massive coquina walls were well suited to absorb and repel the shock of the enemies' cannon balls. The castillo commanded the northern approach by land, the harbor, and St. Augustine itself.[8] Construction began in 1672. It took 23 years for completion, and was named the Castillo de San Marcos. This remarkable citadel still guards St. Augustine today.

In addition to the grand coquina fort anchoring St. Augustine, a second shelter was established for destitute refugees. The Spanish Crown decreed that if Negro and Indian slaves who were fleeing the English colonies — mainly South Carolina and Georgia — would embrace Roman Catholicism, they would be granted their freedom in the name of the king. This freedom sanctuary was named Fort Mose. Two miles north of the City Gate, it was located in the middle of a plantation where small farms had been established. A Franciscan priest was present to teach the faith.[9] This is considered the first free black town in the United States, although free and enslaved Negroes had already been living in St. Augustine for 125 years before the establishment of the sanctuary policy.[10]

In 1702 the governor of South Carolina, James Moore, determined to retaliate against the Spaniards for their conduct of freeing Negro and Indian slaves, invaded Spanish Florida with a large force of Carolinians and Indians. He destroyed as many Catholic missions as he could find, and then proceeded to sack St. Augustine but failed to reduce the fort, where everyone had taken shelter. His expedition was unsuccessful, as Fort Mose would be reestablished.

Next in the sequence of hostilities was the War of Jenkins's Ear, 1739–42, which spilled over into Spanish Florida and the colonies. British violations of trade agreements with the Spanish in the Caribbean led to seizure of a British ship and rough handling of her seamen by the Spanish. "One Robert Jenkins claimed the Spanish had cut off his ear in 1731 [eight-years earlier!], and he publicly displayed the missing part to prove it."[11]

England's Admiral Edward Vernon advocated armed aggression against Spain by attacking Spanish possessions in the Caribbean. In North America, General James Oglethorpe of the Georgia colony invaded Florida in 1740, establishing a camp on the St. Johns River's south shore. He captured two Spanish outposts, Fort San Diego and Fort Mose, and then besieged St. Augustine for more than a month. His stratagem was unsuccessful, as the town's citizens fled to the shelter of their grand fort. When they refused to surrender, the English attackers faced short food rations and were obliged to return to Savannah. Oglethorpe did get satisfaction in 1742 when his forces crushed a Spanish landing force in the Battle of Bloody Swamp at St. Simons Island, but he failed in another attack on St. Augustine in 1743.[12]

Fort Matanzas. Some 20 miles south of St. Augustine lies Matanzas Inlet. Too frequently, enemies used this "back door" to attack the town. In 1742 the Spanish finally plugged the route by building Fort Matanzas, today a part of the U.S. National Park system. (Photograph by Ken Barrett, Jr.)

The present line of defense was east and north of the walled city; the western flank was the natural barrier of the St. Johns River, and the fort at Picolata. From the very beginning the Spaniards discovered that the river running south of the town served several purposes. It provided them with an alternate avenue to exit to the Atlantic Ocean, and it was an inland waterway leading south to Mosquito Inlet, 60 miles south of the town. If the Matanzas Inlet was left unguarded, any enemy could sneak into the inlet, sail up the river, and attack the town, as the evil pirates had done. In 1569 the Spanish erected a wooden watchtower at the inlet.

"The watchers looked out for ships approaching especially from the south. They could not prevent entry through the inlet because the tower was manned by a minimum number of soldiers with no cannon. They warned the authorities by using their water carriage, two canoes for transportation and communications." In addition, a second watchtower was erected on Anastasia Island; in this instance the watcher signaled the fort by colors.[13]

The naming of this river and inlet occurred back when Captain Menéndez de Avilés was founding the village around 1566. As the French colony on St. Johns Bluff starved, French Huguenot Jean Ribault, attempting to save the colony with reinforcements, was blown off course by storms and shipwrecked south of St. Augustine at the inlet. Answering the opportunity, Menéndez lured the French to surrender by promising them freedom. As they came ashore, Menéndez put them in small groups and methodically murdered the soldiers and sailors in the sand dunes, and so named the inlet and river "Matanzas," which in Spanish means "slaughters." Menéndez finished off the French ambitions in the south at Cape Canaveral, killing the enemy, including Jean Ribault. Of course the French would have done the same to the Spanish.

The signal towers seemed adequate for the next 170 years. The War of Jenkins's Ear erupted in 1739, and General James Oglethorpe's siege of St. Augustine in 1740 convinced the Spanish garrison that Matanzas Inlet should be fortified. Placed on a small island close to the entrance of the inlet, the fort was constructed of masonry with sides 50 feet long, parapets made of wood filled with earth, three embrasures facing the inlet capable of mounting nine cannon, with a possible capacity of 50 men if necessary. Thereafter, Fort Matanzas was never challenged, by land or sea, until the American Revolution.[14]

The Treaty of Paris 1763, and the Changing of the Guard

The French and Indian War between the English and French colonists in North America was the last of the colonial wars, also called the Seven Years' War (1756–63).[15] "By the year 1758, England had sent troops and ships to North America in readiness to launch her great offensive against France for control of the New World. In three successful offensives, English commanders in the northern colonies and Canada wrested control of the continent from France, eliminating the threat of French expansion eastward into the Appalachian mountains, as border troops destroyed French forts, gradually reducing the French and Indian threat.

"This murderous conflict between French and English colonists and their Indians ended in an outstanding victory for the British and American colonists, but at the expense of great loss to frontier settlers. It also placed the British government deeply in debt, leading to King George III's efforts to tax the 13 colonies, which helped bring on the Revolution."[16]

Fearing a British victory, Spain had entered the war belatedly in order to protect her New World possessions. Britain declared war on Spain in 1762, first taking the French base of Martinique, and then capturing Spain's Havana, Cuba, thereby gaining control of the major islands of the West Indies. In the best interest of all countries, a treaty was proposed.

In 1763, the Treaty of Paris ended the French and Indian War. Signed by England, France and Spain, the treaty formed four new royal British colonies: Quebec, Grenada, West Florida, and East Florida. In general, its terms eliminated France and Spain from America, leaving only Britain and its colonies. In summary the treaty proclaimed: France ceded to Britain all claims to Canada, Acadia (Nova Scotia), Cape Breton, and the islands in the St. Lawrence River, while retaining fishing rights off Newfoundland. France also gave Britain her territories east of the Mississippi River, except the Isle of Orleans. France ceded to Spain the Isle of Orleans, and all her territory west of the Mississippi. This was a massive land deal in the New World that benefited the English and the Americans.

Furthermore (and almost unbelievably), Spain gave all of her Florida land that she had held for 200 years, in return for and exchange for Havana. A year earlier the British had captured Havana, Spain's crown jewel seaport for Spanish galleons en route to and from Mexico and elsewhere in the Caribbean Sea. Spain bargained away her huge stake in the New World in order to regain Havana.

The Florida territory Britain acquired was more land than could conveniently be administered as a single unit under British standards. Therefore, London decided that this new territory in the British Empire should be divided into two additional American colonies, East Florida and West Florida, which became the 14th and 15th Continental British colonies south of Canada.[17]

East Florida colony comprised most of what is Florida today, except for the Panhandle. East Florida was separated from West Florida by the Apalachicola River, with a northern boundary extending to the Altamaha River, south of Savannah, Georgia.[18] The capital of East Florida colony would be St. Augustine.

The West Florida colony, much larger than East Florida, included parts of Alabama, Mississippi, and Louisiana, bordered on the Gulf of Mexico and Lake Pontchartrain to the south; its western boundary, the Mississippi River; and the northern boundary, 31° latitude. The northern boundary was adjusted to 32° in 1764, to please speculators who had an eye for the lush land around Natchez, Mississippi. The capital of the colony would be Pensacola, Florida.[19]

King George III's British empire could benefit enormously from the two new colonies. "The Crown offered land free but for registration and surveying expenses. Major entrepreneurs who promised to import agricultural laborers could apply for large tracts, tens of thousands of acres. Veterans and immigrants with no other qualification than a family could get smaller acreages. News of these opportunities, together with apocryphal testimony to the healthiness of the climate and optimistic forecasts of the commercial prospects in both Floridas, appeared in newspapers on both sides of the Atlantic. In London, an East Florida Society formed to lobby to secure major land grants for its members."[20]

The news of the change of flags after 200 years had quickly come across the Atlantic from Spain after the signing of the Treaty of Paris. St. Augustine's 3,500 Spanish residents, although permitted under the treaty to remain in East Florida and retain title to their lands and homes, and to practice their Roman Catholic religion, instead decided to exit the new colony and emigrate to Cuba or Mexico before the stipulated 18-month grace period of evacuation expired.

Spanish Governor Melchor Feliu, concerned that Catholic Church properties in St. Augustine were in danger of being confiscated when British authorities arrived in East Florida, met with Juan Eligio de la Puente, the province's royal engineer, who carefully prepared a map of the town's 300 lots and structures.[21]

De la Puente then began a systematic disposal of government, church, and personal real estate. "In an effort to keep the Church property in St. Augustine from being seized by the British, he conveyed it to a John Gordon."[22] John Gordon, an English Catholic from South Carolina, prospered in the mercantile trade, and for the past decade had been trading in St. Augustine despite terms of a Spanish-British trade agreement which banned trading between the two countries. Being of the Catholic faith, Gordon was privy to the fact that much profit was to be made with the coming of the British to St. Augustine and the East Florida colony.

"Gordon proceeded to pay $1,000 for the Spanish bishop's house; $1,500 for the Franciscan convent; $300 for the new unfinished parish church and its site."[23] Gordon's vision was that as the British migrants arrived in St. Augustine, property values would increase in price, and being a good capitalist, he would be rewarded handsomely for his ingenuity.

Gordon was not the only British merchant in town doing business with the Spanish. Jesse Fish, a native of New York and also a British citizen, had resided in St. Augustine since 1735 in the employ of W.W. Walton and Company, which had gained lucrative contracts with the Spanish government to supply it with provisions for its garrison. Over the years, Spain was tardy in maintaining supplies for its residents. Thus, men like Gordon and Fish bridged the gap with their contacts with British colonies. As one might expect, Fish, Gordon, and de la Puente were friends. When St. Augustine was threatened by famine during the French and Indian War, de la Puente and Fish went to Georgia with a company of mounted Spanish dragoons to meet with Gordon, who made arrangements for shipments of provisions and other goods desperately needed in St. Augustine.[24]

Other than church and government buildings, there were 300 dwellings in St. Augustine. De la Puente began planning the sales of properties before the deadline for the departure of Spanish residents; if he had not done so, the titles to their dwellings would have reverted to the British government on their arrival in town.[25] De la Puente had the

Spanish owners of unsold properties give deeds of transfer to him; de la Puente in turn deeded them to Jesse Fish, who took over the deed at a nominal price, thus becoming titular proprietor of 185 unsold houses and even a larger number of vacant lots in St. Augustine.[26]

Before leaving St. Augustine on August 1, 1764, de la Puente had made arrangements with Luciano de Herrera, a St. Augustine native who intended to remain in St. Augustine under British rule, to collect money from Mr. Fish as he sold the properties, and transfer the funds to Havana in gold, silver, or letters of exchange.[27]

It was a certainty that Jesse Fish and John Gordon would team up to purchase the larger tracts of land in the East Florida countryside. Fish remarked, "I had long known that many of the Spanish inhabitants had good and indisputable titles to large tracts of land in this province. I advised my friend Mr. Gordon, then in Charlestown, South Carolina, of the favorable opportunity to make purchases. He immediately traveled here to purchase sundry valuable tracts of land." Fish and Gordon purchased millions of acres of land from the Spanish, on which the only human inhabitants in recent years had been hunting parties of Creek Indians. Method of payment for these land purchases with John Gordon were in exchange for cash, merchandise, and Negroes.[28]

On the other hand, Jesse Fish did not have the wealth that Gordon had, and pretty well established a paper empire of bills of sale for houses and lots of ground in St. Augustine, with the assumption that once the town filled up with British prospects who would purchase houses, he would be able to repay his obligations from the increase in property and lot sales. For that day and age, it was a bold entrepreneurial stroke rivaled by few others.

On schedule and beginning in August 1763, Spanish transports sailed from St. Augustine nearly every day with human cargo of Spanish residents and their possessions. By January 1764, the last Spanish ship departed; aboard were the governor, his advisors, the parish priest, and the last of Spanish residents and free Negroes. Not everybody left; Gordon and Fish were on duty, Francis Xavier Sanchez and Manuel Solona would remain, as well as St. Augustine merchant Luciano de Herrera.[29] Outside the walled city it was a different story. Not bound by any old or new paper treaty were dozens of Amerindians, runaway slaves, frontiersmen, traders, and "Crackers" (impoverished whites). All of these denizens professed no allegiance to any form of government, Spanish or English.

For several weeks the town was quiet, awaiting the arrival of the English. First to come on the scene was Major Francis Ogilvie, 9th Regiment, with his troops fresh from their mighty victory over the Spanish at Havana. The new assignment was a comedown for the victors, as they viewed essentially an old 18th-century European walled town. Fires, rot, termites, destructive sieges by the French and English, and the torrid weather, had destroyed most traces of 16th- and 17th-century St. Augustine. Rectangular in shape, the town boasted its central plaza with narrow streets, and little else except that grand old Castillo de San Marcos, attacked many times but never conquered.

Repeated pirate, English, and Indian attacks had aroused the Spanish government early in the 18th century to provide funds for an earthen wall to be erected beyond the fort, according to standards of the times. "By 1734 an earthen wall, planted with yuccas (Spanish Bayonets) and reinforced with a wooden palisade and ten masonry or earthen redoubts guarded the town on three sides, and the Matanzas Bay secured the fourth. Three parallel defense lines covered the exposed northern land approach. The Cubo line, the town's northern boundary, ran from the Castillo de San Marcos fort to the San Sebastian River. The principal town gate, at the site of the present-day City Gate, permitted access through the Cubo line. Less than one-half mile farther north lay the hornwort (water), or barrier line, and just over a mile beyond stood the Fort Mosa line. Constructed primarily of earth and wood, and containing moats, drawbridges, and redoubts defended by artillery, these elaborate defenses, in conjunction with the Castillo de San Marcos, had not allowed an enemy to set foot in the town since the 1702 English siege."[30] For the present, these defensive positions lessened in value since there was no longer a need for defense from British colonies to the north. Minimum maintenance was so ordered.

As more British troops arrived, a major misfortune was in store for Gordon and Fish; the first incoming inhabitants were British soldiers, not British colonists. Because there was not enough space in the fort to billet the British garrison, the overflow of the regiment would have to be quartered in empty, for sale, Spanish houses. It was February, and these gruff fighters, upon debarking, proceeded to demolish many of Jesse Fish's houses for firewood to warm themselves and for cooking. In addition, troop quartering practice, which required remaining residents to quarter British officers, was unpopular. Fish's for sale inventory evaporated. But not all was lost as incoming British officials of the Crown were exasperated to discover these two men held title to almost all the land of the East Florida colony, land the officials had envisioned for plantation development.

The government officials refused to recognize the legitimacy of Fish's and Gordon's titles until His Majesty King George III approved of such transactions. This jurisprudence was practiced throughout both colonies for the next 20 years. "Claims to private possession of huge tracts on the basis of purchase from departing Spanish owners were given short shrift by the British government on the grounds that such purchases, though permitted by peace treaty, were invalid, since the supposed sellers, mere transients like all the Spaniards in Florida, could not possibly have obtained legal title to such large estates. John Gordon carried on a fruitless campaign for years to obtain recognition of his title to these lands."[31] Nevertheless, the lieutenant governor and then the governor would live in houses as tenants of John Gordon.[32]

The governor proceeded to give the Catholic bishop's house to the Church of England, appropriating the convent to provide quarters for soldiers. The Chapel of Our Lady, belonging to the convent, went with it.[33] The stalemate between the two parties would continue for the next two decades. Over the long run Jesse Fish managed to make a comfortable living. In the account book of Mr. Fish, which is preserved in the Library of Congress, are recorded the names of 90 persons who bought houses and lots from him.[34]

2

The Floridas: East Florida Colony and West Florida Colony

East Florida Colony

The new Florida colonies were established under different circumstances and terms than the original 13 American colonies. With the latter, English rights had been encouraged and fostered by the American settlers for over a hundred years. The newcomers to America cleared the land, developed villages, built homes, charted roads, constructed churches, and became farmers or resourceful merchants, all under the direction of the Crown. Currently they were arguing they were better Englishmen than the English themselves. With this evidence of industriousness at hand, the Crown decided that to make a go of the two new colonies being created by the treaty, planters and speculators must be attracted from other colonies such as Georgia and South Carolina, and even from England and Scotland. Parcels of land in tracts of 20,000 acres were offered, with stipulations that the land be developed and occupied by white Protestants, and they produce a cash crop such as indigo, with usually a 10-year contract before ownership.

Slowly, St. Augustine was becoming a British colony as reinforcements continued to debark for the next six months, bringing in additional civil officials, artisans, merchants, and finally, wives and children of the soldiers. In August 1764, 44-year-old veteran officer Lieutenant Colonel James Grant joined as governor of East Florida Colony. He had been in America for six years, first accompanying the 77th (Montgomery) Highlanders in 1758, whose duty was to fight in the French and Indian War.

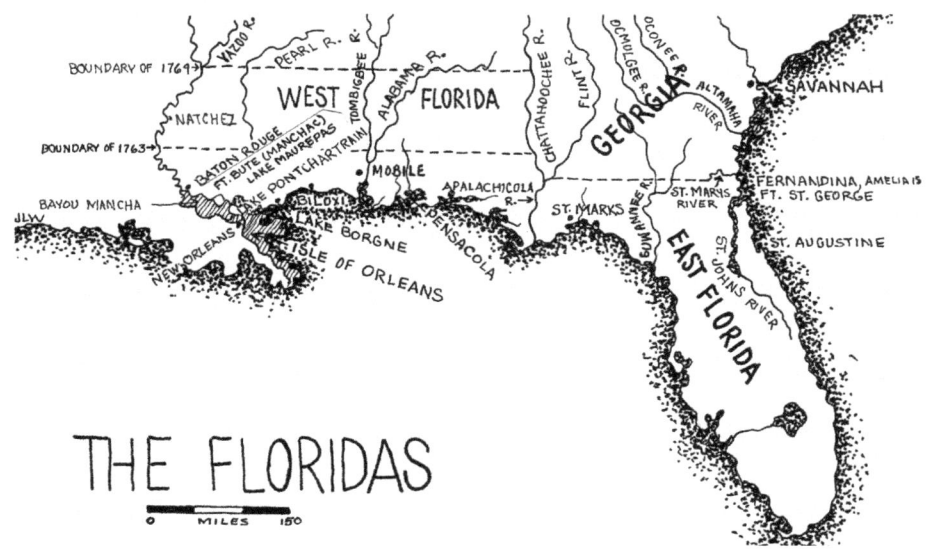

West Florida and East Florida

Over 6,500 British regulars, Pennsylvania and Virginia militia, including Colonel George Washington, moved against the French forces at Fort Duquesne (Pittsburgh, Pennsylvania), in September of 1758. General John Forbes led the British expedition toward the fort, the advance British party was defeated, and its commander, Major James Grant, and 19 other officers were captured and imprisoned in Montreal, Canada. Colonel Henry Bouquet, second in command of the expedition, fought off a furious attack by the French and Indians in October; and in November, with the fort facing starvation, Bouquet succeeded in destroying the fort and attaining the release of Grant.

Major General Jeffery Amherst, delighted with the win over the French in Canada, continued the war with the Indians, who had lost their French support. The year 1760 found Lieutenant Colonel Grant's Montgomery Highlanders and the South Carolina militia on an expedition into Cherokee territory at Echoe, North Carolina, where he won a skirmish with the Cherokees. The following year General Amherst ordered Grant to Charleston, South Carolina, to support local provincial troops raised by Thomas Middleton, Henry Laurens, and John Moultrie as they started up the Santee and Congaree rivers. Colonel Grant picked Lieutenant Francis Marion of Captain William Moultrie's militia to push through the mountain pass, resulting in the

Cherokees' breaking and retreating. Colonel Grant ordered Echoe to be torched, as his victorious force moved down the Tennessee and Tuckaseegee valleys, burning out 15 Cherokee settlements, including their fields of corn. Thereafter, Grant's forces returned to Charleston.[1]

Lieutenant Colonel Grant's military career entered its next phase as commander in chief and governor of East Florida Colony. James Grant had studied law, and he seemed sensible, able, industrious, relatively good-humored, and hospitable in his civil capacity.[2] He invested money of his own in land development and encouraged the ventures of others.[3] At Charleston he invested in land as well as cultivating some influential South Carolinians. He was also noted for his love of good living, and drank Madeira "till we were jolly."[4]

When Governor Grant arrived in St. Augustine he found only a garrison force of 200 soldiers. The absence of a civilian population forced the postponement of his own inauguration, until qualified individuals from South Carolina and Georgia could relocate to St. Augustine to serve on the first governing council. After urgent letters were sent to acquaintances in South Carolina, along with the promises of land and fame, Governor Grant recruited the following council: John Moultrie agreed to become lieutenant governor; his brother James Moultrie accepted the position of chief justice; two other South Carolinians, John Ainslie and John Holmes, took seats on the council along with the new attorney general of the province, James Box, a prominent barrister from Georgia.[5]

The usual oaths of the colonial officeholder quite effectively precluded the participation of any person who acknowledged the jurisdiction of the Holy See of Rome or the House of Stuart.[6]

Two months later, with the booming of new cannon from the renamed fort, Castle of Saint Mark, amid volleys from muskets, Lieutenant Colonel James Grant was installed with appropriate ceremony in the "fourth year of reign of Our Sovereign Lord George the Third, by the Grace of God King of Great Britain, France, and Ireland, and Defender of the Faith."[7] Grant moved into the former Spanish governor's house, a two-story coquina structure with a balcony overlooking the west side of the plaza. The adjoining bishop's house served to hold Anglican services and housed offices of a land surveyor, a customs officer, a secretary, and a naval officer.

Overall plans for development of the colony hinged on persuading established planters from South Carolina and Georgia to relocate to East Florida. Grant's new lieutenant governor, John Moultrie, was such an individual. He was the eldest son of Dr. John Moultrie of Charleston and a brother of William Moultrie. He had graduated from Edinburg, had come home in 1753, and became a prominent and wealthy doctor, plantation owner, and citizen. Moultrie took up almost 20,000 acres in land grants.[8] Becoming one of the first proprietors and planters, "...being honored with the appointment of lieutenant governor, he broke up and dismantled his plantations in South Carolina, and moved all his Negro families into Florida."[9] Moultrie's 180 slaves already knew how to clear virgin lands and plant rice, indigo, and provisions crops of corn, beans, and potatoes. John Moultrie would establish two plantations.

Bella Vista was a plantation situated on the Matanzas River about four miles from St. Augustine, either by the King's Highway or by water. Moultrie's residence included a stone mansion, other necessary buildings for a hundred people, pleasure gardens containing a bowling green, laid walks planted with many trees that yielded olives, dates, oranges, lemons, limes, figs, chaddock vines, white mulberry pomegranates, peaches, plums, and bananas. He had 100 acres of hard marsh, fish ponds stocked with fresh-water fish, 300 acres of land well cleared, cultivated and well fenced, planted with 170 acres of corn, peas, potatoes, and rice. Moultrie also owned a tract of land on Woodcutters' Creek, about five miles from St. Augustine, containing 1,500 acres well stocked with fine pines and cypress, with 25,000 trees boxed for turpentine. Lastly, he owned a tract of 1,000 acres 20 miles from St. Augustine, being a neck of land on a navigable river and the seashore, all good oak land, quarries of fine stone on the riverbank for building and lime. To handle this wide variety of agricultural products he had 140 head of working oxen.

Rozetta Plantation was Moultrie's second tract. Situated on the Tomoka River, it contained 2,000 acres, a neat dwelling house with ten rooms, kitchen, pantry, pigeon house, rice barn, a rice-pounding machine, Negroes' houses, and a kitchen garden. Two miles north of the above on the Mosquito River he had 1,500 acres for an orange grove. On the same river he had 2,500 acres, of which 1,000 acres was fine marsh for planting rice, the remainder of acreage being pine land. While staying in St. Augustine he had a town lot on the bay of St. Augustine near Fort Saint Marks and three houses thereon.

"Moultrie's presence did encourage other successful Carolina planters like William Drayton, Duke Bell, and Francis Kinloch to establish Florida plantations."[10]

Among the many reasons St. Augustine had not flourished under Spanish rule was its inferior harbor located approximately a mile and a half east of the town. The shallow bar at the channel's entrance, eight feet at low tide and thirteen feet at high tide, plagued ships. The sailing ships dared not enter except when there was an easterly wind and a half-flood tide. British authorities imported pilots to steer incoming ships across the channel's dangers. Even one of the leading planters, Andrew Turnbull, had a 16-oared boat built for assistance of shipping in crossing the bar.[11] Of consolation to the British, if friendly vessels had difficulty entering the harbor, so did enemy warships.

Things were different now that the British had taken over East Florida. Commerce was open to the rest of the American colonies, especially Savannah and Charleston. Mail would flow into the colony, supplies of all natures for construction and operation of plantations would find their way to St. Augustine. The British army, officials, and orders to the governor came by water. To facilitate navigation, Governor Grant added a 60-foot-high wooden tower to the old, masonry, Spanish lookout tower in place on Anastasia Island, now under the ownership of Jessie Fish. "A small cannon perched atop announced the approach of every sail, and upon hearing the cannon St. Augustine's residents instinctively looked across Matanzas Bay to the two flagstaffs on the tower. An ensign raised on the northern or southern flagstaff indicated the unknown vessel's direction of approach."[12]

The king had not appointed a provost marshal for the colony, so Governor Grant appointed Alexander Skinner to be sheriff and clerk of accounts, thereby carrying writs of election, summoning all juries, and publishing proclamations.[13] With the arrival of more troops and increased use of the seaport, the town suffered its share of crime and reprobates. "Located conveniently by the fort and the Saint Francis Barracks, public houses dispensed brandy, shrub (fruit juice mixed with rum or brandy), cider, wine, the standard fare, plus tankards of fiery Jamaica rum were consumed in large quantities. Skinner and his constables had a dangerous job as it was risky to apprehend an armed off-duty redcoat or a drunken Indian with a new steel knife at his side."[14] He also was responsible for the lookout tower on Anastasia Island, and for providing lodging and food for visiting Indian chiefs and local rangers.

Accompanying the first British soldiers to reach St. Augustine was a young engineer from Sauchope, Fifeshire, Scotland. Only 21 years old at the time, James Moncrief was already a graduate of the Royal Military Academy in Woolwich. Moncrief played an important part in the history of the new colony as an engineer, building contractor, bridge and road builder. One of his earliest achievements was to supervise the construction of a 900-yard causeway through Jenkins Creek and the swamp west of the town's barrier wall. The causeway led to a bridge spanning the San Sebastian River. Moncrief designed the bridge and had it constructed of Florida pine on the decking and cypress for the underwater pilings.[15] R. McDonald was paid an allowance for attending the Indian Ferry on San Sebastian Creek.

Moncrief then selected the route for a road to run south from San Sebastian Creek. Governor Grant struck a deal with a group of local Indians to open such a road, which originally was an Indian path. A workforce of 20 Indians blazed a road to Oswald's plantation at Timouka, and from there to Dr. Turnbull's plantation at New Smyrna. This road was referred to as "Indian Grey Eyes Road." North of St. Augustine, Moncrief plotted a road to the ferry crossing at Cowford on the St. Johns River. Crossing over the St. Johns, the proposed road would continue north to the St. Marys River. This was at least a 60-mile distance from the capital and would entail raising a lot of money for clearing the land, building bridges, and leveling the road with a proposed width of 16 feet. For the time being, Indian and cattle paths would have to suffice.

Governor Grant did much to advertise the advantages of his new colony for the production of fruit, vegetables, and indigo. To support his contentions he formed two small farms soon after he arrived in town. Grant's farm extended west as far as the road running from the City Gate toward the St. Johns River, and the property extended northward to the ruins of old Fort Mozo (Fort Mose). Following his own advice in letters to new landowners to purchase "country born" Negroes first, and then acquire "new Negroes" at a lesser price,[16] he made several purchases of families of seasoned workers. By November 1764, they were already at work on his 308-acre farm.

Planting at Grant's two farms was largely for experimentation to see what could be grown in Florida. His first love was vegetable gardens with rows of table corn, carrots, English peas, broccoli, radish, spinach, lettuce, asparagus, red beet, watercress, turnip, etc. The provision crops were also grown: corn, oats, red peas, sugar cane, coffee, cotton, and various grasses. The 1766 crop was an immediate success. Grant ventured further by acquiring a 1,450-acre tract six miles north of St. Augustine. He purchased 40 more Negroes, especially those who were familiar with the cultivation of indigo plants that yield a blue dyestuff, then to be processed into blue dye. This was quite an undertaking for the governor, so the "two little farms" adjacent to the town were divided into small tracts and sublet to a succession of small farmers.

The greatness of Governor Grant was his ability to solve problems, whether military, political or personal. The absence of would-be land developers was troubling to him in that they received the land grants but made no effort to occupy the tracts. He was convinced that the key to profitability was a stable labor force, which could only be accomplished by relying on enslaved Africans. He considered Parliament's requirement that Florida land grants be settled with Protestant white families to be unworkable. "The obligation of introducing such a number of White people (one person per 100 acres within ten years) was a great discouragement and to most people an absolute bar to settling the land." Grant believed, and said so many times, that unless enslaved black men and women were permitted as substitutes for whites, "the province can never be settled by British proprietors and must remain as it is until there is an over swarm of Crackers" to take up the premises.[17]

Grant's new indigo plantation, known as Grant's Villa, was situated on the peninsula between the Guana and North Rivers, located six miles north of St. Augustine (today, Guana River State Park). He realized that indigo held great potential as a profitable export crop for East Florida, but few planters were taking advantage of that potential. Indigo, a vegetable dye, was much in demand in the 18th century, when clothing of this hue was especially fashionable. The British government offered a bounty for the production of the dye in the British-American colonies. Otherwise the source of most dye was the French West Indies. Since England was at war with France through a good part of the 18th century, it was imperative that she not buy this commodity from her enemy.[18]

Alexander Skinner, the provost marshal, sheriff, and the colony's Indian agent, was hired as resident manager, a position he held for two decades. Numerous overseers and planters trekked to Grant's Villa to observe the process of cultivating indigo weed and manufacturing the dye, and returned to their own estates to implement the techniques they learned. In a few years, indigo dye became East Florida's most valuable export crop during the 1770s.

Governor Grant continued in his high-fashion planning and operation of the colony, never letting personal investments consume all of his time. In April 1771, the Court of Vice Admiralty was created and signed by Governor Grant. This court exercised jurisdiction over all maritime cases and law, having control over naval affairs. Robert Catherwood was named judge of the Court of Vice Admiralty.[19] Catherwood supplemented his salary from fees earned by handing down condemnation verdicts. Similar courts were located in Boston, Philadelphia, and Charleston. They were very unpopular because their purpose was to enforce British revenue measures such as the Navigation Acts.

After the king made numerous land grants, plantations appeared along the St. Marys River, the Nassau River, and the St. Johns River. With the open harbor at St. Augustine, soon East Florida was beginning to supply many of its own needs for provisions and to export considerable quantities of furs, lumber, turpentine, resin, tar, shingles, indigo, rice, coffee, molasses, tobacco, and oranges. Missions were built, trading posts established, and barter with local Indians quickly grew up.[20] During the French and Indian War, some Indian tribes, especially the Choctaw, had been allies of the French and were suspicious of English professions of friendship. Rumors circulated that without the French to check them, the English would enslave the Indians in the Floridas.

"More than any other single factor in averting a war between Indians and whites in the Floridas was the diplomatic skill of John Stuart."[21] Another Scotchman, Stuart was a failed Charleston merchant who, while serving as a captain of South Carolina militia at the fall of Fort Loudoun in 1760, was made a prisoner of the Cherokees, but was saved from the stake by "Little Carpenter," one of the principal chiefs. "His knowledge of the Cherokee and his friendships among them, together with his quality and his experience, secured him the Southern Indian superintendency in 1762."[22] Governor Grant knew him from his Cherokee expedition in 1761. "The chief aims of the Indian congresses Stuart organized in the early 1760s were to legalize cessions of territory to the British with clearly defined and well-understood boundaries and to establish mutually agreed on trade regulations."[23]

It was long argued by English expansionists that the Indians would rush to ally themselves with the English. Since 1583, Englishmen had been able to read a remarkable narrative of the cruelties of the Spaniards toward the Indians, a narrative written by a Spanish priest, Bartolomé de Las Casas, himself an eyewitness. Las Casas's work, translated as *The Spanish Colonie, or Briefe Chroncile of the Acts and Gests of the Spaniardes*, convinced many English politicians and promoters that the Spaniards had prepared the way for their own destruction by alienating the native populations — where, indeed, they had not completely eliminated them. Las Casas's vivid description of his countrymen's cruelty became a potent piece of propaganda.[24]

Putting this theory to the test, Governor Grant and Stuart convened the first congress with local Indian leaders at Fort Picolata on the St. Johns River to fix the boundary between Indian lands in East Florida. A remote Spanish outpost which guarded the road to St. Augustine, Picolata was located 18 miles west of the capital, and was connected by an old Indian path that led to the east bank of the St. Johns River.

In the Spanish colonial era of the 1600s, the site served predominantly as the location of a Jesuit mission which attracted Spanish settlers to the valley, where, on both sides of the river, large parcels of land were granted for horse and cattle ranches. Haciendas often worked by Indians sprang up along the riverbanks, spawning the early cattle industry. The Indians used this part of the St. Johns, at a narrowing of the waterway, as a crossing place of their trail that ran between the Atlantic coast and Apalache, present-day Tallahassee.[25] Governor Grant felt that the outpost as a defense position was no longer needed for protection from an invasion by an enemy from the Atlantic Ocean; now the colonies, especially Georgia and South Carolina, could commence trade with East Florida using Picolata as the back door to St. Augustine.

Stuart was good at "paleface" bargaining, but Governor Grant was likely to be a poor guesser as to what was in an Indian's mind. Would the Indian be bold, reckless or silent, as the occasion may demand, or would he be foxy or secretly positive? The outing was pleasant, as the Indians agreed to surrender the region east of the St. Johns River, while generous land grants to the Indians by Grant served to open as well as secure the frontier west of the river. The three-day meeting concluded with numerous gifts being exchanged by both participants.

In London, in April of 1764, the Lord Commissioners of Trade and Plantations informed the Society for the Propagation of the Gospel that the commissioners approved having able and worthy missionaries to go and reside in East and West Florida, and would give assistance for the transportation of their families, provide parsonages for their reception, and houses of worship and the furniture therefore. The Rev. John Forbes, M.A., was assigned to St. Augustine, while two other missionaries were sent to Pensacola and Mobile in West Florida.

The Rev. John Forbes and his wife, Dorothy, arrived in late 1764. He conducted the first service in a building that stood on the site of the old Spanish bishop's house. He was given a seat on the Council of East Florida, and served under Governor James Grant and Lieutenant Governor John Moultrie. Soon St. Peter's Church was erected on George Street. After the death in 1772 of the Rev. John Frazer, the Protestant minister at New Smyrna, the Reverend Forbes visited that colony at intervals by request of Lieutenant Governor Moultrie. He also became acting chaplain to the garrison in St. Augustine. Governor Tonyn appointed the Reverend Forbes to serve as judge of the Court of Vice Admiralty.[26]

James Grant (1720–1806), first governor of East Florida. (Reproduced by permission from the St. Augustine Historical Society.)

Documentation of the land grants, owners, and plans for development of same were recorded by the Spanish over their tenure, as well as the British. An engineer's map, drawn with precision of scale, captured the lot designs, the names of owners of lots and blocks, plus their environs, providing graphic evidence of the population of the British in East Florida. By 1770 the Privy Council had issued 227 land grants, embracing nearly three million acres.

"The resulting colonization was slight," lamented Grant. "One reason must be that most of the persons in England who obtained these orders for a thousand acres made little or no attempt to cultivate their lands and settle families upon them." The buyers were drawn from many classes in British public life: titled families, baronets or knights, officers in the army or navy, government officers, doctors of medicine, merchants, and even several members of Parliament.

Then there were the disappointments. Take the scheme which for a time looked hopeful to Grant. Two Bermudians, Ephraim and John Gilbert, petitioned Grant for 40,000 acres on the St. Marys and Nassau rivers on which to settle 500 families. Warrants of survey were given, and a town named New Bermuda, located on the bluff of the St. Marys River, was planned but never settled. In January 1766, 80 families from Bermuda reached Savannah and Sunbury in Georgia; they were dissuaded from going farther and, while there, were attacked by sickness of which many died, and the whole scheme was abandoned. Accordingly, the expansion of East Florida and its growth of the population came to depend on individuals and families from older and more populous American colonies. By 1771, the colony numbered around 3,000 inhabitants, including 900 Negroes, but excluding garrisoned troops and Indians.[27]

Although there was no local newspaper for the colony, residents of St. Augustine were able to find official notices posted at Payne's Corner at the downtown plaza.[28] For the more prominent residents of the town there was a Masonic Lodge founded by Governor Grant, who was appointed Grand Master by officials in Scotland. Other members of Grant Lodge were Lieutenant Governor John Moultrie, Chief Justice William Drayton, the Rev. John Forbes, and Lieutenant Frederick Mulcaster. The military establishment had its own lodge, the Regimental Lodge of the 14th Regiment. Governor Grant was a bachelor and a gourmet who entertained often and lavishly. He had a small circle of drinking buddies who regularly were sharers of the wicked bottle; they believed social functions were necessary to counter disadvantages of life in an underpopulated frontier town. This small body of intimate friends were fellow Masons.

As we know, the Spanish royal engineer de la Puente, before leaving for Havana, had made arrangements with Luciano de Herrera to remain in St. Augustine to collect any money that Fish or Gordon had from the sale of Spanish properties, and transfer such money to him in Havana. Less expected was that Herrera was a spy for the Spaniards. These subversive duties may have been mandated by Puente before he left for Havana. In gathering and transmitting his information, Herrera made good use of the path to Dr. Turnbull's plantation, knowing that Father Pedro Camps, the priest for the Minorcans at the plantation, frequently wrote the bishop of Santiago de Cuba, sending his correspondence by way of fishing boats out of Mosquito Inlet, at New Smyrna. Herrera used the same tactic, by highway, priest, and fishing boats, to send his own reports to Havana.[29]

Another time, a sailor from Havana visited St. Augustine, bearing special holy oil that the bishop was permitted to send to the Minorcan Catholics. The sailor returned to Havana with letters from Herrera containing military information concerning East Florida, which ultimately reached the Spaniards. For the intervening period, Spain would have to depend on secret informers for confidential military information about British movements in the Floridas, especially the West Florida colony.

The Treaty of Paris was a poor treaty for Spain since it gave the British an extension of her American colonies from the St. Lawrence River to the Gulf of Mexico, and to the west bank of the Mississippi River. The principal world players remained the same: Spain, France, and England with her American colonies.

West Florida Colony

East and West Florida had similarities in early history. In the 1500s the Spanish Empire included the Philippines, Africa, South America, and North America. Explorer Panfilo de Narvaez explored western Florida in 1528; Hernando de Soto discovered the Mississippi River in 1539. Narvaez attempted to colonize western Florida but most of his followers perished. Don Tristan de Luna y Arellano founded a settlement at present-day Pensacola in 1559, but two years later the Spanish settlement was wipeout by a hurricane. The Treaty of Paris would align East and West Florida on paper but the great land distance would preclude any possibilities of cooperation between the two colonial governments. Each colony would stand alone.

The West Florida colony was much larger than East Florida as it included parts of Alabama, Mississippi, and Louisiana. Its western boundary was the Mississippi River and its southern boundary was the

Gulf of Mexico. To the east the Apalachicola River was the dividing point with East Florida. This winding waterway flows south for 90 miles and enters the Gulf of Mexico. Small boats could sail the entire length of the river. London-based *The Gentleman's Magazine* characterized the land as little more than pine barrens, sandy deserts with a good supply of mildew.[30] No mention of the "Garden of Eden."

West Florida was the only British colony west of the Appalachian mountains, so the question of imperial policy toward western expansion, toward the Indians and Spanish commerce, became local issues because of serious and long delays in communication with London and British Honduras, the district headquarters. The British lords were of the opinion that the most suitable form of government for both colonies, one most likely to attract new settlers, was of a governor and elected council who would have the power to legislate by ordinance until such time as an assembly might be called.[31]

After the successful capture of Martinique and the fall of Morro Castle in Havana, both in 1762, the Earl of Albermarle directed Lieutenant Colonel Augustine Prevost, 3d Battalion, Royal American, or 60th Regiment, to proceed to Pensacola, Florida, for occupation by British forces. The veteran officer was born at Geneva, Switzerland, and served under General James Wolfe in the Colonial Wars around Quebec. The 32-year-old Wolfe, because of his energetic performance in the field, was criticized by other veteran offices for his impassioned actions. To this charge, the king of England remarked, "Mad, is he? Then I hope he will bite some others of my generals."[32] Apparently, Prevost's energy and stratagem could be traced back to service with Wolfe; Prevost was now in charge of military affairs in West Florida.

He arrived in Pensacola before the governor. In fact, he presented letters from the court of Spain to the Spanish governor, Don Diego Ortiz Parilla, and demanded and received the surrender of Fort San Miguel. The Spaniards did not leave until September, when 664 of them sailed for Veracruz, Mexico, taking with them 108 Yamasee Indians, who were Roman Catholics. Within a few days of the Spaniards' departure, 200 Choctaw and Creek Indians called on him. Prevost had no presents to give them, but they appeared satisfied with some rum which he distributed. They left a white feather with him as a symbol of their peaceful intentions.[33]

Each of the first governors of the British Floridas put a distinctive stamp on his province. Both were Scots, beneficiaries of the patronage of George III's favorite prime minister, the Scottish Earl of Bute. Neither governor was without merit. Both had reputations for martial prowess, and there was reasonable expectation that combat experience might be useful in the new provinces, since the Spanish and French may resent British rule.[34]

Captain George Johnstone was the first appointed governor of West Florida. A professional British naval officer, Johnstone had seen combat in two major wars but had risen no higher than post captain. Proved of physical courage in combat, unfortunately he was labeled as a man without self-restraint, temper or knowledge, and had been convicted of insubordination and disobedience.[35] Nevertheless, in view of his former gallant conduct, Johnstone was formally appointed governor in 1763, much to the disgust of English politicians who were furious with the king for entrusting this high and powerful political office to a Scottish amateur.

Johnstone and his counterpart in East Florida, James Grant, avidly sought to increase the population in their respective provinces. The matters of proper settlement of the colony and equitable distribution of its lands were subjects to which considerable attention was given in the instructions to the governors. In East Florida, land grants were to attract plantation speculators, whereas in West Florida 100 acres of land would be granted to every person being master or mistress of a family, for himself or herself, and 50 acres for every white or black man, woman or child. The new province was surveyed and divided into townships.

The governor's first duty was overseeing distribution of plots of land. Johnstone decided to hold a lottery for the allocation of plots instead of using his power of office to distribute favors. Johnstone took no lot for himself until 201 lots had been given out. This self-restraint was probably approved, as was doubtless his early summoning of a legislature with an elected lower house first being convened in November 1766.

Also, in West Florida more of the land was granted in comparatively small tracts, distributed according to the family size of the occupant as described, or for military service in the recently concluded French and Indian War. Ex-servicemen received a proportion of acreage to rank. Former field officers were entitled to 5,000 acres; captains, 3,000; subalterns or staff officers, 2,000; noncommissioned officers, 200; and privates, 50 acres. The council committee, known as the Lords of Trade and Plantations, inserted a notice in the *London Gazette* that applications for grants of land would be received.

Later in the year, Major Robert Farmar and his forces came from Havana and occupied Fort Conde in Mobile. He took possession of the river and port of Mobile, including all that France possessed on the east side of the Mississippi River except New Orleans, which came under Spanish control in 1767. Upon his arrival, Major Farmar, as commandant of Mobile, took stock of the new colony. He reported, "The ramshackle town of Mobile might be reconstructed; a wavering, almost disappearing road and Indian ferry across Mobile Bay led to Pensacola; the harbor was good, but the bar would have to be removed and a channel made; the soil along the coast was sandy but not unfertile, capable of producing good rice and cotton. Scattered through the country from Mobile west to Lake Pontchartrain there were isolated plantations, most were French but recently taken over by the English." Major Farmar renamed the French works Fort Charlotte and employed Rochon and Company to repair the fort.

The French settlers had not evacuated the province to a man as the Spanish had done, nor had English speculators arrived in Mobile and Pensacola before the troops. "Side by side with the newcomers, the French settlers who stayed on continued their old way of life in Mobile. The French *curé* at Mobile celebrated Mass and ministered to his charges undeterred by the new government."[36] Many of the inhabitants of the former French territory hastened to take the oath of the new allegiance and to secure the quiet possession of their lands. In several instances they purchased the land of departing countrymen.

During these early days, plantations, small farms, and gardens were cultivated; crops of fruits, vegetables, and corn were planted and harvested. Successful beginnings were made in the cultivation of rice and indigo, and the English life had begun in the colony. Reports soon circulated that West Florida was as wealthy in indigo, sugar, cotton, and pine as any West Indies island. Whatever the rumor, a rush for land immediately surrounding Mobile Bay and Pensacola Bay had begun. Maybe this was the "Garden of Eden." Settlers from as far away as the Appalachians began considering these new lands. Most likely because promoters had been recommending these lands of fertility and felicity, the editor of the Annapolis, Maryland, *Gazette*, on July 3, 1766, commented that West Florida was certainly a fertile colony, since "...an unmarried woman of 70 had become pregnant three months after settling in the colony."[37]

It was rumored a company had been formed, of which Their

Graces the Dukes of York and Cumberland were the patrons, and that the prime minister and other magnates were said to have lent their names to the company. Following this news, land speculators and London and Bristol merchants became active, since West Florida was to be governed as a royal colony. The new companies were formed purely for investment and speculation in land.

With the opportunity for profit, a large contraband trade with New Orleans and the former French territories across the Mississippi rapidly sprung up as British vessels began to visit the lower banks of the Mississippi River. "After passing New Orleans ... a vessel would make fast to a tree, where the people of the neighboring plantations came to trade with them. The wants of the colony induced the officials to tolerate the illegal traffic." Farther to the east, both Mobile and Pensacola harbors were surveyed in a preliminary fashion, and pilots established themselves for the time being at the entrance to both harbors by permission of the military authorities.

The growing enthusiasm for the wealth of West Florida proved to be short-lived when Brigadier General Frederick Haldimand, who later was in command of the Southern District under General Thomas Gage, pointed out that Mobile was a hotbed of malarial fevers and the climate required some adaptation on the part of settlers. The use of meat as a dietary staple would have to be limited, the consumption of spirituous liquors reduced to a minimum, sanitary conditions were primitive, and there was a lack of medicine as well as proper hospital accommodation. In addition it was much more difficult to get to West Florida than to East Florida; by land or sea it required additional months of travel and expenses, inhibiting immigration from wherever source. More problems plagued the farmers, who discovered that the soil on the coast and for many miles inland was infertile. Manufactured goods from the other colonies or foreign countries were expensive and also impossible to obtain at times, while off-limits Spanish New Orleans remained the region's commercial center. Nevertheless the offer of free land grants, the once in a lifetime opportunity, did not hold back the settlers from moving to West Florida. Many came by boat or raft on the Mississippi River.

The governor and council addressed security from their external enemies. It was ascertained that the military force in West Florida was extremely deficient. The regiments which were there could not lead to the field 400 soldiers, a disproportioned force to fight against the 10,000 warlike Indians that still lived in the colony. Thus, fortifications were proposed and constructed as follows: three blockhouses surrounding the town of Pensacola, and ordnance and provision storehouses. The fort at Mobile should be repaired and a blockhouse erected opposite the fort of Mobile on the east side of the bay near Red Cliffs, capable of containing 50 men.

A blockhouse for 50 men should be erected at Tanchipaho to prevent the Indian trade in ammunition that was carried on from New Orleans. Fort Bute should be established on a large and extensive plan capable of covering New Orleans, and should contain 300 men. Fort Natchez ought to be put in a respectable condition, for pushing the settlement of these parts and keeping the Choctaws in subordination. There was also discussion on whether the entrance to Lake Pontchartrain ought to be fortified; also, the harbor of Pensacola ought to be fortified to the sea by a battery on Rose Island and another on Red Cliffs.

Various other propositions were aired. Public offices such as a governor's house, courts of justice, council and assembly houses, should be constructed. Hospitals for the sick inhabitants of Pensacola and Mobile, and maintenance of the poor and distressed colonists made a part of the budget. The establishment of public sawmills, naval arsenals, and jails met with approval. Listed as second classification was a unique item: "Four thousand pounds cost for an annual cargo of Negroes to be distributed among the inhabitants who were industrious, for the encouragement of agriculture and trade."[38] The importation of slaves into the colony was in every way encouraged.

There were other conditions of the Proclamation of 1763 that established the boundaries of the Floridas; included was the famous "Proclamation Line" limiting western expansion, with provisions for Indian trade and against the purchase of Indian lands by private persons whether in the new colonies or old.[39] The Proclamation Line drafted by the Earl of Hillsborough established a line along the watershed of the Alleghenies as the temporary western limit of British settlement, placing trade with the Indians under royal control. It confined British Americans to the seaboard and forced withdrawal of colonists already west of this line.

The consequence for East Florida of the Proclamation Line was that the boundary of the Georgia colony was extended from the Altamaha River to the St. Marys River, creating the no man's land

The Proclamation Line. Map by Jean Light Willis.

which became very troublesome. A large proportion of the population of the colony in 1764 was under military command, another body was foreign (French or Spanish), interspersed with a few British civilians of the frontier-speculative type. "West Florida colony had a greater population than East Florida, numbering close on 3,700 whites, 1,200 Negroes, and about 28,000 Indians of the Chickasaw, Choctaw, and Creek tribes."[40]

Under the Proclamation of 1763 the regulation of the Indians was implied; it also demanded regulation of Indian traders, who now had to obtain licenses from the governors. "The powerful Indian nations of the south were close at hand, and were apprehensive for their lands. Traders were constantly pushing northward into the Indian Reserve, which possessed rich stores of furs, wines, and natural food products. The Mississippi River provided a natural outlet for the commerce, and the fact that New Orleans was under foreign control made smuggling so much the easier. West Florida was the natural southern base for all of these ventures, and inevitably attracted in large numbers the very evaders of the imperial laws whom the imperial government was attempting to put down."[41]

The governor was forced to maintain two standards. On the one hand he had to assure the Indians that their hunting grounds would not be invaded by settlers, land speculators or the likes of illegal traders; on the other, he knew it was impossible to hold back for long the tide of frontiersmen in their westward movement. The prevailing feeling in the colonies at this time: "Instead of the colonies sharing in the Honours of Conquest over the French and Indians, Great Britain possessed all the advantages and not an American [was] entitled to an inch of the Indian land."[42]

This Indian Reserve included lands promised to veterans of the French and Indian War. The agitation served as good propaganda for the pioneers in their quest for independence. Both the Indians and the colonists were doubtful of the permanence of Indian territory. Lord William P. F. Shelburne's plan was simple: "The extinction of Indian title to the land by gradual purchase of it by the Crown, the establishment of the reservation, thus regulating the colonists' Indian relations on a continental basis."[43] These were the Crown's instructions to Governor Johnstone.

These orders to Johnstone were contrary to what Major Farmar was doing at Mobile. His orders were to use West Florida as a base for the continental military plan to reconquer the Illinois country for England. The Illinois country, the region between the Wabash, Miami, Ohio, Mississippi, and Illinois Rivers, was inhabited by only a few hundred white settlers, chiefly of French origin, who would hardly fight for Britain and might assist American settlers in securing the land. Its major town was Cahokia (St. Louis). The neighboring Indians would be the chief obstacle to conquest. Control of Illinois country would be valuable to increase trade and dampen the ardor of the Indians.[44] The reference to Illinois country during the colonial period meant all of the Old Northwest Territory, which included the powerful Illinois confederation of Indians. Regardless, this was an ambitious plan covering hundreds of miles into Indian territory, which violated the Proclamation Line.

At this time the council was meeting at Mobile when the governor's feud with Major Farmar began over the Illinois movement. Johnstone, learning that 95 barrels of flour were part of the provisions intended for the army's Illinois movement, objected to the stores being removed. One way or another, the governor practiced obstructionist tactics in an apparent endeavor to hamper the army's Illinois expedition. Both Farmar and John Stuart, Superintendent of Indian Affairs for the Southern Department, explained at length to the governor and council the necessity of putting forth all effort to secure the success of the northern expedition. But Alexander McIntosh, an Indian interpreter, testified that Major Farmar's trading of liquor Major Farmar to the Indians for horses and raw skins, was the principle used by lawless traders. Continuation of this trade under illegal conditions would ruin the entire business. The council, after hearing McIntosh's testimony, resolved that such conduct by Farmar was contrary to the acknowledged regulations of the trade. They therefore resolved that the licenses granted by Major Farmar should be called in at the Creek and Choctaw congresses. The governor and council returned from Mobile to Pensacola; another result of the meeting at Mobile was the passing of some regulations concerning the town of Mobile and the establishment of religious toleration in private life for the French settlers.[45] The primary result of the governor's stay had been the quarrel with Major Farmar.

Although Johnstone had high expectations for his colony, he had become disappointed by the poor quality of immigrants. He hoped to attract settlers from neighboring Louisiana, the French, Germans, and Swiss who had already demonstrated their worth as colonists. Instead, his colony early on seemed to attract Anglo drifters whom Johnstone described as "the overflowing scum of the empire."[46] He, like all of her governors, had to put up with the contentious British Stamp Act, which he enforced despite its being unpopular. "In 1767, Lord Shelburne, who had the policy of 'coercion' of the older colonies, reestablished his faith in the policy of 'conciliation,' and projected a recall of almost all of the colonial governors on grounds that most of the appointments since the conclusion of the late Seven Years' War had been of military men, and that such men were unsuited to a policy of tactful conciliation."[47]

In February 1767, Lord Shelburne wrote to Johnstone, dismissing him on grounds that he had begun an unwarranted war with the Creek Indians, and because of his quarrelsome personality; hence, he was unsuited for such an office as that of royal governor of any colony. It appears that in his dispute with Farmar, Johnstone was in opposition to both the military and the Indian officials of the Crown. He was a good governor in a disjointed colony, living in the shadow of the Indians, Spanish, and French. He left Pensacola, never to return. He was elected to Parliament in 1768, but his lack of qualification for the body found him seeking other positions, first to command a small squadron for service off the Portuguese coast and the Cape of Good Hope, and in 1783 to conduct affairs in India.[48]

In the intervening time, Lieutenant Governor Montfort Browne would be in charge of the colony. His device was to take advantage of his not being an influential absentee landlord. Men such as his brother, the Hannays, the Durnfords, and others who were of gentle or merchant families in Great Britain, whose junior members were officials of West Florida, received grants of various sizes from the king in council, fostering the general policy of the home and colonial government in West Florida of letting out the lands to small proprietors who could and would develop it. Under the supervision of the lieutenant governor, the settlement of Campbelltown, north of Pensacola, was almost entirely made up of 60 French Huguenots who came over, their expenses paid in part by the Board of Trade.

Trade developed considerably in the first five or six years. During most of this period, trade by canoe and pack horse was important and the Indians formed a predominant trading element in the life of the colony. In 1766 the commerce of the colony demanded at least the annual visit of a vessel of 200 tons filled with British manufactured goods, which carried skins back to London.[49]

Montfort Browne was an enterprising official; he attempted to open trade relations with Spain's Havana. "With the advice of Council I sent the sloop to Havana, with a merchant on board, who has been a trader among the Spaniards. They were treated civilly but none were permitted on shore. I received an extremely polite letter from the Governor at Havana in answer to mine. In a short time a Spanish brig headed for Veracruz came in here and purchased $30,000 in goods suitable for their markets, and assured me as this port was now open to them we might depend on the Spaniards coming constantly to this place as it lay so convenient to their ports." Browne closed off the report to the Commissioners for Trade and Plantations with: "I hope my conduct in this as well as in everything else since I have been honored with the Command of the Province will always meet with Your Lordship's approbation."[50]

Neither was the lieutenant governor adverse to filling his land portfolio. Besides taking up several lots in Pensacola, Browne communicated to the council that his brother had received from His Majesty 20,000 acres of land located in any part of the province he pleased, and assigned it to him to take up the land. The lieutenant governor took up 2,600 acres on Dauphin Island, retaining the balance of 17,400 acres unspecified until his pleasure be known.

Unfortunately the settlement at Campbelltown at the head of Pensacola Bay was not a success, even though land was the game; the king had made a fairly large number of grants of 20,000 acres each to various influential members of the court and official circles. Where to locate in this vast colony of West Florida was another story. Late in 1767 two new movements in settlement began. One was the movement into the upper valleys of the Tombigbee and Alabama Rivers. The other was the movement toward Natchez. This movement reached the proportions of a boom in the course of the next five years. "Down the Ohio, the Tennessee, and the Mississippi Rivers settlers came from all the seaboard colonies, while older settlers along the seacoast where the soil was sandy gave up their claims, declaring that their lands were barren, and petitioned the governor and Council for grants of the rich lands at Natchez. These petitions were granted ... but ... exactly one-half the number of acres requested."[51] Without a doubt, during the period of the coming Revolution it was likely that the immigration of loyalists from other colonies, and of "Crackers," constituted a rush to West Florida for safety because it was the only British colony west of the Appalachians and out of harm's way.

It is logical to conclude that West Florida between 1765 and 1770 had been built up under British rule. The population, which had been composed largely of the army, the navy, and trade, was now receiving large numbers of new citizens. The colony boasted sawmills, shipyards, shops, and farms. In the matter of the two major towns, Pensacola and Mobile, both were laid out in town plan by Elias Durnford, Surveyor General of the colony. Social classes based largely on financial standing rapidly formed. The land reserved around the forts was used for the military, and lots were reserved for public buildings and established churches.

Eventually a new governor was appointed to relieve the lieutenant governor as commander in chief. The new governor, John Elliot, arrived in 1769, but hanged himself after one month.[52] Elias Durnford, the surveyor, became the caretaker governor while waiting for his successor, Peter Chester, a professional soldier.

For West Florida the coming American Revolution would not affect its development; instead, covert maneuvering by France and Spain would bring down the colony in the conclusion. For the time being the Florida colonies had survived initial difficulties, and were now discovering some economic viability, although both commanders in chief were disturbed that so few newcomers took advantage of the free land grants. For sure, anyone contemplating a move to the New World would find it easier to choose the mature, developed northern colonies; yet the Floridas were the last chance for good free land in the "Garden of Eden." More time was needed for development.

Both governors had the responsibility regarding external affairs. This meant being apprised of the actions of the Spaniards in Havana who, although they did not at this time enter into open hostilities, continued to spy upon both Floridas. They continued to send their fishermen to the Florida Keys, the Bay of Tampa, and other coastal areas where they came ashore to dry and salt their fish. There were several sources of procuring salt: extracting it from brine wells, or extracting it from inland seawater salt ponds, using the hot Florida sun to evaporate the sea water to gain sea salt. The Spaniards salted and cured quantities of fish, which were bartered with the Indians and traders in exchange for skins and furs that they carried back to Cuba.

Similarly, the Spanish and Indians sought out the sea cow along the coasts and in the harbor. This creature had the appearance of a large seal and grew from eight to thirteen feet in length. It was hunted and killed for its flesh, hide, and oil. In his travels in the Floridas, William Bartram observed, "The Indians call them by the name which signifies the big beaver. The bone is esteemed equal to ivory, the flesh of this creature is counted wholesome and pleasant food."[53] Even with the potential for treachery in the making between the Spanish and the Indians, generally their interaction was limited to local trade. As it was, neither governor could prevent any alliance between the parties because of the distance involved, and thus they were inclined to wink at the possibility.

Due to very little interconnection between the two colonies, cooperation was marginal. It was a long trip from one capital to the other by the sailing boats that took more than a month's time. Both colonies had far-flung Indian territory separating them, so both governors depended on Indian agents, trading post personnel, and missionaries for the latest news. These were the eyes and ears for systematically reporting everything going on in the frontier. There was one overland route available, called the Camino Real, or the Spanish Highway. Its course and distance were, from St. Augustine "...to Fort Picolata on the St. Johns River, 27 miles; across the river by raft or canoe to Fort Pupo, three miles; then to Alachua Savanna, 45 miles; to the Talahasochte on the Little St. Marks River, 75 miles; then down this river to St. Marks, 30 miles; total distance, 180 miles on this ancient highway grown up in many places with trees and shrubs, and in the ever presence of Lower Creek and Seminole Indians who occupied nine towns in East Florida."[54]

Fort San Marcos de Apalache at St. Marks was the last British outpost in East Florida. Situated a short distance from the Gulf, at the confluence of the Wakulla and St. Marks Rivers, it was within about 70 miles of the western boundary of the colony, the Apalachicola River. Over the years the Spanish had constructed three wooden blockhouses or forts here, and each had capitulated to termites and rot. What was left to establish a British presence was a small, primitive wooden structure to house a tiny garrison of 30 men. It was a token needed to support the established trading posts that were now an integral part of keeping peace with the Indians, and to monitor the Cuban trade. James Spalding, who lived on St. Simons Island, Georgia, established five trading posts in East Florida by 1774. Several were located in Indian towns along the Spanish Highway, one being at Talahasochte. Agent Charles McLatchie directed and established sales with the Indians here.

The town contained 30 houses occupied by Indians, plus a spacious council house. "Its inhabitants shaped their large canoes from the trunks of cypress trees, making some that could carry 20 to 30 persons. In these boats they made their hunting and trading expeditions down the west coast of Florida, even to the Bahamas and Cuba, bringing back sugar, coffee, liquors, tobacco, in exchange for Indian furs, deerskins, bear's oil, honey, beeswax, and other articles. In small sloops, the Spaniards made journeys from Cuba to Talahasochte or St. Marks to trade, or to the Bay of Calos to fish."[55]

At this time John Stuart, the superintendent of Indian affairs, was also the commanding officer of Fort St. Marks. Trains of pack horses carried supplies to the Indians and returned laden with beaver skins and other pelts, dried venison, beeswax, honey, and other commodities which the savages gave in barter. Trade goods such as razors, knives, gun parts, glass beads, silver combs and earrings, buckles, and horse tack indicate full participation in the trade economy.

Shortly after England was awarded the Floridas, Governor Grant ordered a company of the 9th Regiment be sent to Fort St. Marks from St. Augustine. Captain James Harries set sail from the harbor at St. Augustine, traveling by way of the Bahamas to Pensacola, arriving at St. Marks in January of 1764 during a serious storm. To save his ship and men, he cut down the mast, threw provisions overboard including baggage, arms, and ammunition, and limped back to Pensacola. Refitted, Harries returned to St. Marks, finally taking possession of the old wooden fort.[56] At this time the Indian trading post was operated by Panton, Leslie and Company from Charleston, who owned additional trading posts on the St. Johns River, at Pensacola and Mobile. Each trading post store was in a specified Indian village or designated site such as St. Marks. The small harbor sheltered the craft which plied back and forth to St. Augustine or Havana.

Besides the trade economy with the Indians, there were also Indian gifts supplied by the Crown for the governor's use. Alexander Skinner was dubbed Keeper of Indian Presents; he was responsible for the storage and distribution of same. In 1764, Governor Grant depended on the home government fund for a large assortment of presents to be shipped to him from England. These presents were British manufactured products which intrigued the Indian chiefs. They constituted mainly manufactured goods such as blankets, shirts, scarves, guns, knives, and other articles under the listing of "trinkets." The fund also granted the governors leeway for them to provide provisions of rice, flour, beef, rum, and tobacco to the Indians. Over the 20 years England was in Florida, tons of presents were sent to both governors for their discretionary use. Between the trading posts and Indian presents, Grant managed the Indians rather well.

But things would change in 1769, when Grant was advised of a general policy of retrenchment in the imperial expenses of operating the colonies. The government decided that Fort St. Marks, nearly 200 miles from St. Augustine, which was staffed by men who suffered much from sickness, inadequate food and water supplies, and the difficulty of provisioning it, would be abandoned. Of course, the independent trading posts would remain since they were privately owned. The wooden fort would serve as the colonists' shelter if there was an Indian provocation.

The licensed Indian traders and southeastern Indians accepted repeated intrusions by William Bartram, the son of John Bartram of Philadelphia. Like his father, he was a botanist who traveled widely collecting specimens. John Bartram's visit in 1766, with his son William, was climaxed when his son bought a 500-acre plantation along the St. Johns River in the vicinity of Little Florence Cove, north of its juncture with Trout Creek. It was an adventurous purchase; nevertheless, with the help of six slaves given to him by his father, he set about establishing a rice plantation. Having lived a sheltered life in Philadelphia, the young Quaker was definitely a poor candidate for success at a wilderness plantation and, as it happens, it became a dismal failure that he had to abandon in only a few months.

Henry Laurens, a Charles Town merchant and friend of the family, wrote to William's father, John, giving him a report on his son. Laurens described William's location as "...the least agreeable of all the places I have seen, located on a low sheet of sandy pine barren verging on a swamp. The water was stagnated, exceedingly foul and absolutely stank." Laurens observed the younger Bartram to be a man of tender and delicate frame, but a man with no wife, no friend, no companion, no neighbor, no human inhabitant within nine miles, and no boat to the nearest water highway. "He is thirty miles from St. Augustine, seated in a beggarly spot of land, scant of the bare necessities and totally void of the comforts of life." And friend Laurens dared say, "There are discouragements enough to break the spirits of any modest young man, unless his crimes had been so great as to merit a state of exile." The combination of frontier hardship and parental advice apparently convinced William to choose a more promising occupation than a Florida planter. By November 1767, William abandoned his St. Johns River rice plantation and left East Florida for a trip back to Philadelphia.[57]

A determined William Bartram returned to Florida in 1774, as a naturalist engaged by a wealthy London physician, John Fothergill, to travel throughout the American Southeast and record his observations in sketches and prose. These were published under the title *Travels in Georgia and Florida, 1773–1774*. Entering the St. Johns River, he sailed very close to the site of his former plantation, but made no visit to the estate. It is said Bartram had an inventive and cunning mind in securing ingress to wherever he wanted to go — naturally, with the assistance of the governor, traders, or Indians, whichever would accommodate him in his travels. Aside from sketches and prose, he was good in edifying narrative of real or imaginary events.

While accompanying a trader who had purchased some Seminole horses, Bartram observed, "The Seminole horses are the most beautiful and sprightly species of that noble creature, are of a small breed, and as delicately formed as the American roe-buck (male deer)." The Seminole horses are said to descend originally from the Andalusia breed, brought here by the Spaniards when they first settled Florida. He then supplied the method the traders made use of to reduce the wild young horses to their hard duty. "When any horse persists in refusing to receive his load, if threats, or the discipline of the whip, and other common abuse prove insufficient, after being haltered, a packhorse man catches the tip end to one of the horse's ears betwixt his teeth and pinches it, when instantly the furious strong creature, trembling, stands perfectly still until he is loaded."[58] This was the animal control of 1774.

Mankind does not seem to change over the years. Bartram continues: "On my arrival at a trading post, I was surprised to find the store shut up, and guarded by a party of Indians. It was relayed to me that the trader had been detected in an amorous intrigue with the wife of a young chief who was out on a hunt but arrived next day, and upon information of the affair he resolved to exact legal satisfaction, which in this case of Indian justice was the cutting off both ears of the delinquent, close to the head, which is called cropping. About a dozen young Indian fellows, conducted by their chief, paid a friendly visit to the trader at his own house, where he was instantly knocked down, stripped to his skin, and beaten with knotty bludgeons. The trader subtly feigned himself speechless and unconscious, as the executioner drew out his knife with an intention of taking off the trader's ears. The trader instantly sprang up, ran off into the dark swamp, miraculously eluding his enemies, finally making a safe retreat to the house of his father-in-law, chief of the village. The trader was married to the chief's daughter. Throwing himself under his protection the chief gave his word that he would do him all the favor that lay in his power. The next day there was a council of the chiefs of the town to deliberate on the affair. Their final determination was that he must lose his ears or forfeit all his goods at the trading post, which amounted to upwards of one thousand pounds sterling!"[59]

The Bartram tales are relayed to demonstrate what one might expect when traveling in these two new colonies. Bartram always traveled with companions, many of them traders, and at other time with Indians. His caravan consisted of around 20 men and 60 horses, making a formidable appearance, discouraging outlaw gangs. He was never challenged while exploring the two Floridas.

Back in East Florida, Governor Grant received word from London that his nephew, William Grant, had died in July 1770, and that he, James Grant, had inherited title to Ballindalloch Castle and all of its associated properties, establishing Grant as the Laird of Ballindalloch. Caught between the need to personally address pressing issues related to the inheritance in Scotland and his desire to remain in charge of the East Florida colony until it became an unqualified success, Grant began planning for a leave of absence. He advised the Board of Trade of his intention to depart East Florida in May 1771, and return within 12 to 18 months.[60] Governor Grant returned to England, and then divided his time between his castle in Scotland and his townhouse in London.

In April of 1773, Grant won a seat in the House of Commons, ending his governorship and necessitating a cessation of his activities in East Florida. He did not give up his plantation, as income from Grant's Villa continued to be sent to Ballindalloch. Likewise, we will not bury Governor Grant in the cobwebs of history. During his first American sojourn, Grant for some unknown reason developed a vehemently anti–American attitude that grew progressively worse as the Revolution developed. In February 1775, in the House of Commons, Grant proclaimed that the Americans could not fight and that he would undertake to march from one end of the continent to the other with 5,000 men. Grant's military activity would have to wait almost two years to have a go with the patriots, "...where the belief in the brotherhood of man happened to collide with the spirit of the American Revolution, where it was said every major general of the American Army, except Benedict Arnold, was a Master Mason."[61]

3

Interim Governors and the King's Road

Our focus returns to East Florida, where John Moultrie, the noble planter from South Carolina, rather than Dr. Andrew Turnbull, the speculator, would serve as interim governor for the absent James Grant.

"The story of Dr. Andrew Turnbull's New Smyrna settlement has been told and retold, sometimes in legend, sometimes in popularized fancy, or scholarly account. Regardless, there is merit in briefly examining the heartbreak of one of the greatest colonizations ever attempted in North America before the Revolution."[1]

For 12 years, Dr. Turnbull was a Scottish physician in Smyrna, Greece. Considered a world traveler, he predicted that East Florida could produce crops similar to those grown along the banks of the Nile River in Egypt. With such promises in hand, Dr. Turnbull secured two partners, Sir William Duncan and George Grenville, who would speculate and finance Turnbull's experimental plantation in the New World. The British Crown offered up to 20,000 acres of land for each investor. The venture would be named New Smyrna after Smyrna, Greece.

Turnbull's plans were to transport an entire colony of laborers to form a huge working plantation. These settlers would be in the service of Turnbull and his partners as indentured servants for a specified period of time. In the spring of 1767, Dr. Turnbull began seeking settlers who wanted a chance to begin a new life in East Florida. Setting sail for Italy he embarked 110 Italians, and in Greece he took onboard his transports 200 mountaineers. His most successful recruiting was on the island of Minorca. The overpopulated island had been suffering from a three-year famine, plus many Greek families, refugees seeking relief from the Ottoman Turks, had relocated to the island. Always the promoter, Dr. Turnbull began fanning the embers for the opportunity to own land in the new colony of East Florida, and signed on 1,100 Minorcans. Meanwhile, across the Atlantic, Governor Grant issued warrants of survey for the tract of land 70 miles south of St. Augustine, at Mosquito Inlet, now Ponce de Leon Inlet.

Prior to his recruiting campaign in Greece, in November 1766, Dr. Turnbull and his family had sailed to St. Augustine, bringing with them an overseer, six carpenters, and a number of enslaved Negroes he purchased during a brief stop at Charles Town. William Watson, his overseer, proceeded with the carpenters to erect plantation buildings while the Negroes began clearing the land at New Smyrna. Dr. Turnbull also brought a sizeable cargo of equipment and clothing destined for the proposed colony, such as Indian presents of beads and sashes, along with muskets, gunpowder, tools, saddles, bedding, shirts, etc. Everything had to be brought to the new colony, since little was available locally at this early date.

"Turnbull followed Governor Grant's advice and purchased from John Graham, a leading Savannah merchant, 22 additional Negroes, who were sent to New Smyrna to assist the carpenters, clearing land, and planting gardens for food." In January 1767, Grant confirmed for the Board of Trade that Turnbull had a gang of Negroes already at work forming a cotton plantation under the direction of a skillful planter, John Earle from Georgia.[2]

While most of the wealthy British or Scot grantees were content to receive title to East Florida acreage and then wait for others to develop plantations, thus driving up the value of the land, Dr. Turnbull had immediately assumed financial partners and set in motion his plan for a colony of white inhabitants to work the land. They would eventually become owners of the land. Unfortunately the odds for success were zero.

"After a final stop at Gibraltar, eight sailing ships, carrying 1,403 colonists, sailed for East Florida on April 17, 1768. When some of the ships finally anchored off St. Augustine on June 26, Governor Grant praised Dr. Turnbull as a zealous, active and enterprising colonist, characterizing the importation as the largest number of white inhabitants ever brought into America at a time."[3] The poor settlers couldn't care less, since the journey had been filled with so much suffering and death of their people. Already weakened by the many months of famine before signing on with the good doctor, many of his passengers suffered seasickness and scurvy aboard ship, resulting in 148 being buried at sea. Accompanying the Minorcans were two Roman Catholic clerics, Father Pedro Camps, a priest, and Father Casanovas, a friar. As the Greek Catholics were outside the Roman communion but favorably regarded by the Anglican Church, the Rev. John Frazer was appointed as second missionary in East Florida.

The Minorcans' experience was not any different from that endured by tens of thousands of earlier immigrants to America. A transplanted Scot living in Philadelphia described a similar ordeal: "Few sailing vessels in these early years were of more than 150 tons, so passenger space was limited. Huddled below decks in the dark and stinking ship's hold, they endured the rough sea voyage that lasted eight weeks. When one is without money, his only resource is to sell himself for a term from three to eight years or more, and to serve as a slave. Families endured a great trial when they see the father purchased by one master, the mother by another, and each of the children by another. All this for the money that they owe the captain or owner of the ship. And yet they are only too glad, while waiting for passage, that at last they find someone willing to buy them. Young and able-bodied persons who can do efficient work can, nevertheless, always find someone who will purchase them for two, three, or four years, but they must be unmarried. Young married persons, particularly when the wife is with child, no one cares to have them."[4] Dr. Turnbull did not separate the families, although he did have a good number of single men with him.

Once ashore at St. Augustine, the Minorcan clan had to walk overland on an old Indian path for 70 miles to get to their new home, New Smyrna. Governor Grant mused that because they spoke a different language from the inhabitants of St. Augustine, he felt most likely the colonists at New Smyrna would remain together. At the same time he warned that if Dr. Turnbull was not supported, he doubted the experiment at New Smyrna would have any success or profit. Nevertheless, Dr. Turnbull's contract was too good an offer to pass up. The colonists came as indentured servants; they would be expected to cultivate the land and its crops for Dr. Turnbull and his partners, for five to seven years to pay for their passage to the New World and for provisions to maintain their yearly subsistence. In return for their work on the plantation they would receive one-half of the profit from cash crops such as the cultivation of cotton and indigo, but not corn. In addition, after seven or eight years of labor, the adult colonists were to receive 50 acres each, plus five acres for each child in a family.[5]

There were only a few profitable years as the plantations' Minorcan population diminished because of death; the births did not outnumber the deaths. Discouragement, tyranny by overseers and the doctor, famine during the lean years, and being plagued by malaria from mosquitoes all helped doom the experiment. It became obvious that indentured Europeans or others were not a good investment for land speculators. In the southern colonies in general, the Europeans could not stand the hot climate and were severely limited in performing a day's work. Experienced planters were said to buy enslaved Africans, who tolerated the heat, and could be forced to work harder and longer than white indentured servants. The lesson learned here was that plantations had to be empowered by the Negro slave, therefore directly opening the floodgates for the importation of thousands of Negroes into East Florida.

New Negroes straight from Africa often possessed valuable agricultural skills, including indigo cultivation learned in the farm fields of their home countries. The majority of "new Negroes" were men from West Africa, apparently from ethnic homelands near the Atlantic coast from Senegal through Sierra Leone. That West Africans could possess skills at indigo cultivation and processing tint cloth with indigo dye, plus being thoroughly familiar with the entire indigo procedure, made them in demand by the slavers.

Negroes, African-born as well as Carolina-born, were steady, dependable, and capable agricultural laborers whose efforts enriched their owners. Their ranks were field workers, domestic servants, cooks, fishermen, hunters, basket weavers, blacksmiths, sailors, carpenters, coopers, cattle keepers and cowboys, horse tenders, plow and hoe hands. A ratio of one hired white overseer to 70 enslaved Negroes was about the norm for stability on the average size plantation.[6] Additional incentives were employed.

Attention is drawn to the Negro "drivers," who were the production managers, so to speak, of the black field hands, male or female, while still slaves themselves. Their duty was to forcibly work the Negroes faster by verbal encouragement, singing popularized ballads, and sometimes by the sting of the whip, which oftentimes resulted in violence and later a runaway. Extra rations and favors, sometimes the promise of freedom for him and his family, were the "driver's" rewards. In the Floridas the Negroes' lineage is difficult to trace because their locations were unstable, at times almost as vagabonds; they shifted from one plantation to another, often from a colony to the north, and eventually the American Revolution scattered their likes as their owners fled the colonies seeking refuge and safety.

For Dr. Turnbull and his settlers, things went from bad to worse. By 1773, 900 inhabitants had died from malaria spread by swarms of mosquitoes. Politically, Dr. Turnbull had severe reverses as Governor Grant returned to England and was succeeded by John Moultrie, and later by Patrick Tonyn, both cool to Turnbull's colonist idea, which was floundering and failing. Serious charges and rumors began about Dr. Turnbull's operation at New Smyrna. One was that he failed to release some of his colonists when their time was up. Another rumor was that the colonists, being Catholics, would not get title deeds to the land since the terms of Turnbull's grant from the Crown specified Protestants.

Eventually it got so bad that in the summer of 1777, representatives from New Smyrna appeared in St. Augustine to secure release from their indentures. The Court of Sessions declared many of Turnbull's indentured people still bound by their contracts. But Governor Tonyn disregarded its decision and, with his encouragement, most of the Minorcans were removed from New Smyrna to the capital. The governor wrote that the discharge of the colonists would be no real loss to the proprietors of New Smyrna since the cost of their maintenance would always equal the value of their labor. Governor Tonyn assigned lots to the survivors north of St. Augustine, where they built their huts. Several scores lost their lives from exposure during the first rainy season after their arrival there. The men engaged in fishing as a means of subsisting while some joined the militia. Under a civil environment the Minorcans survived and prospered. The Minorcan Cultural Society of St. Augustine is now over 225 years old.[7]

It comes as no surprise to learn that Dr. Turnbull early on began hedging his investment by purchasing Negroes as he needed them. He had already kept the slaves he had purchased in 1766 at Charles Town; with Graham's assistance, the doctor purchased additional slaves for the cotton plantation he was preparing, bringing the total to 51 enslaved black men and women owned by Turnbull at New Smyrna in the early months of the settlement. With a lesson learned, Dr. Turnbull hired

John Earle, a planter from Georgia who brought his own Negroes to New Smyrna on a schooner chartered by Turnbull.

Of course, with the disaster, the partners had to be considered. Dr. Turnbull's partners, Grenville and Duncan, were justified in demanding a return on their investment, approximately 40,000 pounds sterling (in excess of six million dollars in today's currency).[8] Dr. Turnbull did keep the plantation operating with his overseer and Negro workers, providing profits from growing cotton, indigo, and corn. Dr. Turnbull practiced medicine in St. Augustine. During the American Revolution he lived in Charles Town as a loyalist, but never recouped the investment.

Dr. Turnbull's experiment did not discourage the typical plantation being formed in East Florida. His immediate neighbor's day-to-day routine portrays what other planters had to do in hiring Negroes, constructing buildings, planting crops, and making the plantation profitable. Richard Oswald, a land speculator attracted by the generous terms of the Treaty of Paris, was from Glasgow, Scotland. His business career began in London where he became an army contractor and, later, commissary general in Germany for the British forces of the Duke of Brunswick. His agent in America obtained two grants of 20,000 acres each. One, named Timouka, was located on the Halifax and Tomoka Rivers, about 40 miles southwest of the capital. The second grant, named Ramsey, was located on the Mosquito and Indian Rivers. Both grants had the usual proviso that white Protestant inhabitants were stipulated for the settlement.[9]

At the Timouka plantation he established four settlements for cultivation of rice, indigo, Indian corn, and sugar. The settlements were named Mount Oswald, Ferry Settlement, Swamp Settlement, and Adia Settlement. At Mount Oswald Plantation, buildings consisted of a dwelling house, large barn, stable, kitchen, overseer's house, and corn house.

Of the 400 acres cleared, 100 acres were river swamp completely dammed with floodgates and planted with rice. Ferry Plantation, 100 acres of river swamp, was cleared for corn and rice. The 300 acres of Swamp Plantation were cleared for corn. Adia Plantation had poor land and was not cultivated. Oswald discovered that white settlers were difficult to recruit, and hearing of Dr. Turnbull's experiences with white Europeans, he had no choice but to place from 100–150 Negroes on the land to get the job done. Oswald was an absentee owner who managed his plantations through an agent and overseers. In 1777, while in Paris he made the acquaintance of Benjamin Franklin from America, and during the American Revolution the British ministry consulted him about affairs in America. In 1782, Oswald was authorized to take part in drafting the preliminary peace treaty to end the American Revolution.[10]

Plantation development continued to the south of St. Augustine, while to the west and north of the capital city smaller plantations and farms were formed along the St. Johns, Guana, Pablo, Nassau, and St. Marys rivers. A seacoast indented everywhere with estuaries, fertile soil, warm climate, and a labor system based first on indentured whites and then increasingly on African slaves, invited the southern colonists to disperse and take up large holdings; a reasonable number of plantations became the unit of political organization.[11] The plantation system, instead of small township groupings like in the northern colonies, prevailed chiefly because good land was more plentiful and the chief crops of indigo, cotton, corn, and later tobacco, could be grown more profitably on a large scale.

As developed in Virginia, the plantation system resulted in a society made up of several layers or ranks. The African slaves were at the bottom; a considerable bulk of impecunious whites, the Crackers, ill educated, lacking initiative, getting their living mainly from poorer soils and small farms, were next in rank above the Negroes; white merchants, tradesmen, artisans, and free Negroes held a doubtful place; while the planters with their great holdings were dominant politically and industrially.[12]

Upon discovering that the provision harvest fell short of expectations at plantations south of St. Augustine in 1770, Governor Grant urged the Musquito Crackers to travel north to learn how to raise provisions at his plantation. It's a safe assumption that Crackers had come with the British as they were colonizing North America in the 17th century. Shakespeare said, "Never did I hear of any Prince so wild a libertine." The word "Crackers" is not used, but libertine means one who acts without moral restraint, standing in defiance of established religious precepts during the Revolutionary period in Europe. Liberty, which we take for granted, is the condition of being not subject to restriction or control; unrestrained; to be set free with the right to act in a manner of one's own choosing.

"Crackers" was undoubtedly British slang referring to impoverished whites in rural sections of the colonies, whom they viewed as rash, wild, devoid of good sense or wisdom. Today, Crackers is used disparagingly, but during the establishment of the colonies they were poor whites, Scottish, Irish, and English, attempting to get a start in the New World. Did they come across the Atlantic with the British migrants or were they home grown? A little of each.

St. Augustine lost its frontier garrison appearance as signs of growth under British rule became obvious. Vacant houses and empty streets began to fill up, much to the delight of Jessie Fish, as the city became a sustainable seaport for the colony. Government offices established the old town as center of the administrative arm of the colony. "The English sheriff and the English lieutenant reappeared in the New World with their functions and their importance increased; such offices fell naturally into the hands of the larger landowners, members of the colonial gentry."[13] Retail stores opened their doors and featured goods imported from England. Taverns flourished, many in dwellings, serving the seaman and soldier his elixir of life, liquor and beer.

Royal Engineer James Moncrief reconfigured the old Spanish bishop's house, then used as troop barracks, to provide chambers for the Royal Council meetings. One member serving on the council was Dr. Robert Catherwood, who, with his wife Jane, came to East Florida in 1764, and served on the council for 18 years. Dr. Catherwood served as surgeon at the Spanish Hospital on Aviles Street. Later it was converted into a jail. Thereafter he became a justice of the peace, and justice of the Court of Common Law.[14] A John Hewitt was assigned for working and taking care of the fire engine, a hand-drawn apparatus.[15]

An earlier idea by Governor Grant was to have the Board of Trade create a special fund by cutting corners on yearly expenditures. Each year as the colony grew, so did the savings in this special fund. This money was to be used for improvements in the town, many of which had been accomplished. Now Grant and Moultrie agreed that the most important need was a road connecting the capital, St. Augustine, with the colonies to its north, Georgia and South Carolina. Colonel Moncrief had drawn up such plans earlier; now with sufficient funds the task became viable.

Captain Robert Bissett accepted the contract to build the longer and more difficult segment to the south, between the Matanzas and Tomoka rivers, and beyond to Dr. Turnbull's New Smyrna settlement, and then to the Stobbs farm. Captain Bissett was one of the first settlers in East Florida, having formed a plantation to the south, as we know. In fact Bissett had nine different tracts in a state of nature, totaling 9,500 acres. His main tract was about 90 miles south of St. Augustine, fronting on the west branch of the North Hillsborough River.[16] He and his son, Alex Bissett, owned 116 slaves between them. By January 1773, Lieutenant Mulcaster of the Royal Engineers observed, "Bissett has his slaves clearing obstructions from the path and roadway, cutting the trees low to permit carriage wheels to pass over the stumps, digging drainage ditches, and packing the new roadway."[17]

The route north of St. Augustine had been measured previously by Jonathan Bryan, a Georgia planter; he had done so on horseback in 1765. It was a distance of 38 miles from St. Augustine to the narrows of the St. Johns River, where a crossing of the mighty river was possible. This crossing was named, appropriately, Cowford. (This is now located in Jacksonville, Florida, at Liberty Street.) Beyond Cowford, Bryan rode north for 40 miles before reaching the St. Marys River, crossing numerous cypress ponds and the south branch of the Nassau River.[18]

During the winter of 1774–75, the road from Cowford, along the St. Johns River to the St. Marys River, was under construction by Charles and Jermyn Wright, East Florida rice planters and brothers of Sir James Wright, Royal Governor of Georgia since 1764. The governor, located in Savannah, Georgia, was wealthy, worthy, and respected, and a true loyalist to the Crown. Moultrie persuaded Captain John Fairlamb and his nephew, Joshua Yallowly, to supervise the construction. This stretch of the road was accomplished despite haggling between the Wright brothers and Moultrie.

The southern section of the roadway was completed late in 1774, and months later the northern section was completed to St. Marys River. It measured 16 feet across, with ditches, and pine logs laid crosswise in the wet portions forming causeways through the swamps, and cypress bridges across the numerous creeks and streams. The traveler on foot, on horseback or with a wagon could traverse British East Florida from the vicinity of Beacon at the Mosquito Inlet, New Smyrna, to the capital, St. Augustine, and continuing northward to the ferry house at Cowford, across the St. Johns River, and north to the crossing at the St. Marys River. Although some of the workers at certain sections were Indians, the majority of the backbreaking work was accomplished with Negro slaves from various plantations, who were hired out by their owners to build the road.

The Rev. John Forbes praised the road, naming it "King's Highway."[19] Immediately the advantage and convenience of the King's Road, linking the East Florida colony to those of the north, had been established on land. It beckoned commerce from Savannah, Charleston, and Augusta; it became a land entrance for new settlers but, more important, a common frontier between East Florida and Georgia appeared. The colony was no longer dependent on the Atlantic Ocean for its existence, provisions, and egress. Outside the old walled city, commerce of the colony was in rapid growth compared to the century and a half of stagnation under the Spanish. Planters from South Carolina and Georgia expanded their horizons and pocketbooks by exporting their experience and receiving grants to establish additional acreage to their plantation holdings; then, too, the little Cracker with worn-out land figured he might just move a little farther south to exercise his own Manifest Destiny.

The new emigrants from the other colonies did not mind taking a chance. Panton, Leslie and Company was an example. This Scottish firm had its main business house in London, with branches in the colonies at Charleston and Savannah, carrying on trade with colonists and Indians. With the British in charge of East Florida, William Panton moved from Savannah to establish a trading post on the west bank of the St. Johns River. This trading post was a plantation on 300 acres. On it were constructed a wharf with river egress to the Atlantic Ocean, two warehouses, four shades (roofs) for lodging naval stores, a storehouse, 70 acres with a naval storehouse, and dwelling houses. Besides exporting naval stores, lumber, pelts, etc., the firm imported cloths, coarse linens from Ireland, sugar, salt, and other commodities. William Panton also had a house and lot in St. Augustine, and two lots in Picolata Township.[20] He was a British loyalist to the maximum as the American colonies moved toward the Revolution. Undaunted by the threat of war he continued to establish trading posts in the Floridas.

When Governor Grant traveled to England in 1771, he planned to return to his colony within 12 or 18 months. In the interlude, John Moultrie, his friend and a wealthy planter, temporarily moved into the vacant governor's position. In Grant's absence, agents and overseers kept the governor's plantations working and showing profit. Although not in residence, Grant continued to communicate his ideas, plans, and orders of implementation from England to Moultrie at St. Augus-

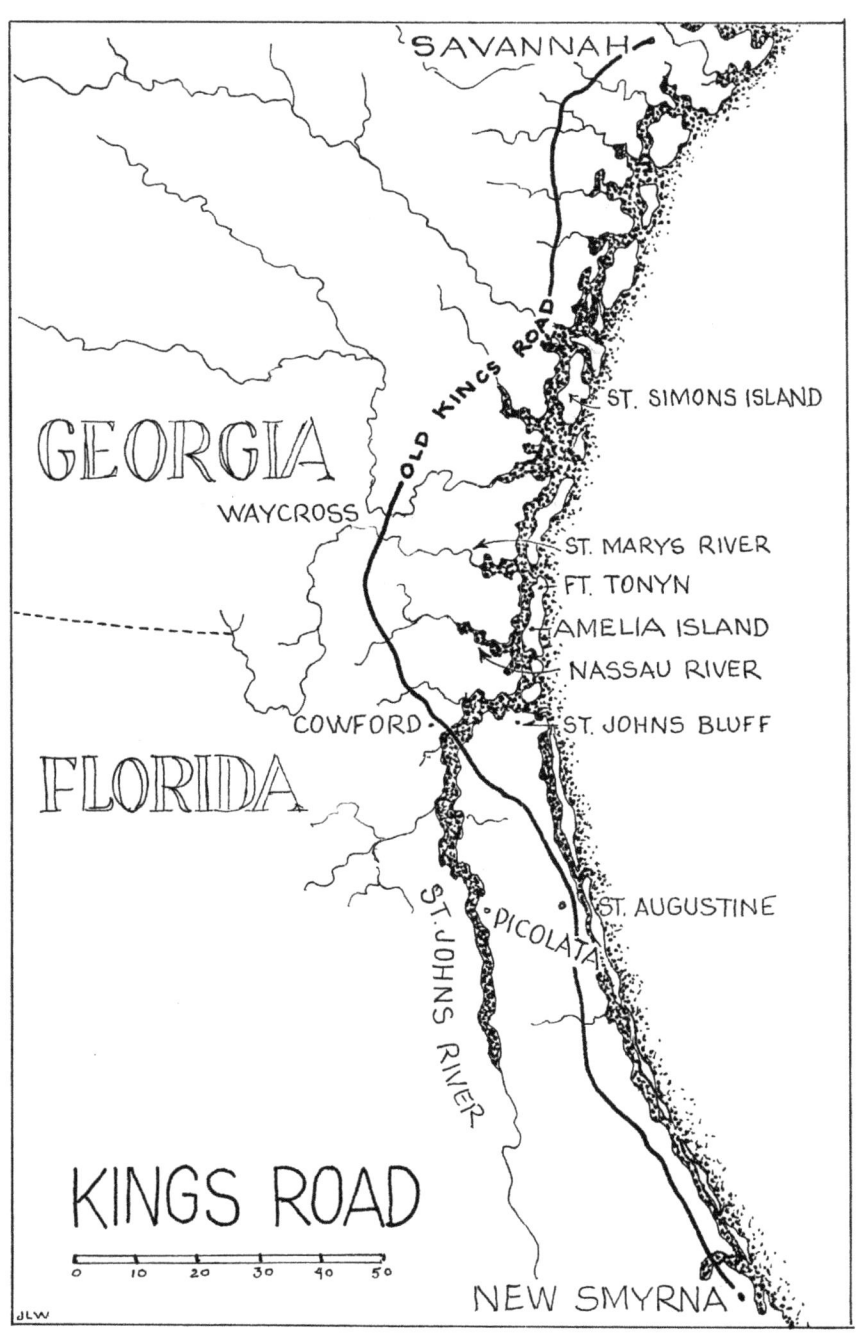

The King's Road in Florida and Georgia. Map by Jean Light Willis.

tine. Time lag on such instructions was two to three months, which pretty much left Moultrie in the governor's chair, supplanting Grant.

The Great Philadelphia Wagon Road

Were the 13 American colonies becoming overcrowded? For nearly 150 years the mighty power of Great Britain was firmly planted in North America. From New Hampshire to South Carolina, the colonies were spread along the Atlantic seaboard, flying the Union Jack from courthouse flagstaffs while sending their products by sailing ships to England. "Except for Pennsylvania, all the colonies hugged the shore. Lying along the coastal plain, most of their land was flat. Settlers looked eastward to the sea, which was the highway linking them to mother England. Their largest towns — Boston, Annapolis, Williamsburg, and Charleston — had grown up close to the ocean, to serve as ports as well as capitals." Toward the west, the colonies ran up against the Appalachian mountain range, which slanted diagonally southwestward from New England toward the Gulf Coast.[21]

It also was apparent that factionalism in the colonies was becoming intolerable. The colonists were split into hostile factions on the grounds of race, religion, social and economic interests, and politics. "In many instances factionalism amounted to regionalism — the New Englanders being opposed to New Yorkers, Northerners being incompatible with Quakers, tidewater settlers being against those living inland." The upper class had almost everywhere entrenched itself so firmly in power that aristocracy rather than democracy seemed likely to be the coming order in America.[22]

In 1751, Benjamin Franklin was disturbed by the newcomers. "Why should the Palatine [German] farmers be suffered to swarm into our settlement, and by herding together, establish their language and manners to the exclusion of ours? Why should Pennsylvania, founded by the English, become a colony of aliens, who will shortly be so numerous as to Germanize us, instead of our Anglicifying them, and will never adopt our language or customs any more than they can acquire our complexion."[23] As the newcomers settled around Philadelphia, resentment against them increased at an alarming rate.

The indenture contract that Dr. Turnbull used in recruiting his newcomers to America was nothing new to him or Benjamin Franklin. Such legal deeds between two parties, binding one party into the service of another for a specified term, had long been used in the 13 colonies. Its primary use was for attracting domestic help for the wealthy, the British military, colonial officials, and all others who imported serfs for one reason or another. These poor whites came from England, Scotland, Europe, and elsewhere, under contract in order to get free passage to the colonies. In exchange they became servants, domestic and menial help such as waiters, busboys, stable boys, valets, cooks, orderlies, handmaids, and servants for all work, for room and board. This arrangement worked fine for 150 years, until the importation of low-maintenance Negro families came on the scene, becoming competition for the serfs. Slowly the poor serfs were turned out into hopeless obsolescence, and with no one to fight their cause, skedaddled where they might survive, becoming the homeless in towns and villages or the squatters in mountains outside the reach of the sheriff.

There were additional matters at hand: how smaller states might secure an adequate voice in the government, where to mark off the three-sided states whose western boundaries had not been defined, and how to treat the Indians. But most of all, the predominantly Anglo-Saxon (with many from New England) families having fourth, fifth, and sixth generations, were running out of suitable land and farms for settlement. These older elements became hostile and aloof to the Scotch-Irish, Germans, Huguenots, Jews, Quakers, Catholics, Crackers, and later immigrants arriving by the boatloads, treating them as refugees. These "kind" would have to go elsewhere to homestead, forcing them westward and then toward the south.[24]

Just beyond the coastal plain called Tidewater, or the low country, was a hilly midland called Piedmont, at the foot of the mountain leading upwards to the Appalachians. This was one of the fertile areas which was destined to become the American frontier. It was the Piedmont which became the main artery of 18th-century settlement. And few trails were more important than the Indian route that extended east of the Appalachians. This ancient Warrior's Path was long used by the Iroquois. Then, by a series of treaties with the powerful Five Nations of the Iroquois, the English acquired the use of the Warrior's Path; after 1744, the British took over the land itself. The growth of the route after 1744 into the principal highway of the colonial backcountry was an important chapter in the development of the South.

Stretching from Philadelphia, Pennsylvania, to its southern terminus at the fur-trading center of Augusta, Georgia, the wagon road passed endless farms, small villages, simple meeting houses, an occasional fort, and of course public houses taking in travelers for the night. These early innkeepers also served in their taverns such refreshments as "wine slings, toddies, and 'Cider Royal.'" Weary wayfarers were fair game for colonial resourcefulness, a traveler surmised: "Of one thing I am certain, the innkeeper wisely concluded no man ever stopped at his boarding house twice, and so he made the most of his charges."[25]

In the road's early days, Philadelphia was the main point of entry from England. Thus the road expanded from its early turnpike status to now being called the Great Philadelphia Wagon Road. The City of Brotherly Love, mainstay of the Pennsylvania colony, was foremost in establishing markets and trade in all commodities. As it expanded, so did the wagon road. From Pennsylvania's capital it went west to Lancaster and Gettysburg, turning south and following the great Shenandoah Valley through Maryland and Virginia, into the Piedmont of North Carolina to such towns as Winchester, Virginia, and Salisbury, North Carolina, an important trading center of the Carolina frontier. The road veered slightly southeastward to the Moravian settlements at Wachovia (Charlotte), and then almost due south to Pine Tree (Camden), South Carolina, and then Augusta, Georgia.[26] Originally way stations for travelers, these villages eventually became trading centers. Learning of cheap land, the Germans and Scotch-Irish began venturing down the wagon road, taking refuge where and whenever they pleased, many squatting in the hills and forests of this new land of promise. "These bold and indigent strangers, when challenged for land titles, replied, '...it was against the law of God and nature that so much land should be idle while so many Christians wanted it to labor on and to raise their bread.'"[27]

Over the decades, much of the road had been cleared to accommodate horse- and oxen-drawn wagons. To maintain the road, county courts appointed overseers who were responsible for keeping up the wagon road at county expense. The farther south one went, the worse the wagon road became because the population of Georgia was too poor and scattered to maintain the road, thus coining the newcomers' phrase, as poor as a Georgian. Nevertheless, the wagon road strongly influenced Georgia's early years.

Because of rapid settlement from Augusta east on the Savannah River, later referred to as "tobacco road," Savannah became the southern terminus of the road. Over this Great Wagon Road, thousands of

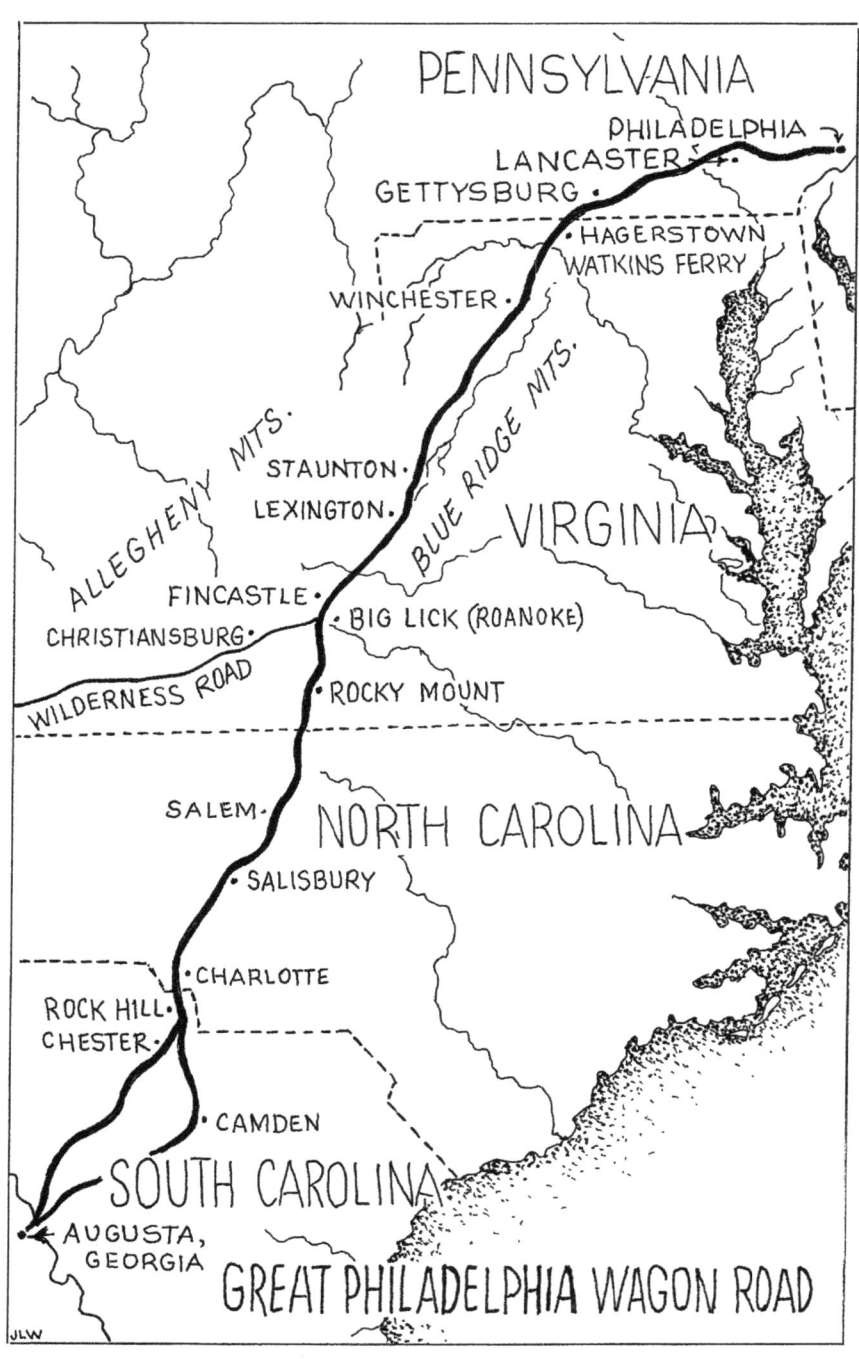

The Great Philadelphia Wagon Road. Map by Jean Light Willis.

English, Scotch-Irish, and German settlers entered South Carolina, Georgia, and south to the new colony, East Florida, and its new King's Road. Likewise, there were many cutoff trails from the Great Wagon Road in all of the colonies. One such example was the Woodpecker Trail that began in North Carolina and traveled south through Surrency, Georgia, into northern Florida at White Springs. In Georgia it was the Wiregrass Trail to the Atlantic coast, terminating south of Savannah.

The Jews were already clearly defined in the 13 colonies, although their status was less than acceptable outside the larger communities, since religion and politics were inextricably mingled in this age as in others. It seemed everyone in the world dreamed of a new life. One such interesting story is about a Scottish baronet, Sir Alexander Cuming of Coulter, who conceived a project to settle 300,000 European Jews on the Cherokee tribal lands in the backcountry of South Carolina. This proposal for a Zion on the Carolina frontier had as its object the relief of oppressed Jewish families in Europe by taking them out of the crowded ghettos and establishing them on land where they could turn their talents and industry to farming and the production of commodities useful to the British Empire. Sir Alexander traveled to South Carolina in 1729, traversed over a thousand miles meeting with the Cherokees, but with no satisfactory ending to his vision. Sir Cuming had to abandon his fantasy utopia for his people because of lack of underwriting for his enterprise.[28]

A new American age was emerging. Nowhere was this felt more keenly than along the wagon and other roads, permitting the poor settlers a new beginning and of course their Garden of Eden — even if it was only 20 acres of land in the shadows of the towering Appalachians.

4

The Georgia–Florida Border Dispute, and the Beginning of the American Revolution

Georgia was the last of the 13 original colonies to be settled. In 1732, 31 years before the Florida colonies, King George II granted a 21-year charter establishing the colony of Georgia, so named after the king. A member of Parliament, James E. Oglethorpe, arrived in America in 1733 with a band of settlers at Yamacraw Bluff, the site of present-day Savannah. Despite an Anglo-Spanish "no trade agreement," English privateers smuggled merchandise to the Spanish settlement at St. Augustine as well as to Spanish colonies in the West Indies. This illegal trading led to war between England and Spain, which was named the War of Jenkins's Ear after the British seaman discussed earlier. Although the war was hundreds of miles from Georgia, Governor Oglethorpe was prompted to invade Spanish Florida and lay siege to St. Augustine. After both sides almost starved to submission, Oglethorpe and his band of militia gave up and returned to Georgia. Although 4,000 settlers were in Georgia the colony was unsuccessful, so Oglethorpe gave up his charter. A determined King George in 1754 reorganized the colony as a royal province, setting the stage for additional newcomers and their dreams.

Undoubtedly, at this time the map makers of Spain and England had difficulty in establishing the Georgia and Florida border. Early Spanish explorers had indicated Spain's boundary in North America extended as far north of Spanish St. Augustine as Beaufort, South Carolina. After the English settled Charleston in 1670, the northern edge of Spain's land claim was moved south of Beaufort by about 30 miles. With the charter of the Georgia colony in 1732, Spain again saw their land claim shrink even more. Spain protested the land grab, citing that Hernando de Soto of Spain was the first white man to visit the Georgia region in 1540 on his way from Florida to the Mississippi River. There was also Pedro Menéndez de Avilés, who drove the French out and built forts along the Atlantic coast in 1566. Regardless, these men had returned to dust, and England in 1721 claimed the Georgia region and built a fort on the Altamaha River.

Augusta and Savannah established the Savannah River as their northern boundary, and the fort on the Altamaha River secured their southern boundary for the colony of Georgia, although its land mass extended to the St. Marys River. England politely marked this area off as "disputed land" located between British Georgia and Spanish Florida. This buffer zone encompassed thousands of square miles of forests, swamps, coastal wetlands, and rivers. This became a foreign territory, almost an asylum, a no man's land. Settlers moved in, of course, but mainly it became an attraction for felons, runaway slaves, escaped convicts, squatters, mixed-breed people, rustlers, smugglers — nothing short of a festering fleshpot. Some ranches and plantations developed over the next 40 years, with open range for the cattle. For the most part it was so remote the tax collectors on both sides avoided this banditti territory with its unknown occupants.

The Treaty of Paris, in 1763, addressed the dispute by royal proclamation: the Florida–Georgia boundary would be the St. Marys River. The King's Road over the St. Marys River was extended to Fort Barrington on the Altamaha River. Still, marauding ruffians from Georgia continued to cross the St. Marys River border into Florida, extending the no man's zone to the St. Johns River. Lieutenant Governor Moultrie of Florida adroitly characterized these raids: "Georgia began to plunder us, we retaliated, the common frontier quite abandoned on both sides, as horses, cattle, and people moved away."[1] Even though the Treaty removed the Spanish and replaced them with Englishmen, two British colonies with a common boundary continued to violate the other side. The explanation was that many of the Georgia colonists wanted to be free of British rule. After the Revolutionary War began in 1775, many Georgians who had been neutral joined the movement for freedom and became patriots. They seized power temporarily in Georgia; therefore, British Florida was now their enemy. There would be no tranquility here for the next eight years as the Revolution's encroachment moved to the southern colonies.

In St. Augustine, Anglican priests regularly conducted services from the former Spanish parish church, a schoolmaster was employed to tutor the children, shopkeepers sold their wares, and finally, scales were used in the public marketplace at the plaza. A not too active Lieutenant Governor Moultrie spent part of his time at Bella Vista, south of the town on the Matanzas River, supervising planting and overseeing plantation operations.

There never was any question about Moultrie's doing a satisfactory job in Governor Grant's position, but in actuality Moultrie lacked Grant's affable personality and ability to soothe passions with eight kind of wines, a full table, and appropriate words. He was not a politician like James Grant. Moultrie clashed repeatedly with Chief Justice William Drayton and Dr. Turnbull. In Grant's absence from East Florida, Lieutenant Frederick Mulcaster sent letters to him in England providing detailed information on issues and activities in the colony. Nonetheless, in ten years of existence, East Florida had been ruled by two despotic military governors, Grant and Moultrie, without the benefit of a representative assembly. Even West Florida had formed such a body. Although Grant and Moultrie approved of the autocratic arrangement, it was not allowable and must be changed.

In a disharmonious atmosphere, Lieutenant Colonel Patrick Tonyn was appointed second governor of East Florida in March 1774. Tonyn was born into a family of British military officers and reared in strict military fashion. The son of Lieutenant Colonel Charles William Tonyn, he had joined his father's regiment, the 6th (Inniskilling) Dragoons in 1744, and in May 1751, became a captain in this unit. After seeing action with them in Germany, he became a lieutenant colonel of Douglas's 104th Foot.[2]

St. Augustine residents' initial impression of the new governor was hardly flattering. "Startled by the large entourage that Tonyn brought along to East Florida, about 20 white servants as dirty a set of fellows as you could wish to look at — they got all hands drunk the second night after they landed. The whore he brought was handsome enough, she had three children with her and is big with a fourth. She is called Mrs. Tonyn." Soon after the March 9 inaugural, residents of St. Augustine realized that Tonyn lacked the sociability and tact necessary to promote social and political harmony. "He neither drinks nor gives claret — he has no wine of any kind, he has not seen Company six times since he has been in the Province. He hangs at home miserably, no method, bad servants and a dirty table cloth ... [are] all the comfort he seems to have, except the comfort of a more dirty whore."[3]

Intolerant and short-tempered, Tonyn demanded strict deference to class and rank, and treated any questioning of his authority with rigid military disdain. The new governor consulted early and often with Lieutenant Governor Moultrie. The colony's two top-ranking officials routinely expressed trust and respect for one another in their official correspondence.

Governor Tonyn solidified his base in London with former governor Grant by letter and inquiry of how Grant wanted the royal cause upheld. "He also sent praise for the King through his correspondences to the Board of Trade. He mentioned that St. Augustine residents were steadfastly loyal to the Crown and had great veneration for the brilliancy of His Majesty's gracious protection."[4]

He also pointed out the fact that the East Florida colony sent no delegate to the First Continental Congress in Philadelphia in 1774, instead burning effigies of John Hancock and John Adams. St. Augustine's loyalty was partially responsible for General Thomas Gage, overall British military commander stationed in Boston, to assure that the few redcoats available in America could best be employed in the most rebellious colonies. Even before the outbreak at Lexington, he ordered 100 men from St. Augustine to Savannah to help Georgia's royal governor, James Wright, maintain order.[5]

At this time, letters conveyed across the Atlantic by service of His Majesty's Post Office were leisurely in their journey, which seldom took fewer than two months for delivery. East Florida was a part of the southern postal district organized in 1764 under a deputy postmaster at Charleston, South Carolina. Mail from England was sent directly to Charleston by packet; and mail for Savannah and St. Augustine was sent overland from Charleston by a post rider traveling by horse, a hazardous journey. On the way, he picked up news and passed it on to the authorities. This ride took fewer than 21 days for the round trip, depending on the weather. The express waited only two days in St. Augustine before beginning the return journey, little time for Governor Tonyn to compose an answer to some weighty dispatches on the problems facing his colony.

On the eve of the American Revolution, St. Augustine was a garrison town. The white population consisted of the army, royal officials and their dependents, a few substantial planters, a good number of merchants and artisans, transient sailors, and Indians living outside the city gate. "Debates over parliamentary sovereignty and taxation without representation had little meaning. Monies raised through customs duties and sale of stamps were expended in America; East Florida got more than its share, a fact well appreciated by the citizens of the town."[6] North of East Florida, colonists believed that grievances were such that the only recourse was to take up arms in defense of their liberties. This willingness to fight, after a 170-year relationship, contained many facets of revolution, and although the East Florida colony never participated, nevertheless at present its people were affected, being quickly absorbed into the whole bloody affair.

The population of the 13 colonies had increased rapidly over the years, and by 1775 it reached nearly 2,500,000 inhabitants. Steadfast among the most popular reasons for leaving their homeland: land ownership, freedom from unjust taxation, economic opportunities to make a living, freedom of worship, freedom from British occupation forces, and freedom from England.

The principals in the Revolution were: the patriot who loved, supported, and fought for his rights and the colony, sometimes called a Whig, or supporter of the war against England, a rebel; and the loyalist, who maintained loyalty to the lawful British government, sometimes referred to as a Tory for his belief in the Conservative Party in Parliament.

As to the events of the last decade, Governor Tonyn had only a cursory review of the rebellion now at hand. Although it was not his decision, necessity dictated that he familiarize himself with what had transpired over the last ten years in the northern colonies. Here is what became known to Captain Tonyn. The battles for control of Canada and the Ohio River Valley, in 1758, between the French and Indian allies, and the British and American militia, had been concluded with the Treaty of Paris 1763, ending the Seven Years' War. At this time Captain Tonyn was fighting in Germany, so his knowledge of the affair was limited. Among other things at the conclusion of the war, France signed away her rights to all North American lands east of the Mississippi River, except New Orleans.

With the French and Indians defeated, American colonists who participated in the conflicts hoped for unbridled western expansion across the Appalachian mountains. Instead, the British stepped in to regulate what they saw as the eventual colonization of the American West — and began taxing the colonists to help erase England's war debt and pay for protecting the western frontier. It was hard for the militiamen to understand why their role in Britain's victory was not rewarded. They became resentful since Americans had remained loyal British subjects for the war and felt they were partners in the victory. When the British government continued to treat them as subjects and not partners, to be taxed and regulated, the colonists felt betrayed. What occurred over the next 12 years was that the early resentment of the patriots eventually turned into a rebellion and then a full-fledged fighting Revolution.

So it came about that the patriot and loyalist factions in 1763, just as East and West Florida were being added to the list of colonies, began a year-in, year-out antagonism against one another. The first such important act was the British decision, in 1763, to keep a standing army in North America. The troops were left over from the French and Indian War, and the British government did not consult the colonists about this move. An additional proclamation that aroused further American discontent recognized the Indians as owners of the lands they had occupied. It also prohibited settlement west of the Appalachian mountains, the Proclamation Line. The colonists came to believe that these limits were unjust and illegal. The next year, in 1764, Prime Minister George Grenville ordered customs officers to strictly enforce the laws regulating colonial shipping under the Navigation Acts.

Grenville also pushed through Parliament the Sugar Revenue Act. This law to protect the colonies from the British West Indies, levied a three-penny tax on each gallon of molasses purchased from the French or Spaniards, and brought to America. Two years later the duty was reduced to one penny a gallon on all molasses. In 1765, the wrangling became downright ugly. Parliament passed the unpopular Quartering Act, requiring colonists to provide quarters, fuel, candles, cider or beer, and transportation for British troops stationed in the colonies. The colonists felt this was taking money from them without their consent.

The second act that Grenville pushed through Parliament was the Stamp Act, requiring colonists to buy tax stamps and place them on newspapers, playing cards, diplomas, and legal documents. Colonists referred to the stamps as "badges of slavery."[7] They refused to allow stamps to be sold, crying "that taxation without representation is tyranny!" The Sons of Liberty, a secret colonial society, sprang up to protest and nullify the Stamp Act. They were the radicals who would lead the colonies into revolution against the mother country. In the name of liberty, they were responsible for many acts of mob violence against loyalists. The favorite ritual was to tar and feather the Tory. To swell their ranks, a day of mourning was called, bells were tolled, flags hung at half-mast, and business was suspended. The merchants of New York, Boston, and Philadelphia united to halt the importation of goods from England. Faced with this defiance, Parliament repealed the Stamp Act in 1766. The repeal was received with the greatest joy in the colonies. But the damage had been done.

A call went out from New York requesting a meeting of all colonies. The First Colonial Congress took place, with its themes the declaration of rights, grievances of the colonies, and taxation without representation. They would not have to wait long to be tested by the British. Chancellor of the Exchequer Charles Townshend persuaded Parliament to place duties on tea, paper, lead, and paint imported into the colonies, assuming that the colonists, who felt internal taxes to be unconstitutional, would have no objection to taxes for revenue collected at their ports. The colonists considered the Townshend taxes to be the same as the hated Stamp Tax. They held a second boycott, refusing to buy British goods. The British Parliament got the message and repealed the Townshend duties in 1770—except for the tax on tea.

Serious unrest developed in Boston at the same time. British troops garrisoned in the city had a fatal clash with townspeople: when a mob of men and boys threatened the outnumbered soldiers, the British troops fired into the crowd, killing three men and wounding eight others. This was labeled the Boston Massacre, the first powerful influence in forming an outspoken anti–British public opinion. The bad feeling which was rapidly growing between the colonists and the mother country continued early in 1772, when the armed schooner *Gaspe,* stationed in Narragansett Bay, Rhode Island, to enforce the revenue laws, discharged its duties in a most insulting and arbitrary manner, with the result of being boarded by patriots, who, after sending the crew ashore and wounding the commander, set her on fire, burning the ship to the water line. In New York the citizens had erected a "liberty pole" in the city, only for it to be cut down by British soldiers. Committees of Correspondence formed at Boston to explain to other towns the rights of the colonies, and to show how Britain had violated these rights. Men such as Samuel Adams, James Otis, Patrick Henry, and Thomas Jefferson, who were considered colonial agitators, organized public opinion against the British.

By 1773, East Florida had been a colony for ten years. The happenings a thousand or more miles away, although most likely known by Governor Grant and other aristocrats, had little effect on their daily lives since it was a foregone conclusion that Parliament was proper in supporting King George. The English were worldwide in their holdings and colonies; officers such as Grant and Tonyn supported British policy and enforced it to the maximum. Yet the American turf was wearing away.

Just how naive did they think the colonists were? The Tea Act enabled the English East India Company to pay the Townshend tax and still sell tea cheaper in the colonies than could the Dutch, who had been smuggling tea into the colonies, without tax. Colonial leaders, tempted by lower-priced English tea, soon realized they would lose their argument against taxation without representation. Thus in December of 1773, a band of colonists disguised as Indians raided British ships in Boston Harbor, lifted boxes of tea from their holds, and tossed them overboard. The affair was witnessed in silence by a large crowd on the shore, as 342 chests of tea were broken open and their contents poured into the water. When the destruction of the tea was completed, the "Indians" and crowd dispersed to their homes. This event was recorded as the Boston Tea Party. Paul Revere was dispatched by the patriot leaders to carry the news to New York and Philadelphia. There, the people would not allow British tea to be landed, and at Annapolis, a ship and its cargo were burned. As far south as Charles Town, tea was hidden and stored in damp, dark cellars, and later sold to help finance the patriots' cause in that colony.

Incensed, the British Parliament passed a bill closing the port of Boston to all commerce and transferring the seat of government to Salem. In addition, Parliament ordered the royal officers to quarter the troops sent from England at the people's expense, thus encouraging the military to acts of violence and oppression. The liberties of the colonists were placed at the mercy of every petty official bearing a royal commission. These outrages were resented by the whole country while evidence of sympathy poured in from every quarter. Salem refused to allow the establishment of the seat of government as the English proposed. With the closing of the port of Boston, large numbers of people from Boston were thrown out of employment, leaving families helpless. Soon various colonies came forward promptly to their relief by sending provisions and other necessaries of life, and money was subscribed in great amounts from other colonies. Cheered by these evidences of sympathy, Boston resolved to hold out to the end.

North Carolina sent a money contribution of 2,000 pounds. South Carolina sent to Boston 200 barrels of rice to help out. Georgia and Florida sent nothing. The time was at hand to choose sides: are you a patriot or a loyalist? It was encouraged by a general congress of all the colonies to take united action for the redress of grievances, and a committee was appointed to correspond with the colonies for the purpose of such a meeting to be held in Philadelphia in 1774. All colonies responded to the First Continental Congress except Georgia, where British governor Sir James Wright prevented the colony from choosing delegates to the congress. Florida did not respond since its governor, Captain Patrick Tonyn, only reached Florida on March 1, 1774. It is doubtful an invitation was extended because East Florida's inhabitants were mostly loyalist in sympathy; West Florida was considered west of the Appalachian mountains and out of the jurisdiction of the other colonies' proposal of liberty for colonies east of the mountains.

The First Continental Congress met in Philadelphia in September 1774, at Carpenter's Hall, to defend American rights, denouncing many laws passed by Parliament since 1763. The 55 members agreed not to import any goods from Britain or Ireland after December 1, 1774, and not to export anything to the British Isles or the West Indies after September 10, 1775. At this meeting, the move for full independence from Britain began to develop. Patrick Henry would sound the rallying cry, "I know not what course others may take; but as for me, give me liberty, or give me death."

After a few months the British Parliament declared Massachusetts, Rhode Island, and Connecticut to be in rebellion. It passed the Restraining Act, barring colonists from fishing on the Grand Banks of Newfoundland, decreeing that trading was to be done only with Britain, and ordering General Thomas Gage to arrest the colonial leaders in Massachusetts, break up the mobs, organize a Tory militia, and send troops to Boston. On April 18, 1775, while the British made their way from Boston to Concord to destroy some military stores of the colonists,

Paul Revere rode across the countryside warning, "The British are coming, the British are coming!"

The British redcoats were challenged by a company of farmers who attacked them from both sides, inflicting on them a heavy punishment. These "Minutemen" and redcoats clashed at Lexington, Massachusetts, and Concord, New Hampshire. On June 15th, George Washington was named general and commander in chief of the American forces. Two day later, the British redcoats drove the Americans from Breed's Hill in the battle of Bunker Hill. On July 3rd, General Washington arrived in Cambridge and took command of the Continental Army, which consisted of 14,000 raw recruits with the rudest implements of warfare.

Patriot General Richard Montgomery led an expedition against the Canadas, captured Fort St. John and Montreal, together with 11 vessels laden with war stores, in November 1775, but the American forces failed to seize Quebec. In this unsuccessful battle, Montgomery was killed. Earlier the Quebec Act had been passed by Parliament, granting unusual concessions to the Roman Catholics of Canada in order to attract them to the royal cause.

At this time the colonists had more than enough manpower to defend themselves and secure their freedom from England. The patriots did not have to transport supplies or their manpower over the Atlantic Ocean. They knew the terrain and could easily retreat to many places not familiar to the British. In the early years their weapons consisted of muskets, Pennsylvania rifles, and a few cannon. What they lacked far outweighed what they had: no trained army except the colonists' militia, the Minutemen; still to be recruited, the Continental Army and Navy; very little gunpowder, uniforms, shoes, outerwear, food, medicines, wagons, oxen, mules, horses, tents, and no money to purchase any of the above. The British officers were content to think this was going to be an easy shoot.

One such display of confidence was personified in John Murray Dunmore, the governor of Virginia, a nobleman and an extreme loyalist. Fearing the worst from the Virginia patriots, he had General Thomas Gage, the British commander at Boston, send him a detachment of 160 men, the 14th Regiment at St. Augustine. The detachment arrived at Williamsburg just in time, as Colonel William Woodford led a patriot force of "shirt-men" (militia riflemen) and North Carolina forces against Norfolk. At Great Bridge, Virginia, Dunmore and his

East Florida forces, plus an assortment of loyal Virginians and black Ethiopians, skirmished with the patriots, and in a 25-minute clash, were defeated, causing the Dunmore forces to retreat and take refuge in British ships in the Norfolk harbor.

Governor Dunmore, along with his Tory soldiers, suffered from cramped accommodations and lack of provisions on the ships in the harbor. His appeal for provisions was greeted with rifle fire from the enemy. Without any conscience, at 4:00 A.M. on January 1, 1776, he ordered British naval guns to shoot into Norfolk while British landing parties set fire to warehouses near the waterfront. Retaliating patriots burnt the home of a prominent loyalist. Between them, the two parties destroyed Norfolk: Virginia's largest town at 6,000 inhabitants, Norfolk went up in flames on a windy New Year's Day.

Dunmore finally landed, and built some makeshift barracks with a view to maintaining a British presence in his own colony. Colonel Robert Howe's Continental troops made it impossible for Dunmore to maintain his location. With his collection of soldiers and British refugees, Dunmore returned to the ships, eventually establishing a new base on Gwynn Island, Virginia, Chesapeake Bay. Loyalist Dunmore fought a losing battle here, also struggling with the ravages of smallpox among his troops. Undaunted, he sailed up the Potomac toward Mount Vernon to fight another day.[8]

Elsewhere, General William Howe replaced General Thomas Gage as commander of the British forces in Boston. Continental forces under General George Washington then fortified Dorchester Heights; Howe's cannon could not elevate sufficiently to hit the patriots' works, located on high ground. Disgusted, Howe realized the occupation of Dorchester Heights made Boston untenable, and on March 7 he decided to evacuate Boston.

While these historic happenings took place in the years 1775–76 within the northern colonies, the citizens and army in East Florida felt well isolated as it appeared the patriot movement would not be strong enough to challenge their rights as Englishmen. The *South-Carolina Gazette and Country Journal* brought by the post rider would be sufficient for current events. This belief was shattered in March 1776, before the Declaration of Independence was signed.

Esek Hopkins, a successful sea captain and privateer in the Seven Years' War, was placed in charge of the Continental Navy at the end of 1775. In the first planned major operation of the navy, acting on intelligence that the British were assembling vast quantities of stores in the West Indies, he sailed for the Bahamas with eight ships and attacked the island of New Providence (now called Nassau). Captain Samuel Nicholas, senior Marine officer of the American Revolution, led the first action in which American Marines ever participated as an organized unit. They captured Fort Montagu, netting over 100 cannon and mortars, plus a large quantity of stores that Washington's army found invaluable. Governor Montfort Browne was captured in the raid and returned as a prisoner of war.

But all of this was in violation of Hopkins's orders. He had been ordered to clear the Chesapeake of Dunmore's fleet, drive the British from the Carolina coasts, and then run the Royal Navy away from Rhode Island. However, Hopkins, a privateer at heart, discovered a discretionary clause in his orders that authorized him to use his judgment in adopting whatever other course of action appeared to be more promising. He got off course and ended up where the booty was, Nassau. There is no happy ending when you disobey orders; his fleet began to evaporate as personnel melted away because of sickness, failure by Congress to pay him for his privateering, and bad morale. Esek Hopkins was through as America's first admiral. The silver lining to the story: John Paul Jones succeeded him as commander, and went on to be the top American naval commander. Six months later Governor Browne was exchanged for General William Alexander.[9]

Within a few days Captain Tonyn learned of the incident. This certainly was a bold sign that the war could come to East Florida at a minute's notice and he should prepare for war, as the rebellious American colonies soon would threaten the growing Floridas. Tonyn ordered that a series of redoubts be constructed west of the existing Cubo and Rosario Defense Lines, built around the three sides of the town not facing the harbor, the city wall. He strengthened the line of entrenchment north of town, the Hornwork Line, reinforced the Castillo, and maintained small detachments outside of St. Augustine at Forts Mose, Picolata on the St. Johns River, Matanzas south of the city, the New Smyrna outpost, and the wooden lookout tower on Anastasia Island. "At the lighthouse on Anastasia Island constructed of coquina by the Spanish, General Sir Frederick Haldimand in 1769 had the structure raised 60 feet higher, with frame work; and had a cannon planted on top, which was fired the moment the flag was hoisted for a signal to the town and pilots that a vessel was in sight. The lighthouse had two flagstaffs, one to the south and one to the north; on either of which the flag was hoisted, to the south if the vessel was coming from there, and to the north if the vessel was coming from that direction."[10]

General Haldimand was at St. Augustine with Grant, and later became second-in-command to General Gage in New York. Although he never spoke or wrote English well, the Swiss soldier of fortune was an exceptionally good commander in the Colonial Wars and in Pontiac's War. Unfortunately for the British, London authorities did not want a Swiss officer to succeed Gage in the command of British forces against the Americans. The authority in London that Tonyn had to report to was George Sackville Germain, British Secretary of State for the American Colonies and also Lord Commissioner of Trade and Plantations. In 1770, he assumed the name Germain on inheriting property from Lady Betty Germain, whose will had included this stipulation. Germain is charged with most of the British errors of strategy during the Revolution, although an impartial reexamination of the evidence shows that he has been overdamned.[11]

As always, personality conflicts with Generals Howe, Carleton, and Clinton, and Germain's attempt to control the war from London, weakened his authority. Throughout his term of service Germain tried to direct military operations from Whitehall, despite changing situations and his inability to supply the British generals with needed reinforcements. Germain and the king believed that loyalists formed half of the colony's population, and all that was necessary was to aid them in their struggle against the Revolutionists.

Germain also believed that the operations in the south would win support of the loyalists in these colonies, thereby turning the tide in that section. He was persuaded that Charleston, Georgia, East Florida, Nova Scotia, and Penobscot (Maine) might be held by the troops in those regions, where recruits could be collected.[12] All of the correspondence and orders between Germain and Tonyn reflected these sanguine expectations. Beset by multifarious problems of conducting the war in the northern and middle colonies, Germain came up short with replacements and additions for his redcoat commands.

With the outbreak of hostilities at Lexington in April of 1775, the British ministry decided to increase their armed forces in the colonies to 40,000 soldiers. Although many individuals were recruited for the British regiments, the results in general were a failure. In this emergency the ministry resolved to employ German mercenaries, which was nothing new in Europe, for subjugation of the colonies. The Duke of Brunswick was the first German prince to conclude a treaty with the British to supply these forces. Under the arrangement, the duke was paid money for each man he supplied, while the British provided the mercenaries the same terms as British soldiers: billeting, food, medical treatment, and monthly pay.

The Duke of Brunswick drafted men from six duchies (states): Brunswick, Hesse–Cassel, Hesse–Hanau, Anspach–Bayreuth, Waldeck, and Anhalt–Zerbst, reaching a total of 29,867 mercenaries drafted for American service. Styled as Hessians by the Americans because three successive commanders in chief of the duke were Hessian, their appearance upon reaching American shores was greeted with a roar of righteous indignation by the colonists for employing Germans to subdue their revolution.

Of course they all did not arrive at one time, but the Germans in the early battles were noted for unwonted cruelty. At Philadelphia, of the June to December 1777 siege, British General William Howe's civilian secretary, Ambrose Serle, commented, "Hessians are more infamous and cruel than any. It is misfortune we ever had such a dirty, cowardly set of contemptible miscreants." The chivalrous patriots soon realized that the Hessians, well drilled and disciplined in the tradition of Frederick the Great, turned out to be poor fighters because it was not their cause. They faulted and failed at Trenton, Bennington, and Springfield, New Jersey. By war's end, 7,754 Hessians had found graves in American soil and 5,000 had deserted, the balance were wounded or captured as POWs. In retrospect they lost their luster on the battlefields, but were not hated as bitterly as the loyalists and their redcoats.[13]

One of the most serious weaknesses the colonists faced at the outset of the war was the lack of central government, but for the war they united politically. The First Continental Congress met in September 1774. The Second Continental Congress in May 1775, at Philadelphia, led to Thomas Paine's *Common Sense* pamphlet, 47 pages of ideas put into the words that a great many patriots had been forming in their own minds. Upwards of 500,000 copies were sold. "Paine was the first publicist to discover America's mission."[14] On July 4, 1776, the Second Continental Congress, by a unanimous vote, adopted the Declaration of Independence from England, which was received with joyous outbursts throughout the colonies. The new states would select their own governors and some of the social distinctions were abolished. The founding fathers actually were committing an act of treason when they signed the document, and their names were held secret until January 1777, as redcoat forces were sent in pursuit of some of the signers.

The English took few prisoners, and those taken were treated harshly. Loyalist prisons filled up rapidly, and the rebels had none. Both sides used prison ships, which were horrible with overcrowding, poor sanitation, and inadequate food and medical care. "In the end the British prison ships probably killed more American soldiers than British rifles, total estimated 7,000 to 8,000."[15] Problems of prisoner exchange stemmed from the rules of the game; only officers could be exchanged. Later a tariff was worked out on the basis of how many privates were equivalent to various ranks, such as two privates exchanged for a sergeant, 16 privates for a captain, etc. As the war dragged on for seven years, patriots were taken to prisons in England.

In East Florida, Fort Saint Marks in St. Augustine would be used as a prison for the colony. The first incorrigible rebel patriots to arrive in St. Augustine were some of Patrick Henry's Virginians whom Dunmore, the royal governor, wanted to get rid of quickly. At His Majesty's pleasure, 27 prisoners were detained in a stronghold awaiting parole or exchange. The Revolution escalated and so did the number of prisoners sent south to St. Augustine.[16] The presence of large numbers of prisoners there later in the war became a problem of housing, and maintenance, because of an excessive number of prisoners to exchange.

In 1769, when St. Augustine was designated Southern District Brigade headquarters instead of Pensacola, General Frederick Haldimand became concerned about inadequate space for officers' quarters. At the time he ordered Captain James Moncrief, engineer, to supervise the conversion of the unfinished bishop's house to barracks. In addition Moncrief drew up plans for conversion of the monastery into quarters for officers. He also designed a troop barracks to accommodate 267 men by adding wings to the northern and southern ends of the rectangular stone chapel located adjacent to the monastery. Delays in construction, and shortage of satisfactory manpower and supplies, carried on for several years before the St. Francis Barracks was finished and occupied.

The decision to make St. Augustine a brigade headquarters necessitated construction of another barracks to accommodate troops from two additional regiments. To avoid repetition of the problems experienced with the St. Francis Barracks, Moncrief's plan called for a wooden structure to be prefabricated and erected on land purchased from Jesse Fish. As a first of its kind in the Floridas, "a Pile of Barracks" was prefabricated in New York and shipped via boat to St. Augustine in 1769. Three stories high with porches, the impressive wooden building was 208 feet wide, with wings on each end that were 82 feet long and 38 feet wide. Open porches edged the floor on all sides, erected on a brick and stone foundation south of the St. Francis Barracks. It took eleven months to complete the job, in 1770. Much like the wooden Spanish forts in the previous century, the wood, if other than oak, deteriorated quickly from the damp climate and termites. By 1790 only a part of the building remained, finally burning out in 1792.[17]

The Declaration of Independence eliminated colonial control by England of the 13 original colonies, but one colony, East Florida, stood steadfast and loyal to the Crown. East Florida had sent no delegates to Philadelphia for the First or Second Continental Congress meetings because they had not been invited.

In the early summer of 1776, 200 Hessian recruits stepped ashore at St. Augustine wearing knee-length, brick-red woolen coats with blue facings, white linen breeches and waistcoats, cocked hats, and freshly-tarred black gaiters, and carrying large haversacks and 15-pound "Brown Bess" muskets with foot-long bayonets. British transports with additional reinforcements continued to arrive, and by fall 1776, 760 mercenaries were on hand to help defend the province or be forwarded north as replacements.

5

The Southern District Brigade and Headquarters, St. Augustine

At Southern District Brigade headquarters, Tonyn had limited control of the garrison's military establishment, arriving and departing as ordered by superiors such as Generals Haldimand, Germain, and others. During the summer of 1776, the garrison at St. Augustine had small detachments from the 14th Regiment doing outpost duty, plus an incomplete detachment of Royal Artillery with three companies of the 16th Regiment. These foot soldiers were made up largely of recruits from England and Hanover, since temporary British forces hardly afforded a satisfactory total for defending the overwhelming frontier and river borders of East Florida. Tonyn had to contend with possible attacks by land from patriot rebel forces now overrunning Georgia, by sea from privateer attacks, and on the St. Marys River no man's land from robbers, rustlers, and undesirables. The Royal Navy added little to St. Augustine's strength at this time. At best, one 20-gun sloop manned by 160 men was based at St. Augustine, along with sister sloops in the Bahamas and Georgia to curb smuggling.[1]

There were, of course, minor incidents that troubled the governor. To the south, Spanish raiders in the vicinity of the Halifax and Tomoka Rivers forced Moncrief to abandon his southern properties and move more than 80 slaves to a tract on the North River 18 miles from St. Augustine.

The closest hostilities occurred off Anastasia Island early in the war, when a rebel privateer, the *Commerce*, seized the *Betsy*, a British merchant ship waiting to cross the bar. The *Betsy* was freighted with a large shipment of gunpowder for the garrison and the Indians. Waiting for favorable winds and tide, her captain anchored outside the bar, giving the South Carolina privateer time to sail up from the Matanzas Inlet and surprise her at daybreak. Crewmen who otherwise might have been inclined to fight were bribed 100 pounds by the Carolinian captain. Pounds sterling proved effective in the submission of the *Betsy*. The lookout on Anastasia Island watched in dismay as the powder was transferred to the privateer for the benefit of the patriots' cause. "Without a shot being fired in protest, the guns aboard the supply ship were spiked and 111 barrels of gunpowder were transferred to the privateer *Commerce*. Governor Tonyn ordered a tracking party to pursue the *Commerce*, but she had too much lead time and escaped in the inland waterway on her way back to South Carolina."[2]

Knowing things were not going to improve, Governor Tonyn wrote to Lord Germain in London in August, stating he had called the inhabitants of the province to a meeting at the Statehouse to discuss the responsibilities of citizens during the crisis. He requested all males of the province to embody into a battalion of militia, whereupon all in attendance were in agreement. The militia, under Tonyn's control, would be composed of 11 companies, two from residents along the St. Johns River area, four from St. Augustine, one from New Smyrna, plus four black companies from the plantations, with white officers. Tonyn appointed John Moultrie colonel, Robert Bissett lieutenant colonel, and Benjamin Dodd major. What services this militia actually performed is uncertain, though it was claimed later that on an occasion or two, when the regulars had to encamp, the inhabitants as militia performed guard duty, patrolled, and did other duty without receiving any pay, rations or arms from the government.[3]

Faced with many controversial situations, the loyalists and patriots had begun feuding as far back as 1770. Neighbors became enemies. Tens of thousands of British loyalists had lived in the colonies all their lives. Now the talk of Revolution was put to the test by the Sons of Liberty, the secret colonial society that sprang up back in 1765 to protest the Stamp Act. They assumed many different names, but were the radicals who led the colonies into revolution against the mother country. In the name of liberty they were responsible for many acts of mob violence against loyalist citizens. Tar and feathers were the fate of those whose conception of liberty did not suit their own. Committees of Correspondence were created in 1772 to coordinate activities of colonial agitators and to organize public opinion against the British. They also were active in furnishing men and supplies to the Continental Army.[4]

At first confined to the northern colonies, their sting movement traveled toward the southern colonies, finally in South Carolina and Georgia. If a loyalist knew what was good for him and his family, he made plans to move out of harm's way. As loyalists left their homes and began to trickle into East Florida, Governor Tonyn made it known in Savannah and Charleston that loyalists were welcome in the East Florida colony, where no secret organization such as the Sons of Liberty existed. It was his duty to protect British subjects.

In addition Tonyn continued to be concerned with the disruptive frontier between East Florida and southern Georgia, which the refugees did little to stabilize. Law-abiding folks called these less than desirable newcomers low people, riffraff, Virginia Crackers, and unsavory refugees from the northern colonies. In South Carolina in 1766, these undesirables had formed organized outlaw gangs and were cooperating with other criminal bands as far north as Pennsylvania. The Great Philadelphia Wagon Road also became a highway for crime.[5]

After the home guard had been established, Tonyn's next organization was a provincial corps known as the East Florida Rangers. This was a cavalry operation consisting of 130 male inhabitants of East Florida, and loyalist refugees from Georgia and South Carolina. They were engaged to serve for three years, organized into four companies, receiving clothing, provisions, and one shilling a day. The Rangers were charged with scouring the woods for the enemy, obtaining intelligence, foraging, and driving cattle and horses from the disputed border area, cooperating with the Indians, defending the outlying plantations, and in general performing services that the regulars were incapable of doing. The Rangers were under the orders of Governor Tonyn and not the regular British officers. Tonyn wanted a cavalry he could control and which could carry forth fierce retaliatory raids against the enemy, soldier or civilian. It was a mixed-race corps of white and black men dressed in frontier garb. The 116 uniforms provided each consisted of a hat, hunting shirt, belt, breeches, shoes, buckles, blanket, and leggings. Each soldier was responsible for his horse.[6]

Tonyn appointed a loyalist refugee, Thomas "Burnfoot" Brown, to the rank of lieutenant colonel and commander of the East Florida Rangers. Brown had denounced the patriots as savages because he declined to sign a revolutionary petition at Augusta, Georgia. A mob of Liberty Boys struck him down, scalped him, and then tarred his legs and held them over a fire. Losing two toes in the incident, he was carted through Augusta. The next morning he swore to the Liberty Boys that he repented of his past conduct and promised to support the American cause. "He was then supplied with a horse and chair to ride home." However, he at once proceeded to the Saluda River in South Carolina to join General Robert Cunningham, with whom he had planned the capture of Augusta for the Crown. On August 4, 1775, as published in the *Georgia Gazette*, Brown was singled out as "hostile to the rights and liberties of America." At this, he made his way from South Carolina and soon appeared in St. Augustine.[7]

Two other East Florida Rangers were Daniel McGirth and his brother James from South Carolina. Daniel was a scout for the South Carolina patriots' Rangers when his superior officer coveted McGirth's favorite mare named Gray Goose. The officer trumped up a charge on McGirth, had him tried by court-martial, and took pleasure in seeing McGirth whipped and imprisoned. The McGirths were a tenacious lot who managed to escape prison, steal Gray Goose back, and ride with Captain John Baker's gang to the St. Marys River. While Baker's command was encamped at night, the McGirths, who were performing guard duty, stole the horses of their comrades, fleeing over the St. Marys into East Florida, and later joining the East Florida Rangers. Daniel was appointed lieutenant colonel, and his brother James a captain.[8] Daniel McGirth acquired a plantation on the St. Johns River, and rented a house in St. Augustine.[9] Daniel McGirth and Thomas Brown would ride high in the saddle for Tonyn and his East Florida Rangers.

On the west bank of the St. Johns River lived the Seminole Indians, who might lend some military assistance to the loyalist cause. Tonyn was a strong supporter of the idea and claimed to have the friendship of the Indians. Hoping for the success James Grant had achieved at Fort Picolata in 1765 and 1767 with the Indians, Tonyn called another Indian congress at Fort Picolata, scheduled for December 1775. Heavy rains turned roads to mud and forced the Indians to take lengthy alternate routes, arriving at the Cowford ferry crossing on the St. Johns River, 40 miles south of Fort Picolata. Governor Tonyn boarded His Majesty's schooner, the *St. Lawrence*, and sailed downriver for the congress, which was held at Cowford from December 6–8. Unlike previous congresses that focused on peace and land cessions, this meeting was to establish an alliance between Creek, Seminole, and British forces loyal to His Majesty. Tonyn treated Pumpkin King and Long Warrior to a cruise on the *St. Lawrence*, and they were given commissions as captains of their towns. Chief Cowkeeper did not leave his village in Alachua, but sent a promise to meet with the governor in St. Augustine as soon as the Creeks from Georgia had cleared out of East Florida, as he was not fond of them.

At the congress, Tonyn persuaded the Alachua Seminoles to fight alongside the East Florida Rangers and provincial forces. They were recruited to scout, guide, and fight for both military units. Alexander Skinner, the keeper of Indian presents for the colony, and Tonyn's principal agent in Indian affairs, distributed gifts to the Indians of beef, rum, and potatoes, along with firearms, gunpowder, and manufactured trinkets. In turn the Indian chiefs presented Tonyn with ensigns of the eagle tails, deer skins, and a tobacco pipe. The governor was impressed with the Seminoles. Soon after, British officers with 70 men, 25 Crackers, Chief Cowkeeper, and Seminole warriors traveled north of the St. Marys' Florida border, driving cattle away from the Georgia estates.[10] It hadn't taken the governor very long to test his personal cavalry.

The months following the signing of the Declaration of Independence brought an artificial peace to the Floridas, although Georgia border warfare and a few isolated incidents with privateers continued. West Florida had its own problems as Spain began rattling the sword. But there was no serious military movement made by the patriots in South Carolina and Georgia. Every American state promptly acquired a bill of rights as well as its own constitution. All power was vested in and consequently derived from the people. The South Carolina government meetings were divided between Columbia and Charleston, a two-headed affair. Sparsely populated Georgia's capital was at Savannah for nine months of the year, and three months at Augusta.[11] It seemed that each state, unprepared for self-administration, would need a year or more to get its affairs into alignment with the federal government.

So what could Tonyn expect from his allies or enemies? Hard to tell, but becoming the lone colony in the south loyal to the Crown, Tonyn would be the southern anchor for future British military operations. As for Georgia and South Carolina, both in flux with internal affairs, they quite likely and quickly would become his enemy.

The state of Georgia had been carved out of the South Carolina land grant. Its first governor, James Oglethorpe, had retired after 21 years of service and was replaced by Sir James Wright, former lieutenant governor of South Carolina. Wright was wealthy, worthy, and respected, while retaining his loyalty to Britain. By 1765 his circumstances would change.

The Stamp Act, in 1765, designed to raise money for the cost of maintaining British soldiers in America, brought about great unrest in Savannah. Wright defied a body of 300 armed countrymen who gathered in Savannah to halt the sale of stamps; fortunately for the governor, public opinion among the loyalists rallied to his defense and the issue was settled. For the next ten years he performed his duties capably and without further serious challenges, until the news of Lexington and Concord in 1775. Aroused by the events, the public endorsed the "Liberty Boys" of Savannah, who started defying Wright's royal authority. They seized 500 pounds of gunpowder from the provincial magazine, spiked a battery of cannon, and erected a "Liberty Pole," which they paraded under with muskets.

On June 13, the patriots called for a provincial congress to meet on July 4, 1775, to take control of the colony. Georgia's revolution lockstepped with the meeting of the First Continental Congress in Philadelphia. Governor Wright remained another six months hoping for armed assistance needed to restore his authority. In January 1776, two patriot warships and a troop transport arrived at Savannah and promptly arrested the governor to keep him from rallying the loyalist nucleus of the regular army. After being held incommunicado by the patriots for a month, Wright escaped, taking refuge on a British warship. He made an unsuccessful attempt to retake Savannah but finally gave up hope of restoring loyalist control to the capital. He sailed to Halifax, North Carolina, and two months later he sailed for England. The patriots' coup was completed.[12] For the time being, Georgia would serve as a military and buffer outpost for South Carolina.

Tonyn's concerns about Georgia were justified. East Florida was in danger of a rebel attack, but he could not expect any help for the time being from the loyalists in Georgia while it was under control of patriot rebels. Even though the royal governors of four southern colonies (Virginia, North Carolina, South Carolina, and Georgia) had been removed by the revolution in one way or another, there remained considerable pockets of loyalist citizens, strengthening the idea of a possible invasion of several states from Florida by British forces. Georgia, for instance, with a scattered population of 4,000 settlers, might be recovered. South Carolina, on the other hand, would be difficult.

The Palmetto State had become a royal province in 1719, its capital being Charles Town. It was one of the wealthiest colonies of the 13, and had a population of over 12,000 settlers of all classes. The elite who controlled the state owed their wealth to growing rice and indigo with the labor of 100,000 black Carolinian Negroes. Farther to the west, South Carolina's backcountry began 50 miles inland, stretching to the foothills of the Appalachian Mountains. Until 1730, this vast area was populated by Catawba and Cherokee Indian tribes. In the 1740s and 1750s, hundreds of settlers every year poured into the Carolina backcountry via the Great Philadelphia Wagon Road. The sudden influx of settlers through South Carolina's back door disrupted the orderly plan of settlement that had been initiated earlier, and encroached into Indian territory.

In 1760 the Cherokees, urged on by their French allies, launched an attack on the frontier settlements, forcing families to abandon their cabins for the safety of scattered British forts. British forces eventually came to their aid and defeated the Cherokees. In 1763, the Indian nations of the Southeast signed the Treaty of Augusta with Great Britain, with careful delineation of Indian territory. Shortly, the frontier along the Great Wagon Road attracted lawless individuals who terrorized the law-abiding farmers of the backcountry. The settlers' appeals for protection from these culprits went unheeded by the Charleston authorities. By the fall of 1767, vigilante groups scattered throughout the backcountry began cooperating with one another, calling themselves Regulators. Their goals were to regulate society, and create law and order on the frontier by ridding the backcountry of highwaymen and petty thievery. In June 1768, the Regulators passed their Plan of Regulation. For the next three years, backcountry loyalists enforced these rights and were in control of South Carolina from 50 miles inland to Cherokee territory.

No sooner had the frontier begun to calm down than a number of extra-legal organizations came into existence, such as the ones calling themselves the Moderators, who were in opposition to the Regulators. Fortunately, a military truce occurred between the two parties. It coincided with the constitutional dispute between the colonial assembly and loyalist officials, resulting in a government shutdown. At this point, royal Governor William Campbell fled Charleston for the safety of a British warship in Charleston Harbor. For all practical purposes, royal government ceased in South Carolina; an independent government of patriots had succeeded.[13]

In retaliation for the loss of the royal province to the patriots, London came up with a plan at the end of 1775, an invasion of South Carolina to restore the royal governorship and British authority. A fleet consisting of two 50-gun ships, four frigates each of 28 guns, and several smaller vessels under the command of Commodore Sir Peter Parker, transporting 2,500 redcoats under the command of General Charles Cornwallis, set sail from Cork, Ireland, on December 1775. They were to rendezvous with General Henry Clinton's British forces in America, who set sail from Boston in January 1776, with 2,800 forces. The two liberators were to meet at the mouth of the Cape Fear River, in North Carolina, for the retaking of Charleston.

Weather delays caused Clinton and his forces to be a month late in reaching Cape Fear River, arriving March 12. Here he was joined by two former governors, William Campbell of South Carolina, and Josiah Martin of North Carolina. It was alarming to Clinton that Parker's "Irish fleet" was not waiting at Cape Fear. Sir Parker's armada had been scattered on the long Atlantic crossing, finally reassembling, and arriving on May 31, 1776. Before proceeding against Charleston itself, it was thought advisable to destroy the works on Sullivan's Island, situated ten miles south of the city, at the entrance to the harbor. By now the attack was hardly a surprise to the patriots, who were commanded by Colonel William Moultrie. He was the brother to John Moultrie, lieutenant governor of East Florida, and a staunch loyalist. Colonel Moultrie's joint force of militia and Continental Army were already waiting on Sullivan's Island. General Clinton's information made him realize the folly of the invasion, but Commodore Parker talked Clinton into another ambitious plan; Clinton was to go ashore while Parker's fleet shelled the harbor defenses on Sullivan's Island. The attack was made on June 28.

Moultrie's Americans had fortified Sullivan's Island, which was defended by 375 regular soldiers and a few militia.[14] Clinton made his move, debarking his forces at the inlet at low tide on Sullivan's Island, and then to his mortification found it underwater at high tide, rendering his attack useless. On schedule, Sir Parker's Irish fleet went into action with a savage shelling of the patriots' batteries on the island, which replied with equal shelling of the invaders; the whole harbor seemed to be in flames. But the day would not belong to the Irish fleet, as their luck ran out. Three of the ships ran aground, putting them out of action. Commander Parker's flagship, the *Bristol*, was raked with 70 hits. On two occasions the cannon fire swept the quarterdeck clear of all sailors except the brave commodore, whose staying power was rewarded with his breeches being blown off by one blast.[15] At the height of the battle, South Carolina's flag (indigo blue with a silver crescent in the upper left-hand corner) was shot from its staff. Ignoring the danger, Sergeant William Jasper leaped upon the rampart, picked up the fallen flag, and tied it to a gun plunger, heartening on his comrades.[16]

For ten hours the contest was terrible as ship after ship poured in upon the fort its tremendous broadsides. The firing ceased between nine and ten in the evening as the Irish Navy, defeated, slipped their cables to the outgoing tide, drifting and then disappearing. General Cornwallis and his forces had no opportunity to participate in the day's fiasco; ship and personnel sailed for Staten Island. The siege of Sullivan's Island and Charleston was over, and the capital was safe for the time being. Great credit was given to Colonel Moultrie and his men; the fort thereafter was called Fort Moultrie.[17] The king's military forces may have accomplished something if they had shown some speed in the attack to catch the patriots unaware of their presence. As for the Irish fleet, having consumed three months in crossing the Atlantic, they arrived five months too late.

These patriots were daring fellows as depredations again began occurring around the St. Marys River. The settlers near the border were forced to drive their cattle back across the St. Johns, and Tonyn sent several small boats with a force of regulars, Rangers, and Indians to reinforce the outpost. The armed schooner *St. John* of the Royal Navy, which was already on the river, was attacked by three armed vessels from Georgia, compelling it to retire, and the inhabitants of Amelia Island had to flee to the mainland. Later on, another raid by an American party from Georgia on two plantations of Captain Benjamin Dodd, one on the St. Marys River and the other on Trout Creek, resulted in the withdrawal of the British outpost of 100 men to the south side of the St. Johns.[18] Attacks by both sides set in motion the shifting history of the no man's land between the St. Marys and St. Johns rivers.

A committee of prominent Georgians prevailed upon General Charles Lee, the American general in command of Charleston, to secure approval of the Continental Congress for an invasion of Florida to capture St. Augustine. A reconnaissance force led by Captain John McIntosh of the Georgia Line, traveling across the debatable border land of previous decades, attacked the British fort on the St. Marys River maintained by Jermyn Wright, brother of the exiled royal governor. Jermyn held over 11,000 acres in Georgia, and six plantations, including this one of 140 acres on the St. Marys River. Mr. Wright and a number of other loyalists had a stockade around Wright's mansion house that was defended by many Negroes.[19] The Tory stronghold was attacked several times but this nest of villains, as they were referred to by the patriots, could not be removed, and the patriots, with few casualties from the sortie, returned to the north.

The undaunted General Lee assembled a larger force at Savannah; 260 soldiers of the Continental Line, a contingent of Virginia and North Carolina militia, resumed the invasion of Florida. Colonel William Moultrie, brother of John Moultrie of St. Augustine, commanded the expedition as it moved south. The summer heat, the swamps of the Ogeechee with swarms of mosquitoes and biting green flies, made the march very difficult. Camp sickness from fever, no medicine chest for the little army, and then a climbing death rate caused the expedition to go no farther south than Sunbury, Georgia, some 25 miles south of Savannah, where they called it quits and returned to Savannah.[20]

Almost day-and-dating the southern failures in Georgia, the patriots in the North, under Generals John Sullivan and William "Stirling" Alexander, suffered a defeat at Long Island, New York, by the forces of Generals Henry Clinton and Charles Cornwallis. By a masterly retreat, George Washington succeeded in saving his army from a total rout. On September 16, 1776, the British took possession of New York City, and on October 28, the patriots retreated from White Plains, New York. During the fall and winter, the Continental Army suffered a series of reverses and hardships, while General Washington had all that he could do to keep his limited forces of 3,000 men from utter destruction. Thomas Paine summed up the fearful test at hand: "These are the times that try men's souls." On a bitter cold December 8, Washington and his ragtag army crossed the Delaware River at Philadelphia, while the British attempted to follow but could not get any boats for the crossing. They waited for the river to freeze over to pursue Washington's Continental forces. Congress, fearing a British attack on undefended Philadelphia, adjourned in a hurry and traveled to Baltimore, Maryland, for the next three months.

These early victories led the British command to believe that the Revolution was coming to an end. General Cornwallis turned over the army to a subordinate, no less than General James Grant, former governor of East Florida who had returned to active duty. Grant had reached Boston with General William Howe, and now succeeded Cornwallis as commander of the outposts the British left in New Jersey as they withdrew the bulk of their army to New York.

Grant still had it in for the Americans; he penned Hessian commander General Johann G. Rall: "You may be assured that the rebel army in Pennsylvania at Valley Forge, have neither the shoes nor stockings, are in fact almost naked, dying of the cold, without blankets and very ill supplied."[21] Five days later, Washington and his resolute force crossed back over the Delaware, attacking General Rall at Trenton, New Jersey, and annihilated the Hessians on December 26. The actual crossing took place in the dark, in a driving sleet storm, starting on Christmas night and finishing early the next morning. The sentries' password was "Victory or death." Washington followed through with success at Princeton, New Jersey, on January 3, 1777. Strange as it may seem, Grant's inattention to affairs and his losses did not turn out to be crucial to his position. He continued to write letters to Governor Tonyn and to his overseer at his St. Augustine villa plantation.

At St. Augustine, the British Royal Navy began showing its presence as smaller ships called at the port. The *St. John* and *Hinchinbrook* periodically anchored in the bay, while the *Lively*, *Perseus*, *Dauphine*, and *Galatea*, each manned by 160 men and mounting 20 carriage guns, patrolled the coast. As the Revolution progressed, the Royal Navy grew stronger in American waters; three-masted frigates, armed with 32 guns on two decks, served by 200-man crews, cruised the southern ports. All good and well, as the vice-admiralty court at St. Augustine reaped the rewards of captured booty, oftentimes foreign merchandise, powder, foodstuffs, and, very often, slaves.[22]

PART II

Florida in the American Revolution, 1776–1783

Prologue: Accept or Oppose the Idea of Independence?

    The effective collapse of British authority in America posed a question that most colonists had previously managed to avoid: Would they accept or oppose the idea of independence? There could be no loyalists until there were rebels, and there were no rebels until after 1773. Not until independence was perceived as the chief point of contention could anything resembling a loyalist party emerge. When it appeared the radicals decided that the connection with England should be abandoned, the loyalists broke with their countrymen. Thus there was no fixed time prior to July 4, 1776, at which the two sides can be identified, as most Englishmen were horrified by the idea of independence.[1] After the outbreak of armed fighting the issue arose.

    Afterwards, many loyalists were drawn to Tory military organizations, only to be singled out by patriot committees as enemies to the American cause. There are many stories about the emotional atmosphere engendered by the patriots among the loyalists. Lieutenant Governor of Massachusetts Thomas Oliver, being pressed to resign his position, at first absolutely refused, "Although," he observed, "the crowd swore they would have my blood." But then he considered "the distresses of my wife and children, and thus, nature, ingenious in forming new reasons, suggested to my mind the calamities which would ensure if I did not resign." Hurriedly he signed the resignation the mob's leaders thrust upon him.[2]

Names were proposed and they became objects of mob violence. Many British officials thought it best to flee to where they could be protected by royal troops in Boston, New York, and Philadelphia, which towns became islands of protection for the time being. Others set sail for Canada or London, hoping to ride out the unpleasantness and return to America at a later date. It is thought that over 7,000 faithful to the Crown left America at this time.

Southern colonies continued the harassing and passed provincial laws for anyone who aided British forces or criticized the Continental Congress. Local committees became responsible for enforcing the laws and conducting investigations of individuals charged with opposing the Revolution. Loyalty oath statutes were enacted in most states by 1777. When the local militia was formed, if you did not join the ranks you were a marked man. Once a person had been declared an enemy to the freedoms and rights of America, he could be subjected to all sorts of ingenious pressures designed to make him abandon his beliefs. The enforcers were the Sons of Liberty, who with the threat of a dress of tar and feathers, could put an individual to flight.

Despite their status as slaves, the Negroes became involved in this freedom issue. Not every patriot went to war. At the time a substitute system was practiced in the northern colonies, which permitted a man to send a Negro in his place in the ranks. George Washington's little army averaged 50 Negroes per battalion. Not so with the southern colonies, where they opposed the use of slaves to fight their battles. In 1779 the American Congress sent John Laurens south to enlist 3,000 slaves whose owners would be compensated at the rate of $1,000 a slave, but the planters of South Carolina and Georgia refused to sanction the plan. "So ventures which might have given a powerful impulse toward gradual destruction of slavery failed."[3]

Seeing the political and military advantage of bringing Negroes into their ranks, the British Army promised freedom to all slaves who would serve with them. This offer helped them acquire experienced laborers to construct forts for defense while costing the planters plenty for loss of their slaves. This strategy mostly backfired in East Florida, where the Negroes became booty for anyone to steal for resale to other colonies, usually in the West Indies.[4]

Slowly the shooting war of the Revolution moved south as the Continental Army, the regulars of the American Army as distinguished from the state militia, had strengthened their ranks. The Boston phase of the Revolution had ended, and now a collection of Continental officers moved to do battle with the British force in the Carolinas and Georgia. The curtain would come down on West Florida first as the Spaniards made their moves. In East Florida, Tonyn observed the country was filling up with strangers as the refugee movement from the north accelerated.

6

The Fighting Begins in the South, with the Invasion of East Florida

The Fighting Begins in the South

The Second Continental Congress adopted the Declaration of Independence on July 4, 1776. Ties between the colonies and the mother country had now been cut.

The British officers in East Florida during the Revolution were exceptionally able men. The present governor and commander in chief of East Florida, Patrick Tonyn, was promoted to full colonel in 1777, and moved up to major general in 1781. He was assisted by two Swiss brothers, Augustine and James Marcus Prevost, who handled the British troops in the field. Tonyn's own militia, especially the East Florida Rangers led by John Brown, were very effective in action along the Georgia-Florida border that embraced the disputed land. They commanded men loyal to England regardless of race or color. Any patriots had long fled the colony lest they become guests in the fort.

The Revolution in the northern colonies had little effect on the Floridas at this time. In the year 1777, General George Washington gained victory at Princeton, New Jersey. These were small armies fighting: at Princeton the British loss was 100 killed, 300 prisoners taken, while the patriots had fewer than 100 killed. More important to the patriots, Marquis de Lafayette from France arrived in America in April and entered the American army. He was not yet 20 years old, spoke a few words of English, and had never heard a shot fired in anger. History would record him as a symbol of liberty, enamored of American ideals, and spending $200,000 of his personal fortune in support of the rebels. Lafayette deserved the symbol of being the outstanding liberal of his day.¹

During 1777 the French supplied America with more than 20,000 muskets and 1,000 barrels of gunpowder, while Spain limited herself to furnishing secret subsidies to the colonists, $200,000 to Hortalez & Cie (a fictitious firm used to buy European war supplies for the patriots), plus another $197,230 in war materiel, and other subsidies of about $645,000. The French subsidies were almost $2,000,000, and loans over $6,000,000.²

St. Augustine was now the main station in the British Southern District and headquarters for all British brigades and various militia. Governor Tonyn was relieved to see Colonel Augustine Prevost arrive in the capital from West Florida with six companies of the 60th Regiment. At the outbreak of the Revolution, Prevost was ordered to Europe to enlist men for the 3rd and 4th Battalions of the Royal Americans. These new troops were sent to West Florida at first; he then repaired to East Florida with six companies, as colonel commandant of the 4th Battalion.³ The regiment adopted a service uniform of green instead of the typical British red coat, with the rifle as its weapon instead of a smoothbore. The Royal Americans had served with distinction with Wolfe and Prevost in Canada, and were considered a corps d'élite.⁴ Augustine Prevost's brother, Major James Marcus Prevost, was with the regiment. For the balance of the war the 60th would be supported by local militia, East Florida Rangers, and Negroes, comprising the town's main line of defense as well as offense.

Patrick Tonyn, second governor of British East Florida. (Reproduced by permission from the St. Augustine Historical Society.)

From his St. Augustine headquarters Colonel Prevost ordered his regulars to posts on the St. Johns River, stationing the Ger-

6. *The Fighting Begins in the South, with the Invasion of East Florida* 99

man recruits in the capital to work on fortifications, all the while receiving training and learning to speak English. Prevost's actions duplicated Tonyn's strategy, resulting in antagonism as to who was in command; most troubling was the existence of Tonyn's East Florida Rangers. This mounted group of 130 cavalry was organized into four companies independent of Prevost, and riding for the governor for the past year. In the future they would have to cooperate with British forces when necessary.

At the beginning of the new year 1777, it was decided that the forces in East Florida would invade Georgia for a foraging expedition in order to replenish supplies in the colony, which were running low. After some bickering between Tonyn and Prevost, Lieutenant Colonel Lewis V. Fuser was chosen to lead the raid. The force consisted of 73 British regulars and 100 East Florida Rangers under Colonels Brown and McGirth, a battery of field pieces, and a body of Creek Indians.

Moving north from St. Augustine by the King's Road, the force passed through Cowford at the St. Johns River, then marched to the St. Marys River, where they stopped at the house of Captain Taylor. They fortified the area, and named it Fort McIntosh, probably as a bit of humor, as they were marching to attack the patriot fort in Georgia with the same name. That Fort McIntosh was so named for Lachlan McIntosh, Continental general of Georgia. This fortification was located on the northeast side of the Satilla River, about halfway between the present-day towns of Waycross and Jesup, Georgia. It was a stockade work, 100 feet square, and had a bastion in each corner and a blockhouse in the center. It was garrisoned by 60 Continentals under the command of Captain Richard Winn.

After a 100-mile march, the loyalist forces had reached 45 miles into Georgia country. The mounted East Florida Rangers were the first to reach the fort. They launched an attack that lasted five hours. Colonel Brown demanded an unconditional surrender with the alternative of death for the entire garrison, to which Captain Winn replied that he was "bound in honor not to comply." With night approaching, the Rangers withdrew while Captain Winn sent a mounted man to Fort Howe, about 28 miles to the northeast, with a request for reinforcements.[5]

During the night the British regulars arrived and Colonel Fuser took command. The attack was renewed, and again in the afternoon Fuser made another demand for the fort's surrender. Captain Winn, devoid of any replacements, conferred with Colonel Fuser between the fort and British lines, and articles of capitulation were agreed upon; finally the garrison marched out and laid down their arms. Four patriots had been killed, three wounded, and 68 captured, at the cost of one Indian wounded on the British side.[6] Lieutenants John Milton and William Caldwell were taken as prisoners, while the other soldiers were paroled, not to take up arms in the American cause until regularly exchanged. Milton and Caldwell were confined in the fort at St. Augustine for nine months, until exchanged.

Meanwhile, Colonel Fuser occupied Fort McIntosh, but three days later, hearing that an American army was on the march to intercept him, he burned the fort. The expedition went about its business, intercepting and taking with them 2,000 head of cattle that had been brought in by the East Florida Rangers, who were experts in such matters.[7]

Early explorer Ponce de León had introduced a few cows during his expedition of 1520. Subsequently, with Franciscan missionaries and early Spanish rancheros maintaining cattle herds, plus the animals that fell into Indian hands, the Florida peninsula showed a marked increase in the number of cattle on the open range. Later they were referred to as "Pine Woods" cattle because they had to make do with whatever grew in the thick, desolate pine barrens of Florida. They weighed about 800 pounds on the hoof, and would yield about 300 pounds of meat that closely resembled venison in flavor. Naturally, they were sought after by Indians, Georgians, rustlers, army commissary agents, and ranchers because they were open range or free for the taking. The Floridians and Georgians recycled these animals for years. Driving these cattle back to St. Augustine took skill, especially at Cowford where they had to swim the herd across the St. Johns River. But they made it, and the cattle were scattered to various farms, and butchered for their beef and byproducts.

The peace was not expected to last long in Florida, as word arrived that Button Gwinnett of Georgia, commander in chief of the Council of Safety, had issued a proclamation inviting the people of Florida to repair to the American standard.[8] His proposal had some merit, since there were those in Florida who proposed to Tonyn that he capitulate to the Americans, agreeing that East Florida would assume an attitude of neutrality in the war, provided the Americans would not molest this colony. Tonyn argued "...that having the St. Johns River as a strong defensive line, the Floridians and the King's troops could prevent the patriot force from crossing it."[9]

The first large-scale invasion by American forces into East Florida began as Colonel Samuel Elbert with two battalions of the Continental Line and Colonel John Baker's Georgia militia began their march toward St. Augustine. The Continentals were the regulars of the American Army created in 1775 by the Continental Congress. They were made up of riflemen of the Boston Army scattered in Massachusetts, Connecticut, Rhode Island, and New Hampshire. In addition to these forces, Congress authorized the raising of Continental troops in other colonies. Georgia raised two infantry regiments in July 1776.

Not having the authority to draft men for military service, the Congress and states used various bounties to induce enlistments, especially when it became clear that the Revolution was not likely to end so speedily as was at first imagined. General Washington recommended recruits be offered at least 100 to 150 acres of land, a suit of clothes, and a blanket for enlisting, with pay varying to men who would enlist with a good firearm. The longer the war lasted, the more the bounties were increased in land and pay. In addition, 10,000 militia were put in the field by the states of Virginia, North Carolina, South Carolina, and Georgia.[10]

Colonel Elbert's Continentals marched south out of Savannah, traveling about 25 miles to Sunbury, Georgia, then took boats to the St. Marys River. He was to be joined by Colonel Baker and his 109 mounted Georgia militia at Sawpit Bluff at Rolfe's sawmill on the Nassau River, eight miles north of the St. Johns. Baker's militia overland advance was impeded by swamps and high water, plus a brush with some Indians. Baker reached the rendezvous at the appointed time but found Colonel Elbert's force had not arrived. Impatient, Baker sent his brother, Major William Baker, with 40 riders to reconnoiter the country as far as Cowford, the St. Johns River crossing. The patrol discovered that the British knew of their approach; Tonyn's men had already made preparations to withstand the attack. The patrol returned to camp and two days elapsed with still no contact with Colonel Elbert's Continentals. Baker's men were now in a precarious position at Sawpit Bluff. As the Georgia cavalrymen encamped, a party of Creek Indians stole 40 horses from the camp. Enraged, the Georgia cavalry gave pursuit and in a skirmish that cost Baker two wounded, the horses were recovered and one Indian killed, his body mutilated by the rebel horsemen. This event occurred on the Florida side of the St. Marys.[11] In all likelihood these Indians were part of the East Florida Rangers.

Since the best defense is an offensive move, Major James Marcus Prevost had crossed the St. Johns at Cowford with 100 regulars, Rangers, and Indians, marching 11 miles to Rolfe's sawmill, and encamped. A scout of the East Florida Rangers located the patriots' cavalry and brought back to Major Prevost a horse's ear as proof that he had found them.[12] At daybreak of May 17, Colonel Brown's mounted Rangers came up on the Americans on a neck of land between Trout Creek and a branch of the Nassau River, at Thomas Swamp. In accordance with orders, Brown's Rangers engaged the patriots while the main body of Prevost's regulars moved in three columns to surround them. Brown's surprise at 50 feet turned Baker's column in the direction of Prevost's expected appearance; already shaken by this sudden sniping, the patriots were quickly overwhelmed by the superior Prevost "greencoats" advancing through the heavy underbrush. At the sight of the British bayonets, half of the Georgia militia volunteers fled while Captain Ignatius Few and about 40 patriot Americans surrendered.

There then occurred one of the most horrible events of the war as the Black Creek Indians fell upon their captives. An eyewitness account: "The prisoners were all put to death, including Captain Few, except 16 who were saved by Major Prevost and some regulars." The Indians had been involved in the action two days earlier when they had stolen the horses and the Indian was mutilated at the hands of Americans. Later, Tonyn defended the Creeks: "I must acknowledge that they are very intelligent and useful spies in observing the movements of the rebels."[13] The Thomas Creek (swamp) battlefield remains wild and undeveloped, much as it was in 1777. As for the sortie, its execution in the pine barrens and swamps of Florida lent credence to the cooperating British regulars and Florida Rangers.

Colonel Elbert's Georgia amphibious Continentals from Sunbury did not reach Florida until two days after the battle at Thomas Swamp, landing on the north end of Amelia Island, opposite the mouth of the St. Marys River. Here they were joined by the survivors of Baker's militia, who told their story of defeat. Elbert's excuse for not rallying with Baker was that the St. Marys passage was guarded by two British warships, and the American naval force had been turned back after a warm engagement with the British ship *Rebecca*, carrying ten carriage guns. Elbert also had intelligence from his scouts that the south side of the St. Johns at St. Johns Bluff was armed with cannon; thus he abandoned his attempt to invade East Florida and join Baker as planned.

Colonel Elbert's Continentals went ashore near the present site of Fernandina, Florida, where French Admiral Jean Ribault dropped anchor in the St. Marys River in 1582 and claimed Amelia Island, Isle de Mai, as a possession of France. The ownership of the island had then been juggled back and forth between the French and Spanish, and it was now a part of East Florida. The 650 square miles of land were largely devoted to forestry and agricultural products. Similar patterns of British colonization were apparent at Amelia Island. "Lord Edmont's plantation on Amelia Island contained eight or nine thousand acres of land. A town was laid out at the northern end in 1770. The land was under the care first of Martin Jollie, later of Stephen Egan, who was visited there by William Bartram. Indigo was raised successfully, and Bartram describes the island as excellent hummocky land, suitable for cotton, corn, and also every other esculent vegetable. Other plantations were small, made up of local grants, seldom exceeding one thousand acres."[14]

Colonel Elbert sent a patrol to the south end of the island, and a skirmish ensued with a party of British forces which had advanced to meet them. Patriot Lieutenant Ward was killed and two of his patrol were wounded. In retaliation, Elbert ordered every house on the island to be burned and all the cattle destroyed. The colonel believed that he could not advance into East Florida without the British having timely notice from friends among the American informers. Lacking provisions, and learning that the mouth of the St. Marys was clear of British ships, he proceeded sailing up the St. Marys, searching for foraging parties of Floridians, keeping them for a time out of Georgia. He abandoned the failed expedition, and marched back to Savannah while his ships returned to Sunbury.[15]

A written statement of the facts of this escapade sounded the signal of what was in store for St. Augustine, East Florida, and Governor Tonyn. Turncoat white Americans traitorously switched allegiance and ravished those who remained loyal to the Crown. The humble memorial of William Chapman follows in a digest form: "William Chapman and his sons were induced to purchase in 1773, 40,000 acres in the Province of East Florida. They engaged proper agents, hired vessels, purchased implements, utensils, cattle, clothing, and sent over to said intended settlement. In February 1774, Chapman and his sons purchased 12,000 acres of land from Wm. Knox, Esq., situated on the River St. Marys on the northern boundary of East Florida. Chapman and his sons erected buildings, cleared land and established a rice plantation in a likely way of reaping adequate profits. When in consequence of the unhappy dissentions at that time prevailing in America and the refusal of Chapman and his sons to join the revolters against his Majesty's Government, they found it necessary to take flight in the night of May 22, 1776, to Amelia Island, with such of 35 Negroes and effects as they could carry off in the plantation boats, but leaving behind the stock of cattle, hogs, and other valuable effects. In 1777, afterwards the revolters (Colonel Elbert) came over to Chapman's plantation, set fire to all the buildings, destroyed their crop of rice, drove off their cattle, and carried off or dispersed the Negroes; Chapman and his sons did not remain long on Amelia Island as the ravages of the revolters forced them to retire to the St. Johns River and to settle a small tract which they bought near Picolata Fort with a view of subsisting themselves and Negroes by the cutting of lumber and raising naval stores until such time as the hoped for success of his Majesty's Arms should enable them to return to the Plantation on St. Marys River which was capable of bringing in a very ample income."[16] Within a few short years of arriving in America, Chapman and his sons were transformed from being profitable planters into refugees of the war.

This and many other factual narratives all had the same ending, financial ruin by insolvency in East Florida. Chapman and his family were close to the border, crossing over quickly. But loyalists in North Carolina, South Carolina, and Georgia had a long trek overland on the King's Highway, or along Indian and traders' paths, or by water, by whatever mode they could make it safely to get away from the patriots. Abandoning their homes or farms, and moving by foot, horse, wagon, or boats, they traveled south to the King's refuge in East Florida. Fort Tonyn was established at the St. Marys River, most likely in the vicinity of the King's Road crossing, as loyalist refugees flowed toward the border to take up arms for His Majesty's cause in East Florida.

By way of the Broad and Saluda Rivers in South Carolina, 350 loyalists arrived at Fort Tonyn. Of these descendants of the Palatines, 150 were mounted. They were conducted to St. Augustine, where they presented a memorial to General Prevost, saying they were willing to serve under him but wished to remain a part of the troops of South Carolina, choosing their own officers. Prevost embodied 260 of them as the South Carolina Royalists and placed them under the charge of his brother, Major Marcus Prevost, for drill and discipline. They became rifle dragoons and were assigned to duty on the St. Johns River.[17] Colonel Alexander Innes was in command, as arranged previously by Lord William Campbell, the last royal governor of South Carolina.

Shortly after the arrival came an even larger company of loyalists known as the Scopholites, from one of their leaders, Colonel Scophol of the South Carolina militia. They had assembled near Ninety Six, South Carolina, coming from the interior of the colony. The settlement began at the 96th milepost on a trail used by traders with the Indians, marking the distance northward to Keowee, a Cherokee Indian village in the foothills of the Blue Ridge Mountains. The first land battle of the Revolutionary War in the South was fought at Ninety Six in November 1775, when about 500 patriots hastily built a rustic fort of fence and rails, and fought an attack from a large British force of Tories. There were casualties on both sides, the battle ending with a formal truce. The British later on fortified Ninety Six, building a stockade. The present force under Colonel Scophol were an outgrowth of the Regulator movement in South Carolina in prerevolutionary days.

Colonel Scophol's combatants, after crossing the Savannah River some 40 miles below Augusta, Georgia, were joined by a party from Georgia under the command of Colonel Thomas, the joined forces numbering 400–500 men. Passing through scattered Georgia settlements and farms, they plundered and destroyed, seeking sustenance for the journey to Fort Tonyn. They too would be afforded provincial designation.

Political refugees from North Carolina also arrived in East Florida during this time. Colonel Mills of Green River recruited 500 loyalists for the purpose of joining the British at St. Augustine, but Mills and 16 others were betrayed and lodged in Salisbury jail. Doubtless some of Mills's men succeeded in crossing the St. Marys River. Lieutenant Colonel John Hamilton, a merchant of Halifax, North Carolina, took his loyalists to New York, and some months later proceeded to St. Augustine, where he formed his corps, the Royal North Carolina Regiment, partly of refugees from other southern provinces.[18] There were 460 men in eight companies. Governor Tonyn and Colonel Prevost began amassing a larger expeditionary force to invade Georgia.

There now ensued a period of watchful waiting for an encroachment by either side, north of the St. Johns River or south of the St. Marys River, each side expecting an invasion from the other. Elsewhere in the north, the patriots crushed the Hessian forces at Bennington, Vermont, putting English troops to flight. Next came the defeat of the Americans at Brandywine as the British, under General Sir William Howe, advanced on Philadelphia. The American Congress was forced to move hastily to York, Pennsylvania, where it met in the county courthouse for the next year, while the British occupied Philadelphia, the capital of the rebellion.[19] On October 4, 1777, Washington's forces met defeat in the battle of Germantown. In December 1777, Washington's army went into camp at Valley Forge, and his army endured untold sufferings. Confidence in General Washington was shaken, and the cause of the colonies looked dark. The English then had matters almost their own way as they closed out 1777.

But their good fortune ran out in February 1778. France recognized the United States as an independent nation and agreed to a military alliance which included large-scale French aid, including a powerful army and fleet soon to begin arriving in the United States. Hence, France continued its enmity with England, and Spain would follow in this maelstrom of international rivalries.

By this time, American planters and farmers along the Florida-Georgia border deserted their settlements in fear of an advance out of East Florida. In addition, Colonel Elbert received a message from Major James Marcus Prevost, saying among other things that in the future all small parties found in arms beyond the limits of Georgia would be regarded as robbers and murderers. Regardless, Prevost received intelligence in February 1778 that the Americans were preparing for another invasion, despite the strengthening of the British in East Florida by a stream of refugees from the great defection in the backcountry of South Carolina. Scores of small parties of five or six men each were reported in Georgia to be going from Carolina into Florida.[20] While the Continental Congress was discussing plans for the invasion of East Florida by a southern force under Major General Robert Howe and Colonel Elbert, the initial action was taken by the Floridians. Under orders from Governor Tonyn, Lieutenant Colonel Brown, with a scouting party of 100 Rangers and 10 Indian scouts, crossed the border, trudged through southern Georgia to the Altamaha River, swam a quarter-mile across the Altamaha, and traversed many swamps to attack Fort Barrington in March 1778. Taken completely by surprise, the patriots surrendered. Casualties amounted to two Americans killed, four wounded, 23 taken prisoner, and at a cost of one killed and four wounded on the

British side. The fort was then burned down and detachments of the Rangers sent on service in Georgia. Brown and the remainder retired to a post which was established on the St. Marys, Fort Tonyn.[21] The captured prisoners were marched to St. Augustine.

The lot of the Revolutionary War prisoner was hard, as neither the British nor the Americans were prepared to take care of those they captured. The first were the political prisoners, then the fishermen, privateers, officers, and sailors of the navies, and then came the large hauls of men who surrendered and those captured, Whigs or Tories. There was always the chance of being exchanged, but till then — which never seemed to come — they were cast into lockups. Later on, the British used prison ships in New York and elsewhere, and transported some prisoners to jails in England. American military prisoners were packed into improvised quarters and died in large numbers. "Loyalists were subjected to equal horrors in such places as the abandoned Simsbury copper mines in Connecticut."[22] At St. Augustine, Governor Tonyn used the old fort and its dungeon to keep his prisoners that were brought to town. It started out with a trickle of prisoners, but as the Revolution advanced in the South so did the number of prisoners increase. Other facilities would be commandeered as needed.

Invasion of East Florida

The first thrust of the southern invasion of East Florida began at Frederica, Georgia, north of present-day Brunswick. Colonel Elbert, with 300 regulars and two fieldpieces, sailing in three galleys, surprised two armed British ships, the *Hinchenbrook* and *Rebecca*, and effected their capture without the loss of a man.[23] Meantime, three British vessels in service off the East Florida coast intercepted several merchant ships from France, capturing 16 officers and 200 soldiers who were on their way to Washington's patriots. The Frenchmen were landed at St. Augustine and kept prisoners of war in the large Statehouse, while captured seamen were impressed into service on His Majesty's warships.[24]

At the same time, General Robert Howe's marching Continentals were approaching the East Florida border. Robert Howe was the son of a wealthy planter from North Carolina who had taken command of the American Southern Department in October 1777. Howe was not related to the British Howe brothers who were officers. Two regiments were under the command of Colonels Elbert and Charles Cotesworth

Pinckney of South Carolina. Pinckney earlier had served as aide-de-camp to George Washington at the battles of Brandywine and Germantown in the fall of 1777. In addition to the 3,000 regulars, there were 1,200 Georgia militia commanded by Governor William Houstoun. The Florida officers and men were well informed of the enemy's movement since they were fighting on familiar ground. General Prevost's plan of defense was to make no resistance north of the St. Marys but to oppose the passage of that river with Brown's East Florida Rangers and the South Carolina Royalists of his brother, Marcus Prevost.

On June 23rd the Americans crossed the Satilla River and encamped not far from British Fort McIntosh on the St. Marys. Brown's Rangers and Indians advanced to Fort McIntosh when the parties found themselves hemmed in and surrounded by General James Screven with his detachments of Continental regulars. Cut off, Brown and his Rangers were forced into Cabbage Swamp, where they resisted American efforts to ferret them out. In the meantime, Prevost sent forward his brother Marcus with 450 British regulars and South Carolina Royalists to Alligator Bridge, some 18 miles due north of Cowford. From Alligator Bridge, 200 regulars were sent forward to rescue Colonel Brown and his Rangers from the swamp. From this position they were extricated by a body of regulars under Major Graham, and fell back toward the position at Alligator Bridge. Although the Rangers came out of the swamp, many of them had lost their rifles.[25]

Meanwhile the American Continentals entered the Amelia Narrows, near the present site of Fernandina, making junction with the American fleet under Commodore Bowen. There were about 800 men with the naval force, which consisted of five galleys, two flats, two pettiaugers, and several sloops and schooners.[26] It now seemed the Americans were everywhere. While the rescue of the Rangers was being effected, Prevost sent another detachment of British to disperse a party of American troops encamped at Nassau Bluff, on the north side of the Nassau River near its mouth. This having been accomplished, the British party returned to the camp at Alligator Bridge, reaching there at about the same time that the rescued Rangers did. Alligator Creek was east of Callahan, Florida, and the British camp was surrounded by a trench and entanglements of log and brush. As the Rangers were crossing the bridge into camp, a party of 300 American horsemen, which had been sent by General Howe, fell upon them, shouting, "Down with the Tories."[27]

Colonel Elijah Clarke had pursued Brown's Rangers and had attacked expecting to break through a weak point in the British fieldwork; but the horses had trouble getting through the obstacles of logs and brush because the ditch dug was too wide for the horses to jump.[28] There was a short, hot engagement that lasted until Colonel Clarke was wounded; the loss of Clarke seemed to dishearten the patriots as they withdrew with a loss of three killed, nine wounded and one captured. Prevost lost one man and eight wounded. The next day the British withdrew to a strong position on Trout Creek, six miles north of Cowford, leaving a few Indians to observe the American forces. On June 30, Lieutenant Colonel Brown sent word to Governor Tonyn from Alligator Creek bridge that he had met and driven back the rebels with the aid of Major Prevost's regulars.

The people of St. Augustine were so alarmed by the approach of the American forces that many citizens carried their valuables onto ships. In addition the intelligence received by General Howe that the two lines of defense of the city were weak and in bad repair, and that the garrison of the fort had plenty of provisions, but not enough for the population of the town, encouraged him to continue the attack.

General Howe and 400 Continental regulars marked time waiting for Georgia Governor Houstoun and South Carolina General Andrew Williamson to catch up with their militia, which never happened. The jinxed and ill-fated Howe soon recognized there were hopeless factional differences among his chosen officers. Governor Houstoun of Georgia insisted upon his constitutional right to command his militia and refused to obey Howe. Commodore Bowen insisted that his naval force was independent of the patriot army. Far more unforgettable for General Howe was that his army had lost a considerable number killed, wounded, and captured, but his heaviest losses had been due to sickness in the field; more than 300 South Carolina Continentals had died from heatstroke, food poisoning, putrid drinking water, fatigue — yet not one from the shot of a rifle.

The character of land in Florida, Georgia, and South Carolina along the coastal areas was pretty much the same. Once one got off the King's Highway it was tough terrain of oak trees, heavy brush, swamps, rivers, and streams to conquer. Here in the South there was a tropical exposure to sun, heat, violent rainstorms, and no fresh water for man or animals. And when the day was done, there was no safe place to bivouac. If poisonous snakes or alligators didn't find the troopers, biting gnats in the swamps and bloodsucking mosquitoes, vectors of malaria and yellow fever, had to be dealt with. They found no facilities for toilet or bathing, unless they crossed a river. The woolen garments, heavy muskets, and stiff leather shoes made the march that much harder. The British forces had the same experiences. On a move to Sunbury, "The troops several times were forced to subsist on a small supply of rice and oysters which they found in bays and inlets. One group of soldiers lived for three days upon the flesh of an alligator and some Madeira wine from a ship which had been wrecked on the beach. However, when they reached Jekyll Island, they had a treat, horseflesh."[29]

Under such adversity and with the command torn by factions, it is no wonder that after a council of officers it was decided to abandon the invasion. The splintered and dejected Americans crossed back over the St. Marys for a long march home while being harassed with rearguard action by Prevost's men, so ending the last serious attempt by patriot Americans to invade East Florida.[30]

The next move was a strategical expedition by British General Henry Clinton, located in New York, to seize back Savannah, Georgia, from the patriots. General Clinton had been involved in the Battle of Bunker Hill and had distinguished himself at the battle of Long Island; he was one of the Crown's top generals. General Prevost had been notified of the expedition by General Clinton under the date of October 20, 1778. This time of the year suited Prevost; short days and long nights kept the hot weather under control, and was more desirable for the invasion of Georgia by the Florida forces. Although of no consequence to the strategy of General Clinton, this movement on Savannah was something a little different for the Florida Rangers. Up to now this militia had served the colony and Governor Tonyn well in defending their families, farms, and plantations from the trepidations of the American patriots. From all accounts over the two-year period, they mustered over 100 horsemen when called upon, and were considered the governor's cavalry, "split shirt banditti and a parcel of horse thieves and villains."[31] One thing for certain, they always came back to St. Augustine with seizures of cattle, horses or other spoils, with remuneration in mind. Would this sortie into Georgia be of any such personal benefit to them and the governor, or would it essentially be their duty as soldiers of East Florida Rangers to cooperate on such an important stratagem?

Over his term as governor, Tonyn had been accused of many

improprieties which fell under the disguise of perks and capers of the office. It was alleged that he granted lands to some persons not entitled to them and refused grants to others who were entitled. It was rumored that he had borrowed money from many of the inhabitants, giving them bills payable in London that came back protested; that he had obtained receipts for public work done and then refused to pay the workmen; that he had bought up staple provisions and tried to sell them at a double price; that he inflicted cruel punishments on his servants and Negroes; and that the master builder had refused to repair the platform for the guns in Fort George on account of Tonyn's failure to pay workmen.[32]

Whether Tonyn had a material interest is difficult to prove. "The charge Tonyn profited from the sale of the stolen cattle is borne out by one of the officers of the 60th Regiment, who wrote that in one raid the Rangers brought 1,800 head of cattle to the St. Johns, where they were sold by Government or Tonyn to Messrs. Mackenzie and Pontio Sanchez, for 25 shillings per head, who sold the beef at 3d [penny] per pound in the public market."[33] Even early in the autumn of 1778, Negroes, horses, and other property in Georgia were being continually carried off by "Tonyn's banditti," who came from East Florida in small companies; when captured, these raiders claimed treatment as prisoners of war on the grounds they were soldiers in the king's service.[34] Regardless of what we charge Governor Tonyn of doing in those days, it was common practice for officers in authority to receive extra compensation, whether it was skimming cash (very unlikely here) or sharing in the spoils of war. The standard among patriots and loyalists was the same thin line of conscience defining the difference between "foraging" and "plundering."

As commander in chief and later a general, Tonyn kowtowed to no one. He and Prevost were like oil and water; Prevost claimed he was in command of the military while Tonyn refused to recognize his authority. The great bitterness between the two officers never interfered or obstructed field operations, which were outside Tonyn's magistracy. As recently as April 1778, at the time the regulars and Rangers were to march north to resist a threatened attack on the St. Marys River by the Americans, Prevost refused to send an officer to be under Colonel Brown's command, and so ordered the regulars not to cross the St. Johns. Thereupon, Tonyn wrote, "that the public service might not suffer, I give up for a time what I think my right," and told Brown to give up the command, and submit to the orders of Major Beamsley Glazier.

Tonyn was a strong supporter of military assistance from the Creek Indians, while Prevost was skeptical. He did have the friendship of the local Creeks Pumpkin King and Long Warrior, who were in the proximity of St. Augustine. John Stuart, Superintendent of Indian Affairs, Southern District, preferred to keep the Creek, Cherokee, and Choctaw nations neutral and friendly, and not use them for military affairs. According to accounts, the western frontier of Georgia had as neighbors at least 15,000 Indian warriors. In 1777 and 1778, Tonyn wrote directly to Stuart's Indian agents among these nations, requesting them to bring about Indian raids into South Carolina and Georgia as a diversion to a threatened American invasion of East Florida. Only a few hundred Indians were forthcoming, which stirred Tonyn to further condemnation of Stuart. As one might guess, Alexander Skinner, the keeper of Indian presents and commissary supplies, was a busy man under Tonyn.[35]

Stuart was not the only one he harassed, as Dr. Turnbull and others became subject to charges from Tonyn. Tonyn disregarded the Court of Sessions decision that many of Turnbull's indentured people were still bound by their contracts. With Tonyn's encouragement, most of them had removed from New Smyrna to the capital. When Dr. Turnbull returned to St. Augustine from England, the governor alleged that Turnbull was evading the payment of a large indebtedness on the New Smyrna estate, despite the fact that Tonyn had previously admitted that the doctor's reverses there had left him without the means of payment. Nevertheless, an order was issued requiring Turnbull to pay 4,000 pounds bail. Being unable to do so, Turnbull was taken into custody by the provost marshal and kept a prisoner for a year and seven months. The property at New Smyrna was divided among the heirs of the original proprietors, and only a small part of the proceeds fell to Dr. Turnbull who, when released, took residence in Charleston, South Carolina.[36]

7

Battles for Georgia and South Carolina

In 1775, Moses Kirkland, a British informer from South Carolina, sailed to Boston to report on conditions in the Carolinas. He was captured not far from his destination by a Continental schooner. Because he was carrying charts of Charleston and its harbor, he landed in a Philadelphia prison — but not for long. Escaping jail in the spring of 1776, he returned to East Florida, where he was appointed a deputy in the district of the Seminole and Creek Indians. In March 1778, the determined Kirkland set sail from St. Augustine for Philadelphia to submit a plan for the invasion of Georgia and South Carolina; a British drive would sever the vital flow of money and supplies to the patriots into southern ports from French and Dutch islands in the Caribbean, plus recapture Georgia and South Carolina, which could help stem the colonial rebellion.[1]

This time Kirkland reached and completed his assignment, with approval of his invasion strategy from Sir Henry Clinton. The conquest of Georgia would begin as a pincer movement, with American patriots being attacked from the south and the north. General Prevost's East Florida forces would invade Georgia, reduce and capture the seaport of Sunbury, and then continue north to lay siege to Savannah. Concurring was General Clinton's expedition by sea to lay siege of the Georgia capital.

In November, two detachments were sent forward from St. Augustine by General Prevost; the land detachment in the charge of Marcus Prevost, the general's brother, would move north on the King's Highway into Georgia to devastate the country through lower Georgia. There were over 150 cavalrymen: South Carolina Royalists, East Florida Rangers, and grenadiers of 2d and 3rd Battalions, 60th Regiment. At Fort Howe they were joined by Daniel McGirth with 300 provincial forces and Indians. The fast-moving cavalry proceeded to the Sapello River and there waited for the infantry to come up.

The second contingent, in the command of Lieutenant Colonel Lewis V. Fuser, made up 250 men of the 4th Battalion, 60th Regiment. Fuser's forces were to go by inland channel, water route, with the armed flat *Thunderer*, while the privateers *Spitfire* and *Alligator* were to alarm the coast. Eventually the two loyalist forces were to converge on Sunbury, Georgia, and capture the town. Sunbury was a thriving town with a population estimated at about 1,000 inhabitants, and was a busy seaport, a worthy rival of Savannah. A low bluff on the Medway River was fortified and garrisoned by 200 patriot forces at Fort Morris.[2]

Marcus Prevost's forces continued through southern Georgia settlements, taking captives and plunder from the plantations as they went. Near Midway they learned that a small force of patriots was in the vicinity to hinder Prevost's advance. Midway was 24 miles southwest of Savannah and about 10 miles west of Sunbury. The two villages were Congregationalist communities, politically active, and espoused the American cause, since townsmen Button Gwinnett and Dr. Lyman Hall were two signers of the Declaration of Independence.

At Midway Meeting-House, Colonel John White of North Carolina, commander of the 4th Georgia Continentals, had posted 200 men and two cannon at a breastwork south of the church. When Brigadier General James Screven arrived with 20 militia, he ordered the patriot force to advance a mile and half south to establish a new defense line. When the two forces came together a brisk skirmish ensued. Marcus Prevost's horse was shot from under him. Uninjured, he mounted another horse to rally his men, and withstood General Screven's charge. While the Continentals were embroiled in the affair, 27-year-old General Screven was wounded. Two local doctors were allowed to enter British lines that night to attend him, but their efforts were futile; General Screven expired after a few hours, beckoning Colonel White to withdraw his forces through Midway.[3] Prevost sent Daniel McGirth on a reconnaissance to Sunbury to locate Colonel Fuser's forces, only to find that Fuser had not arrived there. After burning Midway Meeting-House, Marcus Prevost and his force retreated, destroying all buildings and carrying off quantities of booty along their march.

The irony of this day is that Colonel Fuser had landed his forces a few miles south of Sunbury at Colonel's Island the day of Prevost's encounter at Midway. Here, Fuser learned that 300 patriots had marched to Sunbury and took refuge in Fort Morris. Leaving 60 men behind with the boats, Fuser's detachment of about 200 loyalists, under the guidance of several East Florida Rangers, moved toward Sunbury. Meantime, Colonel Fuser sent Captain Johnston of the Rangers to Midway, seeking out Prevost's force. The next day the armed vessels sailed upriver to help Fuser's force invest Fort Morris as Captain Johnston returned from Midway with the news that Prevost's forces were on their way to Ogeechee. Without Prevost's men, Fuser in desperation summoned the fort to surrender, but received the reply, "Come and take it." It was worth the try, although history offers hundreds of examples of men fighting well from behind walls, but Prevost forbade the storming of the fort and conducted his forces back to the vessels, sailing back to the St. Johns River. When Colonel Prevost reached St. Marys, he had a public sale of his pillage; Negroes, horses, cattle, poultry brought in 8,000 British pounds. From here Colonel Prevost led his force to the St. Johns River, where Colonel Fuser was waiting. Each charged the other with failure of the expedition.[4] No mention is made of how many shared in the piracy.

With his detachment en route back to St. Augustine from the abortive attempt to capture Sunbury, Colonel Fuser received orders via courier from Prevost at St. Augustine to halt his command at the south end of Cumberland Island, where the St. Marys harbor served a sheltered offshore anchorage for British armed vessels.[5] In St. Augustine, General Prevost incorporated his brother Marcus's detachment with his own forces, leaving behind Major Beamsley Glazier's four companies to guard St. Augustine. At Cumberland Island, Colonel Fuser's forces were added to Prevost's expeditionary legion, including three new companies of New Jersey volunteers under Lieutenant Colonel Isaac Allen, sent by Colonel Campbell. All total, General Prevost's force numbered 900 officers and men, with Marcus Prevost second in command. This small army from East Florida moved north by the inland passage in small boats, accompanied by a flotilla of supply ships which had to skirt the coast and make wide detours to escape American armed vessels patrolling the area. Once again their goal was Sunbury; but this time the Continental Army commanded by General Robert Howe was at Fort Morris at Sunbury, with regulars and militia.

The other part of the invasion, General Clinton's expedition by sea, carried two commanders, General John Campbell en route to take command in West Florida, and Lieutenant Colonel Archibald Campbell, in charge of the Georgia movement. On November 27, 1778, Colonel Campbell sailed from Sandy Hook, Philadelphia, with 3,500 troops escorted by a squadron led by Admiral Peter Parker. On December 23, the expedition anchored off Tybee Island at the mouth of the Savannah River. Although a military engineer, Colonel Campbell lacked information on which to plan his strategy. On Christmas night he sent Grenadier Captain Sir James Baird ashore with a light infantry company. The captain picked up two local loyalists who furnished Colonel Campbell with satisfactory intelligence concerning the state of affairs at Savannah. This encouraging information convinced Campbell that he and Parker could capture Savannah without waiting for Prevost's forces to join them.[6]

Landing two miles below Savannah at Girardeau's plantation, on December 28, two American galleys sounded the alarm of the British egression. On the 29th a British light infantry came ashore and immediately was met by Captain J.C. Smith and 50 South Carolina Continentals posted at Brewton's Hill. After rebel fire had killed three men and wounded five, the British Highlanders drove Smith's outpost back and secured a beachhead for the army. Informed that British ships were at Savannah, General Howe rapidly returned to Savannah with 700 Continentals and 150 militia, leaving Major Lane with 200 Continentals at Sunbury. Howe established his main line of defense half a mile southeast of Savannah to cover the road that led from the enemy landing site. This road crossed a marshy stream by a causeway and was flanked on the river side by the rice swamps of exiled Governor Wright's plantation, and by wooded swamps on the other side. Howe's main line was 200 yards behind the stream. The bridge at that point was destroyed and a trench was dug. Although outnumbered four to one, Howe's patriots appeared to be in a good position that left the British no choice but to make a costly frontal attack.

General Howe's main line of defense was Georgia militia under Colonel Samuel Elbert; South Carolina Continentals under Colonel Isaac Huger; Lieutenant Colonel William Thompson's 3d Rangers; and Colonel George Walton, posted on Huger's right in some buildings with 100 Georgia militia riflemen and a cannon. On the 29th of

December, the main body of Campbell's forces advanced, and then halted and formed on the river side of the road, 800 yards from the American line. In his report General Campbell said, "I could discover from the movements of the enemy that they wished and expected an attack upon their left." When is not known, but the British accidentally picked up an old Negro named Quamino Dolly who told Campbell of an obscure path through the swamps and around the American right, left unguarded by Howe. General Campbell skillfully used a feigned attack by sending the 1st Battalion of the 71st Regiment to join the light infantry and convey the impression that he was strengthening this wing for an attack of the patriots' left.

Unaware of the real danger, Howe began cannonading Campbell's line. Meanwhile, Baird's light infantry and Turnbull's New York volunteers slipped to the rear and circled around to execute the turning movement. Captain Baird reached White Bluff Road undetected and pressed on to wipe out Walton's Georgia unit by an attack from the flank and rear. At the sound of Baird's attack, Campbell had his guns run forward from concealed positions to open on the American line, and his infantry charged. Assailed suddenly, General Howe had no other choice but to order a general retreat across the swamp causeway. His men had to fight their way through British forces. The American right and center got across with difficulty, saving their artillery, but Elbert's Georgia militia were cut off from the causeway and had to retreat through flooded Musgrove Swamp, causing many to drown while others surrendered. At Savannah the patriots lost 83 killed or drowned, and 453 (including 38 officers) captured. The British had three killed and ten wounded.[7]

That night the discouraged forces of General Howe marched eight miles to Cherokee Hill and camped. Crossing over the Savannah River the next day, Howe joined Major General Benjamin Lincoln at Purysburg, South Carolina. Lincoln had just been appointed commander of the Southern Department and arrived at Charleston on December 4, too late to play any part in preventing the British capture of Savannah on the 29th.

The existence of Georgia as an American colony depended on the outcome at Sunbury against the invading East Florida forces under General Prevost. His land forces had been delayed by various causes: poor and limited roads, being encumbered with wagons and artillery, but especially by the inexperience of transporting artillery and other impediments by boat through the inland watercourses of Florida and Georgia. On January 6, 1779, Prevost reached Colonel's Island, a few miles below Sunbury. For the next two days the fort and town were invested by troops and artillery. Major Lane, commander of Fort Morris, once again refused to capitulate, ergo Prevost ordered his batteries to commence firing. After a short but heavy bombardment, the fort surrendered on January 9, 1779. The fort contained about 200 officers and men, and an additional 100 prisoners were brought in from the neighborhood by mounted rangers. The patriot prisoners were ferried to Savannah with the Grenadiers' Royal Infantry accompanying them as escort by the inland passageway. Lieutenant Colonel Allen and his New Jersey volunteers were detailed to garrison duty at Fort Morris, which was renamed Fort George (eventually this fort was renamed Fort Defiance during the War of 1812). Lieutenant Colonel John Hamilton's Royal North Carolina Regiment marched out and arrived at Savannah in advance of Prevost's main body of men.

The balance of the army marched via Midway to Savannah. General Prevost was escorted by a party of dragoons from Campbell's mounted infantry, while the country in front was scoured by East Florida Rangers. At Savannah, Prevost's force was called the Florida Brigade.[8] Prior to Prevost's arrival, Colonel Campbell placed Colonel Innes in command at Savannah in order that he himself could lead an expedition up the Savannah River against Augusta. The Royal North Carolina Regiment of 200 mounted infantry led the incursion as Whig militia at Augusta scattered and evacuated the town. Very much like at Savannah, Tories flocked to Augusta to take the oath, join ranks, and be assigned to patrol duty in the backcountry, and of course the Great Wagon Road would determine the maneuvering of most fighting in the South. The Royal North Carolina force was detached from Augusta, riding toward the frontier of Georgia, disarming patriots, reducing a number of wooden stockades, and doing battle with a body of Americans under Colonel Andrew Pickens, who had advanced against Campbell from the Ninety Six district. By the middle of February 1779, Colonel Campbell had the area occupied as best as possible with limited forces.[9] At Savannah the British forces were welcomed by many merchants, while many upland patriots opposed them.

It was after the occupation of Augusta by Campbell and Hamilton that General Prevost and his men made their belated entrance into Savannah. Soon after the Florida brigade had reached Savannah, Major

General Benjamin Lincoln's forces undertook a counteroffensive to recover Georgia, starting first with Augusta. When General Andrew Williamson's and General John Ashe's forces appeared outside Augusta, Campbell evacuated the town. General Ashe crossed into Georgia and began to descend the Savannah River. At Briar Creek he found the bridge demolished. Fifteen miles below on the Savannah was Hudson's Ferry, a fortified British outpost. While Ashe's men repaired the bridge, General Prevost ordered reinforcements to Hudson's Ferry, choosing his younger brother, Lieutenant Colonel Marcus Prevost, to lead a counterstroke. Prevost, with a body of light infantry and the St. Augustine Grenadiers, executed a wide circuit westward and attacked the American rear, which was backed up against the swamp, the bridge not finished. Trapped, Ashe's soldiers headed for the swamps and the Savannah River, where many drowned but large numbers escaped by swimming or on rafts. Two hundred patriots were killed or drowned and over 170 captured. The British restored their hold on Georgia in March of 1779.[10] Communication was kept open between the British posts and frontier settlements.

Lieutenant Colonel Prevost so impressed Colonel Campbell that when he and Hamilton withdrew, Campbell transferred his force to Prevost and returned to Savannah preparatory to his departure for England. At Savannah, Campbell made Marcus Prevost lieutenant governor of Georgia; he was acting governor until exiled Governor Sir James Wright returned from England in July. In the interim Prevost set up the Royal Government of Georgia. James Robertson, a Georgian banished for refusing to take the oath of abjuration, was summoned from St. Augustine to be his attorney general. At about the same time, his brother Brigadier General Augustine Prevost was promoted to major-general.[11] He now had 2,400 men, including the loyalist regiments from East Florida; also the East Florida navy was put under Prevost's command.

Learning that Charleston was undefended, and with the boundary of South Carolina only three days' march away, General Prevost decided to attempt its capture. Prevost first sent a small force by ship to Port Royal Island, where South Carolina militia drove the sortie away. Not to be denied, the British force had little difficulty in crossing numerous rivers and creeks that were left undefended by the patriots, working their way north toward Charleston. General William Moultrie, brother to John Moultrie, former lieutenant governor of East Florida, hastily built land fortifications and earthen works to defend the city. Once across the Ashley River, Prevost's British forces on May 10 summoned Charleston to surrender. After receiving proposals from Governor John Rutledge about surrendering the town, the British commander said he was not prepared to negotiate over civilian matters, and insisted the civilian authorities as well as the army were to become prisoners of war. Learning from loyalist informants that an American army under General Benjamin Lincoln was approaching, Prevost decided that the American lines could not be forced at this time without a great loss of his men; thus he recrossed the Ashley and encamped, later retiring to the seacoast and occupying Johns Island, South Carolina.

Nevertheless a battle did take place at Stono Ferry, South Carolina. When Prevost withdrew, he left Lieutenant Colonel John Maitland in command of a 900-man rear guard on the islands south of Charleston. To cover Stono Ferry from the mainland, actually James Island, Maitland had three strong redoubts and a bridge of boats connecting this position with Johns Island. Why such a large contingent of soldiers to cover a retreat? In all actuality General Prevost had his hands full, not with the enemy but with thousands of Negroes who had followed his army as they moved north, passing through the richest plantations on the way.

The British saw the political, economic, and military advantages of bringing American slaves into their camp. The British promised freedom to all slaves who served them, hoping to acquire a labor force while ruining the patriot owners. For the time being, thousands of Negroes were camped at Stono Ferry crossing. Unavoidably, camp fever raged among them, and the sick were forsaken and died in the woods. General Lincoln arrived at Charleston and decided to attack this isolated British outpost with a force of 1,200 Continentals. He personally led the main effort of attack; shortly after sunrise Lincoln's columns struggled through the dense woods to open fire on the German rear guard. The veteran Hessians rallied and, with the help of reserves from Johns Island, put Lincoln's army in retreat. American losses in this poorly conceived operation were heavy: 146 killed or wounded, and 155 went missing (deserters). The British lost 26 killed and 103 wounded. Maitland decided on June 20 to withdraw but was delayed by lack of shipping; on June 23 he abandoned his bridgehead and started a slow retreat to Beaufort (Port Royal Island) to join General Prevost. During the three days it took Maitland to evacuate the outpost at Stono Ferry, having to convey across Stono Inlet, there was wholesale destruction of the sick Negro slaves. Many were left behind for want of transportation, others drowned while attempting to cling to boats. When in early July Maitland's caravan joined Prevost at Beaufort, the Negroes were segregated. Here hundreds more died of camp fever. The 3,000 Negroes who survived were shipped to Savannah and East Florida, and some were sold in the West Indies.[12]

At Beaufort, General Prevost learned that numerous inhabitants in the interior of Georgia, including some who had taken the oath of allegiance to the Crown, now infested the lower settlements. He therefore dispatched the East Florida Rangers and other regiments south into Georgia. As they marched south, they pillaged many farms and plantations on their way, and again as in the past, slaves were either carried off or followed the British army. The wanton destruction of property provided a bitter foretaste of Prevost's ability to wage war in the South. While Prevost hastened back to Savannah he left Beaufort under the protection of Maitland. Out of necessity to fill the ranks of his depleting army, General Prevost declared the troops from Florida, all of which were organized, equipped, trained, and sent out from Florida, should no longer be distinct from other provincial regiments. Governor Tonyn consented to this arrangement. Uniting with the regular British army, the East Florida Rangers would serve throughout the balance of the America Revolution in Georgia, North and South Carolina, under the command of General Charles Cornwallis.

As Prevost's straggling forces returned to Savannah, six French vessels appeared off the bar at Savannah, their mission to cooperate with General Lincoln's American patriot force in retaking the city. Although Prevost's army in Savannah numbered scarcely more than 2,500 men, and the besiegers fully 7,000 after Lincoln's army joined the 3,000 French troops on September 23, 1779, the assault which was made on October 9th failed at every point. Defeated, Count d'Estaing reembarked his men for the West Indies, while Lincoln and his army departed for Charleston. Colonel Maitland contributed immeasurably to Prevost's success by making a remarkable march from Beaufort to reinforce Savannah. Ill before he started his movement from Beaufort, Maitland died of malaria a few days after the battle. There was much sickness among the troops in Georgia, malaria being the number one killer.[13]

Prior to the capture of Savannah, Prevost had ordered Lieutenant Colonel Lewis V. Fuser, Commander of the 60th Regiment, 4th Battalion, to return to St. Augustine and become commanding officer in

East Florida. Through the intervention of Major General Alexander Leslie at New York, the Royal American 60th Regiment of 450 officers and men were returned to the colonel for defense of East Florida. Another victim of duty in the South, Colonel Fuser died in February 1780, and was succeeded by Major Beamsley Glazier. Shortly thereafter, General Prevost returned to England and retired, having served 22 years in the West Indies and North America. Governor Tonyn never cared for Fuser or Prevost, and termed them as members of a "desperate faction."[14]

After General Prevost freed Georgia from the prevailing police state, Savannah was once again safely in British control. In the north the Continentals were reduced to a pitiable condition; their treasury was bankrupt and their soldiers were starving and unpaid. Early in 1780 the British were able to launch a major expedition into the Carolinas. The British expedition from New York under General Henry Clinton was so buffeted by storms that it could not come into North Edisto Inlet, just south of Charleston, as planned, but had to reorganize at Savannah. In a plodding campaign Clinton forced the surrender of Charleston on May 12, 1780.[15] The pattern that developed in the rebel colonies was assumed in South Carolina and Georgia, i.e., loyalists from the region fled to British-occupied Savannah and Charleston, just as their northern counterparts had sought refuge in Boston, Philadelphia, and New York City, for the comforting accessibility of the British army.[16] At this time the population of South Carolina was 180,000, and Georgia, 56,000 inhabitants, but no statistics are available for the number of loyalists or Americans. The Negro slave population was 97,000 in South Carolina, and 20,000 in Georgia.

The battle for Charleston, South Carolina, resulted in the surrender of 5,500 officers and men (seven generals and 290 other Continental officers), by General Benjamin Lincoln, did have an effect on St. Augustine. Continental Army prisoners were moved to nearby Haddrel's Point, Charleston Harbor, where they were caged for 13 months and suffered great hardships from disease and lack of food. The cruel treatment which the British inflicted on their prisoners was so damnable, the prisoners elected to join the British army in Jamaica.

An ancillary to the campaign happened at Camden, South Carolina, in August 1780, as a force of 2,000 Continentals were marching toward Charleston in an effort to stop the British in the South, who still controlled 10,000 square miles of Georgia and South Carolina.

General Horatio Gates, Washington's longtime friend, commanded this half-starved force of regulars from Delaware and Maryland. Charles Lee warned his friend to take care lest his northern laurels turn to southern willows. After crossing the Pee Dee River at Masks Ferry on August 3, the Continentals were joined by Virginia militia, still in the field after the surrender of Charleston. The joint force, without a plan or purpose, marched blindly and straight ahead toward the enemy. By an uncanny coincidence, General Cornwallis had left Camden and was marching along the same road with his British force of loyalists.

In the course of Gates's march the patriots found some edible corn and beef to feed their emaciated forces, but there was no rum. There was a supply of molasses, however, and Gates conceived the happy idea of issuing each man a gill of this delicacy as a substitute for rum. The half-cooked meat, and half-baked bread, followed by a mixture of molasses and cornmeal mush, had a gastrointestinal effect on the half-starved troops that would be funny if the tactical results had not been so serious. To spare the details that abound in contemporary accounts, suffice it to say that men were "breaking the ranks all night and were certainly much debilitated before the action commenced in the morning."

The two forces met at a place called Parker's Old Field, in Gum Swamp, on August 16, 1780. It was too late to do anything but fight, so the engagement took place in a sandy area of widely spaced pines. The British deployed in a line perpendicular to the road; the American line was parallel to the enemy's. Although some skirmishing took place, General Edward Stevens, observing the British rushing on, put his men in mind of their bayonets; but the impetuosity with which the British advanced, firing and huzzaing (cheering), threw the whole body of militia into such panic that they threw down their loaded arms and fled; and so it went down the line, with two-thirds of Gates's army fleeing without firing a shot. The Battle of Camden was over. Annihilation of Gates's army was so complete that no records of casualties exist except estimates: Cornwallis claimed 1,000 killed and wounded, and 800 captured. The British lost 66 men killed and 238 men wounded. The unlovely Gates was accused of making about every error possible; the harshest criticism leveled at him was not that he lost the battle but that he fought at all. Cornwallis prepared for an invasion of North Carolina.[17]

But the story continues. Gates's forces of captured men and boys were a miserable-looking group; miles away from their homes, facing imprisonment in a local stockade or on one of those horrible British prison ships, their future looked bleak and their morale was broken. What these patriots did not know was that the British ranks were diminishing every day and there were no replacements to be had to fill the standing British forces in America. In addition, at Jamaica, 3,000 British soldiers were ill, and hundreds had already died from camp fever because the barracks were located in low and unhealthful ground. General John Dalling in Jamaica appealed to Cornwallis for Tory militia from the Carolinas, and then sent an officer to enlist American prisoners captured at Camden. Many patriots, offered a choice between serving under the British flag on the one hand, or imprisonment and probably death through hardship and disease on the other, enlisted in the royal forces.[18] The whole of the Continental troops captured at Camden, after a little hesitation, took service under the flag of the brutal oppressor, and became part of the garrison of British Jamaica. The real clincher in the offer that made taking oaths of allegiance to the Crown a little more palatable was that their service would be against the Spanish and not against their own people, the Americans. With this reprieve they left behind them a South Carolina seemingly conquered, and sailed for Jamaica. How much value there was to the trade-off (Jamaica or prison) is not disclosed, but in February Dalling had a regiment of Americans ready to reinforce Pensacola, and possibly to attack Spanish New Orleans and remove once and for all the threat to British West Florida.

After surrendering Charleston, General Lincoln was paroled to Philadelphia and exchanged in October for General William Phillips and German General Baron Friedrich Adolphus von Riedesel. General Lincoln was appointed Secretary of War in October 1781. Whatever the total, this was the largest bag of American prisoners during the Revolution.

For East Florida, the important Charleston victory was welcome news. The shallow bar at the entrance to St. Augustine required East Florida to rely on the Charleston port for the import of most goods from England and the colonies; from there the cargo was transshipped to smaller vessels for the last stage of the journey to St. Augustine. The goods, imported mostly from other North American ports, comprised virtually every type of commodity. Large quantities of provisions for the garrison were imported, such as bread, butter, flour, port, apples, potatoes, sugar, and civilian imports such as wine, beer and rum, powder and shot, saddles and leather goods, hardware, furniture, dry goods of every sort, shingles, livestock, and Negro slaves. East Florida's exports traveled the same route to Charleston. It took a while for the colony to get their products grown and to market. By now, of the exports from St. Augustine, indigo was probably the most important. Though its production within the British empire was encouraged, the indigo grown in East Florida was of good quality and was said to be the equal of the best Spanish flora-indigo. It was therefore worthwhile for Charleston exporters at times to pack Carolina or Florida indigo in *serons*, or French casks, in order to pass it off as genuine Spanish or French indigo.[19]

The export of oranges, orange juice, and orange peel from East Florida at this time was considerable. Oranges would be packed as apples for transportation, sour oranges squeezed into juice, and the peel dried and used for marmalade or medicinal purposes. The oranges were shipped by barrels, juice shipped by quarter casks, and peel in hogshead. In 1776, 65,400 oranges were exported. Other important items in Florida's economy were skins, timber, and naval stores. In 1776, St. Augustine exported 29,000 pounds of deerskins. There is every indication that the little harbor at St. Augustine was busier than it had been during the years of peace. But a survey of individual commodities exported would tend to show that East Florida's commercial progress, slow as it was, was neither greatly helped nor greatly harmed by the course of the American Revolution.

The Charleston campaign was no pushover for General Clinton. His movement by sea, poor weather, and loss of horses and supplies delayed him, yet he succeeded to capture a place and colony of major importance, wiping out and capturing a huge rebel force. One other credit to General Clinton, or to Colonel Banastre Tarleton's cavalry, was the roundup of the South Carolina rebel leaders. Seldom are officials of government accounted for in campaigns such as the one concluded at Charleston. In an effort to degrade these radicals they were rounded up, arrested, and made political prisoners. Although the *Sandwich* was not a prison ship, they were put aboard and they made their way south along the shoreline, making port at St. Augustine. They arrived in September and November 1780, their numbers given between 58 and 68. We can be sure Governor Tonyn was not ready for them, as his fortress was already teeming with soldiers, sailors, Indians, Negroes, prisoners, and loyalists. Among the American dignitaries were three South Carolina signers of the Declaration of Independence — Arthur Middleton, Edward Rutledge, and Thomas Heyward Jr. Additional patriots were William Johnson, the Rev. John Lewis, Edward McCrady, Alexander Moultrie, John Mowat, David Ramsay, Hugh Rutledge, Josiah Smith, Peter Timothy, Noble Wimberly Jones, and others. They lived in the unfinished statehouse and in private houses in town. Since many were paroled, most of them were given considerable freedom of movement. The prisoners' diet was salt fish, occasionally salt beef, vegetables, and potatoes, and one-quarter pint of rum daily. They were permitted to write home for money to purchase items from local vendors. At the statehouse they slept on mattresses on the floor, and stayed the better part of a year.

The more unruly prisoners were roughed up and thrown into the bowels of Fort Saint Marks, where the cell block was presumably the old Spanish powder magazine, containing no windows and only one door. Christopher Gadsden, Revolutionary statesman, merchant, aristocrat, and the acknowledged leader of the South Carolina radicals, who sat in the First Continental Congress, refused to receive a second parole from the hands of those who had already broken them, and became defiant. Governor Tonyn confined Gadsden for ten months at the fort before he was exchanged. Another at the coquina castle was the young French nobleman, the Marquis de Bretigny, one of Marquis de Lafayette's contemporaries who had been captured at sea off Charleston and brought to St. Augustine. British officers did not like the contemptuous nobleman, so they kept him in the fort's dungeon. After several failures at escape, Bretigny finally succeeded, dressed as a common English seaman. As a rule, most prisoners were not maltreated as in English prisons, and lived in reasonably comfortable quarters. There was some mocking of the captives, such as the guards, when marching at quickstep from the barracks to the fort, passed by the prisoners' residences and statehouse quarters, noisily striking up "Yankee Doodle" with fife and drum. And anytime there was a significant British victory, the cannon at Fort Saint Marks boomed a 21-gun salute. Finally, a remote intimation by the Americans came on the Fourth of July, 1781, when at a combined mess they all sang Thomas Heyward's newly composed ode in praise of America.

> God save the thirteen States,
> Thirteen United States,
> God save them all.

Set to the tune of "God Save the King," it caused great surprise among their British hosts, which was the intention.[20]

There was always concern that the rebels or their French and Spanish allies might strike at St. Augustine by sea. Early in 1779, Governor Tonyn could count on only 250 men in three under-strength battalions of the 60th Regiment, an equal number of local militia, 100 armed Negroes, 200 Negroes working on strengthening the fortifications, and a handful of Seminole Indians. Wartime business was good to the local merchants. Bakers built new ovens to keep up with the growing population; also benefiting were hardware stores, the sale of farm implements, rum and wine merchants, butcher shops, clothing shops, and plaza hucksters with fresh poultry and vegetables. Even the public inns, billiard parlors, and places of amusement such as skittle alleys (a game of ninepins in which a wooden ball or disk is thrown to knock down the wooden pins), and "all beer and skittles" were crowded.[21]

As with any war, there is always great sadness and grieving among the widows and children of fallen soldiers and sailors. At St. Augustine, Ann Cameron had joined her Scottish husband even before the Spaniards had completed their evacuation in 1764. When her husband retired from the Royal Scots the Camerons bought a Spanish house, repaired and improved it, and settled down in civilian life. After the Revolution broke out, Ann's husband joined Colonel Brown's mounted East Florida Rangers and was killed on a Georgia raid, leaving her widowed. With no income, Ann had to go into service as a housekeeper. Dorothy Moore and her husband, a sutler for the British garrison, had arrived in St. Augustine at an early date. After her husband's death, Dorothy provided for herself by renting out the larger of her two tabby houses as an inn.[22] These widows were fortunate that they did not have to change their allegiance to the Crown; elsewhere throughout the 13 colonies, many a loyalist widow traded her allegiance and bed to a rebel patriot in order to save herself and her children from starvation and becoming homeless.

Ever mindful of the underhandedness of the Spaniards, Governor Tonyn kept a watchful eye to southeast Florida, especially New Smyrna, located 70 miles from the capital and the farthest settlement without an established fort. He ordered Major Glazier, who succeeded Colonel Fuser, to detach soldiers to St. Johns Bluff, Anastasia watchtower, Matanzas Inlet, and farther south to Mosquito Inlet where Spanish privateers had entered the Halifax River and plundered a plantation belonging to Captain Robert Bissett. This plantation cultivated indigo and farm provisions. In addition, the Spaniards sent in armed boats that plundered the settlement of Smyrna and carried off 30 Negroes; then proceeded to Lupton, where Bissett's Negroes were working on naval stores; plundered Bissett's house and carried away additional British Negroes.[23] This was probably the same party of Spaniards who in the same year entered the Mosquito Inlet (now Ponce de Leon Inlet), set the torch to William Watson's crop of farm provisions, and plundered his Negroes at New Smyrna.[25] The British sloop *Otter*, armed with 14 guns on the main deck and carrying a crew of 125, was sent to intercept the invaders but was lost in a gale off Cape Canaveral. All hands perished.[24]

Spain's foreign ministers despite his desire for vengeance on England, for the time being limited himself to receiving secret messages from his spies in East Florida and elsewhere. It was no surprise Tonyn had another guest from Havana, Josef Puente, brother of Juan de la Puente, who took up residence in St. Augustine in 1778, under the guise of a botanist. Tonyn became aware of this disguise of Puente and the sub rosa activities of Herrera. Alerted to his dangerous position with the governor, Herrera and his family fled to Havana,[26] while Puente removed himself by fleeing to a northern colony. Tonyn was inclined to believe Spain was biding her time to attack West Florida.

8

Spain Seizes West Florida

Of all the great European powers, Spain required the most cautious and delicate handling. Her wars with England had left her embittered, perilously weak, and terribly poor. The British garrison at Gibraltar was a thorn in her side which she would risk a serious operation to extract. Spain was prepared to encourage disaffection and subsidize rebellion among the Catholics of Ireland.[1] There is no doubt the Spaniards watched the American Revolution without any sympathy for England, relishing the thought that Britain may be removed from the colonies.

General Clinton had ordered General John Campbell to take command in West Florida. Campbell earlier commanded a regiment in the operations against the Spanish at Havana in 1762; he had been in America since 1776, being one of Clinton's commanders on Staten Island for two years. He was being sent to West Florida with orders to attack and capture New Orleans if Spain entered the war.[2] Peter Chester, the present governor and a military man himself, had earlier ordered regulars to regarrison the abandoned fort at Natchez and Mahchac, a tiny trading center at the junction of the Mississippi River and Iberville Bayou, plus construct a new fort at Baton Rouge. Coupling this with the present forts at Mobile and Pensacola, General Campbell would command a superior force in the colony if he could get the conscripts. However, he needed to be ever mindful of the danger from American patriots and the Spanish in control at New Orleans.

Governor Chester had good fortune when Congress forbade the New England colonies, which supplied the West Indies with timber products, the continuance of that trade. West Florida stepped in and satisfied this demand with its wood products such as staves and headers used in barrel making for the rum industry, and other naval stores. As West Florida's economic viability was proven, there followed a rush to acquire land in the rich soil of the Natchez district. A general land rush occurred as Lieutenant Governor Montfort Browne intended to settle thousands of New Englanders in 17 townships at Natchez, and maybe carve a new colony out of the western region of West Florida, with a proposed capital on the Bayou Pierre. These plans were acceptable and timely since they provided new hope with free land grants for displaced loyalist refugees who were forced to leave their New England colonies because of the Revolution. But there was a hindrance; Spain could control British trade from Natchez, including upriver Illinois country, because they by treaty controlled the west bank of the Mississippi and all commerce at New Orleans. With its superior wealth and facilities at New Orleans, Spain also dominated the trade of the Gulf Coast to the detriment of British Mobile and Pensacola. Spanish control of the river mouth began in the late 1760s, about the same time the Natchez settlement started to rise into prominence.

The only American scheme to seize West Florida was through a rich patriot merchant at New Orleans, Oliver Pollock, who gave assistance to the American cause west of the Appalachians. Irish born, this American financier and patriot with his own funds purchased supplies for the colony's revolution, urging an attack upon West Florida by way of the Ohio and Mississippi rivers. He thought 3,000 men were sufficient to take West Florida. Pollock had the ear of Congress since he had established good relations with the Spanish authorities at New Orleans, so much so that he became the commercial agent for the American Congress, procuring supplies and weapons from Spanish creditors for George Washington's army. The American Continental Congress seriously meditated a possible attack in 1776 and 1777, but the idea finally collapsed because the patriots lacked experienced men or means at this time to execute an attack on West Florida, so far removed from the other 13 colonies.[3]

In February 1778, Spain finally began to reveal her intentions of participating in the American Revolution. In a veiled transaction, Spain loaned Pollock $74,087 earmarked to Pollock and Thomas Willing, a captain in the U.S. Navy. The conspiracy that played out was as follows: While Choctaw Indian sentinels on the Mississippi River at Walnut Hills (Vicksburg today) were off duty, Captain Willing, with 27 of his men, floated past unobserved in the armed vessel *Rattletrap* on their way to Natchez Landing. Since he was a familiar personality at his old haunt, Natchez, the settlers were willing to believe Willing's promise that in return for their neutrality he would spare them and not plunder their property. Afterwards, pushing southward, the invaders began their privateering and depredation of British plantations and farms on the eastern bank of the river. This sortie caused panic and terror as far away as Mobile. Finally the raid petered out and most of Willing's crew got back to their territory, but Captain Willing and the vessel *Rattletrap* fell into the hands of West Florida authorities. The captain met such small resistance that an alarmed Governor Chester had his defense of the Mississippi strengthened.[4] There is no telling what happened to Captain Willing thereafter, but Pollock was still free and on the loose at New Orleans.

West Florida, with its far-flung Indian territory, was patrolled, so to speak, by the agent in charge of the storehouses at the trading post. Becoming the eyes and ears of the governor, he systematically kept him apprised of the general situation on the frontier. Naturally, Indian tribes in West Florida had classic reasons to resent the American interlopers who violated the Proclamation Line drawn by British officials. Through the diplomatic skill of John Stuart, Superintendent of Southern Indian affairs, confrontation was averted between Indians and settlers of both Floridas. For 17 years he clearly defined the boundaries and established mutual agreement on trade regulations, endeavoring to keep the Indian tribes neutral when the Revolution began, sincerely hoping they would not war against either side. However, contradictory individuals and ill-boding situations by each side got them involved one way or another in current affairs that really did not affect them one way or another. The British spent a great deal of money in appeasing them with gifts, trinkets, and rum, admitting later it was not worth the investment.

Orders from London in August of 1776, informing Stuart and Governor Tonyn that the southern Indian tribes were to be used as British allies, had led to a congress at Pensacola in May 1778. A tentative agreement's terms proposed that the Indians, in combination with British and provincial forces such as the East Florida Rangers, would fight effectively together against the American forces. They did cooperate, as notably reported, in many engagements, meeting the test, while at the same time not being the effective force to the outcome. With the threat of military activity, Campbell had the opportunity to use the services of 26,000 Creek and Choctaw Indians scattered over West Florida. Could he rally them?

Contingent with the Indian situation, Campbell was apprised of the unstable military footing he faced. In East Florida when Prevost needed military assistance, he relied on the command of New York or London for assistance in receiving replacements, supplies or use of the British navy. Campbell, on the other hand, was limited to assistance from Jamaica, British West Indies, commanded by General John Dalling. Mobile and Pensacola, a thousand miles away, would have to depend on the general's generosity for reinforcements and supplies. The Jamaica base languished in low, unhealthful ground, resulting in a high mortality rate and hundreds on sick call. As Dalling's ranks thinned so did the possibility of receiving any assistance from them.

Queen Anne's War, 1702–13, coordinated the union of Spanish and French dynasties, and permitted Spain to refrain from assisting the Americans directly. Instead, Spain limited herself to furnishing secret subsidies to the colonies in the form of finances, such as the loan to Oliver Pollock, and military weapons, while echoing her desire to recover Florida, Jamaica, and Gibraltar, but mainly seeking vengeance on Britain. In February 1778, His Majesty Louis XVI of France agreed to secret treaties which recognized the independence of the United States, created a Franco-American defensive alliance, and provided for joint prosecution of the common war with Britain until American freedom should be won. In addition, France forever renounced all claims to North America east of the Mississippi, while the new United States undertook indefinitely to help the French defend their West Indian possessions against external attack, meaning England. The Continental Congress ratified the treaties in May 1778.

When informed of the treaties, the British responded with gunfire against French ships, spreading the war from the English Channel to the West Indies, but leaving much of Europe neutral. The art of government, statesmanship, and political maneuvers or manipulation seemed ingrained in the new American Congress when a solution was worked out with Conrad Alexandre Gerard, the first French minister to the United States, who declared that the patriots could expect no help from Spain if they asked for both the Floridas and free navigation of the Mississippi River. Quickly, Congress responded by abandoning any claim to territory below the thirty-first parallel, signifying both Floridas. To help Spain conquer the Floridas, the Americans would be permitted use of the Mississippi River through to New Orleans.[5]

The unobstructed use of the mighty river was of the greatest importance to the new settlers beyond the Alleghenies, who could hardly send or receive their products by land over those mountains. Accordingly, the settlers pressed hard for arrangements which would open the river to Americans. Manifest Destiny was already at work. They wanted to push for the extension of American territory westward to the river and have assurance of free passage through New Orleans, where both banks of the river were under Spanish control. The right to use the Mississippi became negotiable, and new instructions were sent to John Jay, emissary to Spain, to give up the right of navigation, if doing so would secure Spanish goodwill and assistance. As it came to be, Spain allied herself with France by convention, and on June 21, 1779, Spain declared war on Great Britain.

This was noxious news for the Floridas. East Florida had a buffer zone of the two states of Georgia and South Carolina, to help from being accosted by the Americans. At the same time the back door to the colony, New Smyrna, was in easy reach of Spain's Havana. West Florida was thrown into dire straits, with Spanish New Orleans somewhat splitting the colony. Baton Rouge, Manchac, and Natchez were west of New Orleans, while Mobile and Pensacola were much farther to the east, making the colony impossible to defend because of its far-reaching borders. In addition and far more serious was the United States giving up any claim to the territory south of the thirty-first parallel, excommunicating the two Floridas as colonies, rendering them their formal charter as a province of the Crown, and now subject to war with their arch-enemy, Spain. Though American privateers hovered off the East Florida coast and powerful Spanish and French armadas sailed ominously close to St. Augustine, no armed enemy ever set foot in the town.

Politically, the West Indian islands did not ally themselves with the 13 colonies. After France and Spain declared war on England, the conflict spread elsewhere: to Gibraltar, Minorca, the Netherlands, and, closer to the Floridas, the West Indies. American privateers had preyed on the West India trade, keeping a flow of salt, cannon and military stores to Washington's forces. St. Augustine always had a brisk trade with the islands regardless of which flag was flying over the fort. A bit of news at St. Augustine for General Tonyn was that former governor, now General James Grant, was selected to lead a 5,800-man detachment from Clinton's army at New York to the West Indies, in December 1778. Traveling in 59 transports, the armada landed Grant's forces at St. Lucia, a French naval base. These veterans of the fighting in America played utter havoc with the French force, causing them to withdraw to Martinique as the original garrison of St. Lucia surrendered and the British owned St. Lucia. After showing strategic ability as an army commander, Grant sailed for England, where he advanced to full general and became a member of Parliament.

When the British naval blockade cut off normal routes of American patriot supplies from Europe, the colonists turned to Spanish New Orleans as a source of Spanish military aid. Starting in 1776, the patriots were able to purchase weapons, ammunition, blankets, and such critical medical supplies as quinine. These supplies were moved up the Mississippi River under the Spanish flag. Much of this American aid came from financier Oliver Pollock. He not only used his credit, he mortgaged personal property to purchase over $300,000 of vital supplies for the American cause. This amount surpasses the contribution of any other person to the direct cause of the Revolution.

In New Orleans the Spanish were by no means powerful, except for the leadership of their governor, Bernardo de Galvez. The 27-year-old Colonel Galvez was appointed governor of the Spanish province in February 1776. During the next two years the young governor did everything within his power to weaken the British in his area; he seized British ships that had been engaged in the profitable contraband trade. His most notable contribution to the American rebel cause was his support of and trust in the patriots' supply agent, Oliver Pollock. When Spain declared war on England, Galvez proved himself to be even more capable in the field than he had been in covert operations against the British.[6]

West Florida along the Mississippi was vulnerable, and became his early target. The thinly garrisoned settlements scattered along the lower Mississippi where Captain Willing met such small resistance would be the first Spanish sortie. In August 1779, Galvez boldly led a motley force of Spanish regulars from Cuba, some French inhabitant militia, some Americans, and Indians against the British outposts on the lower Mississippi. At the tiny trading post of Manchac, its 23-man garrison could not even delay Galvez with his army of nearly 1,000 strong, and they surrendered. At Baton Rouge there was a newer garrison of 300 soldiers commanded by Colonel Alexander Dickson. The fort had 13 cannon within a redoubt protected by a ditch and chevaux-de-frise (an obstacle such as spikes). Instead of storming the fort, Galvez preferred to reduce it with artillery. After several hours of bombardment, Colonel Dickson surrendered Baton Rouge, giving up the entire Natchez district. This caused the separation of the western part of the colony from Mobile and Pensacola. These early successes in West Florida endeared Governor Galvez to supporters of the Spanish instigation. Time and distance would determine the next move by Spain in West Florida.[7]

The capable Spaniard, Bernardo de Galvez, flushed with success from taking the Mississippi River posts of Manchac, Baton Rouge, and Natchez, intrepidly set his sights on Mobile. Joined by Spanish troops and ships from Havana, he marshaled soldiers to attack Fort Charlotte at Mobile, in March 1780. The defense of the Mobile and Pensacola bases was subsidiary to Jamaica's military operation under General John Dalling. As governor he had sent military expeditions to Honduras and Nicaragua; thus he was in no position to assist the Mobile defenders. Mobile was garrisoned by 300 men. Its commander was West Florida's former acting governor and capable engineer officer, Elias Durnford. Early on he argued that the walls could not survive prolonged assaults by any determined besieger.

The Galvez invaders passed the low, flat Dauphin Island and approached Mobile Bay. On the way, severe storms damaged Galvez's ships, depriving him of valuable supplies. Undaunted, he attacked with a single armed vessel. Although Durnford had four companies of the 60th Royal Regiment in the fort and was awaiting reinforcements from General John Campbell at Pensacola, it was a no-win position, and after two days of fighting Durnford surrendered his fort. The four companies of the 4th Battalion, 60th Regiment were taken prisoners of war and were transported to Veracruz, Mexico, and Havana, Cuba. This was on March 14, 1780. The relieving force from Pensacola was unable to reach the fort in time. Durnford and other officials were pardoned, many being merchants who continued their daily routine. The same applied to the general populace; they had lived under several flags in their lifetimes, and Galvez was just another intruder, "so let's wait and see what happens next" was their attitude as the British flag came down and was replaced by the Spanish flag. Across the bay from Mobile on its eastern approach, Galvez had a Spanish fort constructed for defense purposes.

Galvez proposed to move on immediately against Pensacola, the center of British power in West Florida, but lacked strength for the attempt and was forced to be content for the moment with his conquest of Mobile. He was determined, nevertheless, to have Pensacola. Reinforced at Havana with a large army and fleet, in October he sailed for Pensacola, but an untimely and extremely destructive fall hurricane wrecked the enterprise.[8]

Because of the disruptive hurricane in the fall of 1780, General Galvez had to delay his attempt to capture Pensacola until early 1781. General John Campbell's coastal batteries might keep the Spaniards out of Pensacola Harbor until Dalling's relief ships of the British navy would arrive from Jamaica with their cargo of recycled Americans in British uniforms. As for the present garrison at Pensacola, Fort George was placed on a hilltop and was a great deal stronger than Fort Charlotte was at Mobile. In 1778 when Campbell arrived at Pensacola, he brought with him, from General Clinton's army at New York, "a battalion of Waldeckers (from a province in west-central Germany)" who were unfit in dress, equipment, and discipline; also two battalions of provincial loyalist infantry, raised in Maryland and Pennsylvania from Irish vagabonds who had deserted from the American army and were quite ready to desert from the British. Few of them were suited for duty in the wilds of West Florida. At Fort George they joined "seven companies of the 16th Foot (infantry), made up chiefly of worn-out veterans, plus eight companies of the 3rd and 4th battalions of the old 62nd Royal Americans, composed principally of Germans, condemned criminals, and other species of jailbirds." The 62nd Royal Americans, made up of American loyalists, was recruited from Pennsylvania Germans in 1757; it was later redesignated the 60th Royal Americans, and then disbanded.[9] In addition there were several hundred Creek and Choctaw Indians on hand for service.

General Galvez had collected an overwhelming force estimated at more than 7,000 soldiers, together with a well-armed fleet. Campbell hoped to contain Galvez with his collection of about 1,600 veterans in Pensacola. By prior agreement with General Galvez, Campbell withdrew to Fort George in order to spare Pensacola from destruction. On the 9th of March, Galvez's Spanish squadron appeared before Pensacola and began to disembark upwards of 7,000 soldiers and cannon. Believe it or not, the West Florida British garrison of unconformable veterans seemed invincible, and stoutly defended themselves for two months, the siege making little progress. Finally the Spanish artillery, guided by a deserter from one of Campbell's American regiments, succeeded in dropping a shell into the principal powder magazine. The explosion on the 8th of May rocked the town and demolished one of the principal redoubts; whereupon the Spaniards at once advanced to the assault. Campbell's men met and repelled the first attack. But the Spaniards succeeded in establishing themselves in the ruined fortifications whence they could shoot down any man who attempted to work the fort's guns. It was a standoff, and Campbell's chance of any sort of an escape was doomed when his Creek warriors failed to fight.[10]

All during the siege, which lasted from March 9 until May 8, 1781, General Campbell and Governor Chester looked in vain for English sails on the horizon. Back in Jamaica, Sir Peter Parker, who commanded the king's ships at Port Royal, Jamaica, refused to give high priority to the relief of Pensacola. The invasion of Jamaica from nearby Cuba was a possibility on the Spanish agenda, and although the fall of Pensacola might be thought unfortunate, the fall of Jamaica would be received as utterly disastrous.[11] Further resistance at Fort George was useless; the explosion of the magazine killed 105, while 300 went missing, and the balance were ready to give up. With the deed done, Campbell capitulated; eight companies and the fort surrendered. West Florida ceased to be a British colony, passing once more into the hands of Spain. Of interest, a portion of the 3rd Battalion that came to St. Augustine that year were surrendered at Pensacola. Likewise, John Campbell was exchanged almost immediately and promoted to lieutenant general, and returned to New York City.

These conquests by Galvez did little to further the American cause, but they assisted in later diplomatic relations between Spain and Britain. At present Spain gained control of the mouth of the Mississippi, and on the west bank of the Mississippi the Spanish held military posts at St. Louis, New Madrid, and Arkansas, plus Spain control led the Gulf of Mexico. Galvez went to Spain and gave advice on future policy in West Florida and the Louisiana territory.

Although West Florida was in Spanish hands, Governor Tonyn in East Florida still had a strong relationship with Panton, Leslie and Company, the trading post entrepreneurs. The house of Panton, Leslie and Company survived the capture of Pensacola by Bernardo de Galvez. Its head, William Panton, remained in West Florida although his fellow loyalist employees quickly withdrew. The continued presence of William Panton was so essential for the prosperity of Pensacola and the maintenance of good relations with the Creek Indians that the Spaniards entered into a separate treaty with him by which his trading posts were assured their rights, possessions, and Indian trade through its branches at Pensacola, Mobile, and Apalachee. Such agreements were very rare in these days. In return for these concessions, Panton agreed to act as the financial agent of the Spanish government and to promote goodwill between the Spaniards and the Indians. At one time Spain owed Panton $200,000 for advances he had made to them; and the same for the Indians who amassed such a large debt to his firm. The Indians discharged their debt to Panton by the transfer of a tract of land in Florida 40 miles square.[12] The Southern Indians, Creeks, Choctaw, Chickasaw, and Cherokee had lost finally, and without a real struggle, the balance-of-power position they had so long enjoyed among the French, Spanish, and English.[13]

East Florida

In the winter of 1780–81, crafty Governor Tonyn sent Thomas Forbes, a member of Panton, Leslie and Company, under a flag of truce to Havana to gain information concerning the plans of Bernardo de Galvez, who in March 1780, had captured Mobile. Forbes departed Havana in January and arrived at St. Augustine a week later with the alarming news that the Spanish expedition to take Pensacola was underway. Tonyn transmitted this news to Savannah and Charleston with a request for aid for the defense of East Florida. At the same time, Tonyn made requisition on the inhabitants for 100 Negroes to be employed on the fortifications at St. Augustine, in preparation for an attack by the Spanish invaders. By now Galvez's fleet and troops were at Pensacola in full force, prompting the decision that the Seminoles in and around St. Augustine should be employed for the defense of the colony.

At the meeting of Governor Tonyn and his council in mid–February 1781, petitions for land were received from refugees and long-time settlers. The warrants of survey issued were for tracts ranging from 100 to 500 acres. The board then considered the expediency of calling a general meeting of the freeholders to elect representatives for the purpose of framing laws for the government of East Florida. Though

Florida had been settled for more than 200 years, never before had the citizens been allowed to assemble and enact laws. A royal writ commanded all inhabitants of 21 years of age or over, who possessed 50 acres of land, to appear at the courthouse in St. Augustine to elect 19 "fit and discreet persons" severally possessed in their own right of 500 acres of land within the province of East Florida to be their representatives.

The nineteen members were elected, Lieutenant Governor John Moultrie being president of that body. The general assembly consisted of an Upper House composed of Crown officers, and the Lower House, the 19 elected freeholders. Thomas Forbes and John Leslie of Panton, Leslie and Company, were among the 19 members seated in March 1781.

On April 2, an address of thanks from Governor Tonyn was read to the Lower House in which he said that he had done all in his power to render the province a happy asylum for those gentlemen whose firm attachment to the Crown had led them to relinquish their possessions rather than sacrifice their allegiance, but that what he had done still fell short of their merits and distresses. Copies of his address were ordered to be printed, and one copy was posted at Payne's Corner in St. Augustine, and another at the bluff on St. Johns River.[14] Other measures enacted were a bill for the better regulation of taverns, punch houses, and retailers of spirituous liquors, speedy recovery of small debts, and better control of pilots for regulating the pilotage of vessels into the several ports of East Florida. Also on the agenda was whether local justices of the peace could try condemned slaves and execute them on the spot, or whether the accused must be brought to St. Augustine and undergo a time-consuming trial. Britain had abolished slavery in the mother country in 1772, but not the slave trade to the American colonies. Eventually a compromise emerged; local slave trials were permitted but sentence was deferred until Tonyn and his advisors had a chance to review proceedings in St. Augustine.[15] This Negro bill breathed more humanity than any of a like nature passed in the sister colonies. In June, Governor Tonyn sent a message to the two houses to inform them that West Florida had surrendered to the Spaniards. This was alarming news; would East Florida be subject to attack by the Spaniards? Naturally, the Spaniards had had their eyes on St. Augustine since the beginning of the Revolution. For the time being, a larger problem bloomed — the flow of loyalist refugees into East Florida from the Carolinas and Georgia.

Through the exertions of the Anglo-Saxon settlers who had brought to the colony their advanced ideas of government, agriculture, slaves, and commerce, East Florida was just entering upon a career of prosperity when the America Revolution interrupted the cycle. When tempers flared in 1776, a limited number of the lordly and titled English returned to England in hopes that the breach could be reconciled. As time passed, loyalists in Georgia and the Carolinas took sanctuary in British-controlled towns, although a limited number began to stream down to East Florida. These moves were not for the faint-hearted families, as when they moved they lost their home, land, crops, friends, and eminence. They had very little money, but many of them possessed from 10 to 100 Negroes, enough to start over again. If they could obtain grants of land from 50 to 100 or more acres they had the rudiments to start up in Florida.

In view of the persecution, distress, and ruin of many loyalists in adjacent colonies, the Lower House recommended that a law be enacted to encourage such persons to come and settle in East Florida by affording them a few years' respite from such a debtors' law as bound them in those colonies. The rebellion had made it impossible for them to pay immediately.

Another measure of relief proposed by the Upper House was to compel the grantees of the many large, uncultivated tracts of land to sell or resign them, in order that they might be regranted and distributed in small tracts among a number of poor, distressed, and industrious settlers. They inquired what measures should be taken to break up the large tracts of land. Governor Tonyn, examining some of these large, 20,000-acre tracts that had not been complied with, then declared they were subject to reversion to the Crown. Thus he proceeded to regrant some of them in parcels of from 50 to 500 acres to refugee loyalists.[16]

The military operations in the South concerned Governor Tonyn as the British redcoats failed in their attempt to contain the Continental forces. At Cowpens, South Carolina, Generals Cornwallis and Tarleton, on January 17, 1781, sustained a crushing reverse at the hands of frontiersman General Daniel Morgan. The hours of fighting cost the British 100 killed, 229 wounded, and 600 captured, along with equipment (not easily replaced) including 35 wagons, a traveling forge, 800 muskets, and 100 dragoon horses. Morgan had destroyed a great part of Cornwallis's army, and far-reaching effects were to raise patriot morale when it badly needed raising after the year-long defeats in 1780.

At Guilford Courthouse, North Carolina, on March 15, battle honors went to Cornwallis as he clashed with General Nathanael Greene; nevertheless, Greene's aggressiveness proved him to be the master of Cornwallis. At this time, French Admiral Charles-René-Dominique Sochet Destouches, commander of the French squadron at Newport, Rhode Island, sailed south to support General Lafayette in Virginia. But he was forced to withdraw off Chesapeake Bay by Admiral Marriott Arbuthnot's eight ships, who defeated him in a one-hour engagement. The final battle of the southern campaign before Yorktown occurred on September 8, 1781. General Greene surprised the British army, under Lieutenant Colonel Alexander Stewart, near Nelson's Ferry on the Santee River at Eutaw Springs, South Carolina. Troops on both sides fought exceptionally well as General Greene scored a strategic surprise on Stewart; still, Stewart's British outfought the Americans. There were heavy casualties on both sides. Of approximately 2,200 Americans engaged, over 500 were casualties; the British, starting with 1,800 effectives, lost 693 according to records. By this time the British army in the South was so weakened by losses they had to withdraw to the vicinity of Charleston.[17]

After Eutaw Springs, the British held below the boundary of Virginia only Wilmington, North Carolina, Charleston and Savannah. Greene's patriots were so weakened they could not proceed against any of these three towns; therefore they had to camp on the high hills of the Santee River. Earlier, Major James H. Craig had captured Wilmington with a body of British regulars, the 82nd Regiment. When word was received that American general Arthur St. Clair, with his Virginia, Maryland, and Pennsylvania Continentals, were marching south to give Greene assistance, all the loyalists in Wilmington and the region were asked to leave with Major Craig as they were evacuated to the Charleston lines, and North Carolina was free of the British.[18]

General George Washington's army and the French troops under Comte de Rochambeau moved south from Newport toward New York in the summer of 1781. General Clinton ordered Cornwallis's army, now in Virginia, to the port of Yorktown on the Chesapeake Bay, in case Clinton should need reinforcements in New York. When Washington heard that the French West Indies fleet under Francois de Grasse had sailed for Chesapeake Bay, a battle plan was formulated. Bypassing New York, the Franco-American army would march to Virginia to encounter Cornwallis. If the French fleet could get to the Chesapeake capes before the British, and if the American army could get there before de Grasse's October 15 deadline for leaving the North American theatre, a crucial victory might be won. As history records, both "ifs" paid off for George Washington and the Franco-American army.

One of the climactic military actions of the Revolution was the meeting of the French and British fleets off Cape Henry on September 5. Here the French fleet secured control of the sea off Yorktown, dooming the British land forces. The defeated and damaged British fleet had no choice but to head north, back to New York. Ironically no Americans took part in the naval engagement. The Franco-American army of 16,000 men and officers shelled Cornwallis's position incessantly with 52 pieces of artillery. The storming of two British redoubts on October 14 shut off any slim hope of escape for the British army, and on October 17, Cornwallis sent a message to General Washington asking for a cease-fire so that a surrender could be discussed. On October 19, the British marched out of their positions and laid down their arms; General Cornwallis's army surrendered, ending the American Revolution. The good news spread like wildfire as couriers rushed to the capitals of the 13 colonies. Along the Great Wagon Road, church bells thundered the long-awaited news, and taverns roared with toasts to "liberty" and "Great George Washington." In Philadelphia, celebrating patriots broke countless windows in suspected loyalist houses.[19] As fast as the printers could set and print broadsides, they announced: "By this glorious conquest, 9,000 of the enemy including seamen, fell into our hands, with an immense quantity of warlike stores, a 40-gun ship, a frigate, an armed vessel, and about 100 sail transports." These were posted wherever possible. So the deed was done.[20]

Yorktown did not immediately end the strife. The British still had an army under General Clinton in New York City, and another in South Carolina. The American and British armies remained ready to strike at one another should the occasion arise. It was wintertime, the war was five years old, and both sides were played out from the tumult of warfare, so there was little to do but wait and see what would happen next. General Cornwallis was exchanged for South Carolina's Henry Laurens, imprisoned in the Tower of London. Cornwallis the tactician later accepted a post in India, and in 1797 as the governor general of Ireland.

There was no booming of cannon or ringing of church bells in St. Augustine when the news was received about Cornwallis's defeat at Yorktown. In the midst of this turn of events, notification was received from the war office in Westminster, dated November 1781, that Governor Tonyn had been promoted from the rank of colonel to that of major general. The promotion had been earned and the rank necessary for continuation of his duties in the last existing British colony in North America south of Canada.

By the end of the year Tonyn was still expecting an invasion by the Spaniards. The colony was forever being put into condition for this event. Some heavy artillery arrived from England, and the local militia had been given arms and assigned to town patrol. The town seemed to have sufficient provisions to withstand a Spanish attack. Of course, absent from East Florida were its local regiments and militia in the call of duty to defend the Crown elsewhere. Some saw action at Augusta, Briar Creek, and White House; others fought with Lord Rawdon and Cornwallis at Hanging Rock, Camden, Musgrove Mills, Petersburg, and in most other battles down to Yorktown. Part of the Royal North Carolina Regiment was with Cornwallis when he surrendered at Yorktown. Florida loyalist regiments twice defeated the redoubtable Francis Marion, "the Swamp Fox," once on the north side of the Cooper River and again at the Santee River. Other American commanders who came into conflict with some of the Florida forces were Andrew Pickens, Thomas Sumter (the "Carolina Gamecock"), Horatio Gates, Nathanael Greene, and Marquis de Lafayette.[21]

For certain, Governor Tonyn, now a major general, endeavored to apprise himself of the coming British strategy affecting the American Revolution and East Florida. Three thousand miles away, the *London Gazette* reported the latest disaster of Lord Cornwallis at Yorktown. Unanswerable and irresistible arguments began pouring in upon the members of the House of Commons on how to conduct the American war. To the rescue came General Henry Seymour Conway, whose strategic questions and answers stood in very high esteem. On the 22nd of February he made an address praying His Majesty that the war on the continent of North America might no longer be pursued for the impracticable purpose of reducing the inhabitants of that country to obedience by force. As the House of Commons' members listened, he continued, "Our shores are under constant threat of invasion, we have no spare troops for relief of the Mediterranean garrisons, or for aggressive operations in Europe. We maintain on the other side of the Atlantic a far larger British army than we had when we led to victory in Flanders or Germany."

Lord Sheffield, a specialist in the statistics of foreign and colonial commerce, added that the increase in the national debt entailed on Great Britain by the American war amounted to 45 times the average annual value of British exports to the American colonies. Conway put together a conclusive argument in the form of a resolution to the effect that all who advised or attempted the further prosecution of offensive war upon the continent of America should be considered enemies to His Majesty, and to the country. The center of political interest was henceforward transferred from the House of Commons to the royal closet.

Then the news arrived on March 3 that Comte de Grasse had captured from the British the island of St. Kitts, and that Port Mahon, the capital of Minorca, had surrendered after a prolonged siege, to a French and Spanish army. The government had suffered another crushing defeat. Surprising as it seems, a pamphleteer wrote, "In whatever light we may view the American dispute, there is a point upon which every person in Great Britain is agreed, which is that all our defeats and misfortunes have been owing to the mismanagement of the navy." On March 20, Lord North resigned as British prime minister. Finally King George III submitted to his fate and came to a determination. "He hoped to God, whoever the Minister might be, they would take such measures as should tend effectually to extricate Britain from its present difficulties, and to render it happy and prosperous at home, successful and secure abroad."[22] The king's acknowledgment of the United States as an independent nation was not what everyone wanted. For six years, tens of thousands of patriots and loyalists on both sides of the Atlantic had hoped and prayed for a reconciliation of the nations. The split was conclusive.

General Guy Carleton had been appointed on February 23, 1782, to replace Sir Henry Clinton, and soon was on his way. He reached New York on May 5, immediately undertaking steps to end hostilities while political arrangements for peace were worked out. The Secretary of War in London announced it was the intention of the government to convert the war in America into "a war of posts"; his idea was to keep no regular army in the field, but to keep those posts they had and add others to them whenever they should be found advantageous, still affording the means of attacking the patriots if an opportunity presented itself. When Sir Guy Carleton succeeded General Clinton at New York, he took over the royal troops in America, numbering 31,000 of all ranks, besides 2,300 additional British and German recruits en route to join the ranks.[23] Boston was never retaken, therefore throughout the rest of the war New York City was the major stronghold for the British; Manhattan became the chief haven for loyalist refugees from the northern colonies.

To the south, Charleston, Savannah, and St. Augustine remained in British hands but with few regulars and militia to defend them, and with the possibility they might be cut off by superior enemy fleets, French or Spanish. As a result, on May 20, 1782, Carleton ordered the three garrisons to transfer to New York. The governors, merchants, and property holders got up in arms and complained to King George III about the disastrous effects withdrawing would have on the loyal British subjects if Carleton surrendered these colonies. General Carleton and his commanders in New York were still smarting from the Yorktown defeat by the French and Americans.

Then came word that the British fleet under Admiral George B. Rodney, in a battle off Saints Passage, West Indies, defeated Admiral de Grasse and the French fleet, and captured de Grasse. This stunning defeat of the French fleet and protests to the king resulted in Carleton's countermanding the order for withdrawing the three garrisons ... for now.

One American patriot who escaped from Charleston was Henry Laurens, former president of the Continental Congress (1777). In 1779 he was elected to negotiate a treaty of commerce with Holland, and to arrange for a ten-million-dollar loan. Unable to sail from Charleston because of the threatened British attack, months later he departed via Philadelphia on the brig *Mercury*. The vessel was captured off Newfoundland. Laurens threw his official papers overboard but the British retrieved them, revealing the purpose of his trip. Taken to London, he was confined in the Tower of London, a structure of high, thick, stone walls surrounded by a shallow moat. Political prisoners were held in damp, dark cells. Confined on suspicion of high treason, he was held 15 months. Finally released on heavy bail, he was exchanged for General Cornwallis, who had surrendered on October 19, 1781, ending the Yorktown campaign and virtually ending the American Revolution. Laurens was named one of the commissioners to handle the coming peace negotiations.[24] Henry Laurens had a son, John, who fought throughout the American Revolution, only to be killed at Combahee Ferry, South Carolina, on August 27, 1782, right before the end of the war.

The British occupation of Georgia and South Carolina was short-lived. The large land mass was impossible to control or patrol. The South Carolina militia, often led by General Francis "Swamp Fox" Marion and General Thomas "Carolina Gamecock" Sumter, ran amuck in Georgia and South Carolina, and wrested control of the countryside from the loyalists. These cavalry raids, by a series of small but bloody victories, gained control for the patriots. What next? General Benedict Arnold, through the arrest of Major John Andre of the British army and a spy, was discovered to be an American traitor. Andre was hanged, but Arnold escaped to England, where he died in 1801. There was plenty of news to fill the bulletin board in the plaza at St. Augustine.

9

Boom Towns

The spirit of rebellion hardly had touched East Florida; it was too recent an addition to the empire to have bred an independent colonial identity.[1] One of Patrick Tonyn's actions as governor had been to promise protection to loyalists suffering persecution in Georgia and South Carolina. While liberty-loving pamphleteers were writing about rights of man, thousands of patriot were subjecting innocent loyal persons to every sort of indignity ... there was absolutely no freedom of the press or tongue, save for those that expressed opinions against the British government.[2] As the tide turned against Britain, additional Tory refugees from the southern colonies continued to find their way to East Florida. Traveling the Great Wagon Road, the King's Highway, river routes or by sea, these incoming loyalists settled in or near St. Augustine. Those unable to find accommodation in a town already bursting at the seams with people, spilled over into areas in the northern and southern parts of the colony. Over its short lifespan the colony had made grants of land for the development of towns, mainly along its rivers. Early plantation development by promoters and speculators often resulted in seeding a new town in the colony, and also, some of the most fantastic of utopian projects ever dreamed up took place here.

One of the venturesome players in the early development of the East Florida colony was Denys Rolle, a wealthy landowner in Stevenstone, Devon, England. He and four other gentlemen, seized with ambition for the possible development of the new colony, petitioned the commissioners of Trade and Plantations for an immense grant of land, promising to produce indigo, wine, and silk. To enable their white settlers to clear and cultivate the land, they would introduce a

Swiss engine for removing trees, a drill plow, and other machinery recommended by the Society of Arts. Unfortunately, because of Rolle's disagreement with his partners this proposal was cancelled. Rolle's next visionary scheme was a proposal to establish a colony near St. Marks, West Florida; 100,000 acres were to be settled in succession of 10,000 acres at a time by Protestant white inhabitants in proportion of one white person for every hundred acres, which equaled a density of 200 white inhabitants for each 20,000-acre tract. At this time Governor Grant found guides and hunters to accompany Rolle and his party on their journey to inspect St. Marks. A wavering Denys Rolle decided against St. Marks; instead he proceeded with his party to the St. Johns River. Going upriver he found a spot more to his liking, which he named Mount Royal. He justified the change of plans on the fact that they wished to be near St. Augustine.

Governor Grant was a tolerant agent, agreeing to every conceivable favor Rolle would request. However, when Rolle requested more grants of land, Grant refused. Cantankerous Rolle returned to England in 1766, petitioning the king and complaining that he was reduced from 100,000 acres in a single tract to a tract now of only 20,000 acres. His petition was read and dismissed. Not to be denied, Rolle secured purchase orders while in England for land adjacent to his, from gentlemen who had received earlier grants but had not occupied them. Names such as James Penman, William Cusac, Jonathan Grayhast, William Elliot, and others sold their grants to Rolle. By now Rolle had under control 80,000 acres, 100 nearly contiguous miles up the St. Johns.[3]

Denys Rolle's new spread was situated at Mount Pleasant on the east bank of the St. Johns between Picolata and James Spalding's middle trading post. The village of Rollestown was established, close to the site of the present town of Palatka. The site was stocked with cattle, horses, hogs, sheep, and poultry. He grew corn, oranges, and rice, and produced turpentine. His Negroes numbered 138: 96 working, 32 children, and 10 past labor. In his village, he had a church, a parsonage, and offices in ranges on a 10-acre square, with Negro cabins and their gardens on each side. Rolle bragged that, "before his two-storied house with five sash windows, ships from Europe anchored within a plank's length of shore in 33 feet of water."

His spread had a fitful existence, occasionally receiving a shipload of shiftless settlers. One time Rolle returned with a group of 49 settlers;

they were vagrants, beggars, and debtors from the streets of London, including some fallen women for his philanthropic colony. Rolle always experienced various difficulties because he was an absentee landlord, although the use of Negro slaves brought in some spells of prosperity each year. How did Rollestown do with the influx of loyalist refugees? His fine range was stocked with over 1,000 head of cattle, which was continually reduced by dishonest overseers. In 1782 Denys Rolle claimed, "...restocked cattle again at a vast expense, great numbers have been destroyed by indigent refugees and others in the confused state of the colony before its cession."[4] He had his share of squatters, vagrants, and the less-fortunate seeking a haven of safety from the war.

During the years 1780–82, Governor Tonyn issued many land grants because of the influx of refugees from South Carolina and Georgia, resulting in two new towns' being formed outside the walled city. St. Augustine was limited to those who had a lot of cash to buy or rent houses from Jesse Fish or others. Newly arrived refugees began settling at the mouth of the St. Johns River, then six or seven miles upriver on the south bank at Hester's Bluff, owned by William Hester. In 1779 Hester conveyed his tract of land to Thomas Williamson, who divided the 200 acres into town lots with a frontage of 75 feet and a depth of 120 feet. He named the new village St. Johns Bluff. The lots facing the riverfront were named bay lots; two other streets were named Water Street and Prince Street. These lots were 70 feet high above tidewater and facing east toward the mouth of the river. Without a doubt Mr. Williamson promoted the first Florida real estate boom of record.[5]

Word of mouth and a housing shortage got the village prospering. Within a year numerous frame houses were built. George Tallack, a ship's carpenter, had a frame dwelling house and kitchen, and ran a market on the bay. John McDonald kept a tavern and storehouse, including about eight square feet for a Freemasons Lodge. Stephen White was a public innkeeper and horse hirer who had a large new dwelling house, kitchen, stables, and storehouse. There was Dr. Hugh Rose, practitioner of physic; his dwelling house was from 20 to 25 feet long, two stories high, and with a shingled roof. In addition there was a kitchen, stable, fowl house, front storehouses, an enclosed back garden, and an outhouse. Also, a missionary conducted regular religious services in town.[6]

Governor Tonyn pointed with pride that there were 300 houses at St. Johns Bluff, and that it had a rosy future because it might become a seaport of consequence where provisions were landed and naval stores and other products of the St. Johns River country were loaded on ocean-going vessels. In deference to the governor, it must be remembered that these inhabitants were at the end their rope, so to speak. John McDonald had been confined by the rebels in North Carolina, finally seeking asylum in East Florida. He got as far as the Bluff. Stephen White came from Charlestown; on his way his four Negroes and three horses were carried away by the Americans. While developing a plantation in South Carolina, John Chapman was driven from his land by Americans who plundered and destroyed all the buildings on the plantation, and Chapman went with his Negroes to Amelia Island, East Florida.[7] Benjamin Springer, a planter and dealer, abhorring the idea of forfeiting his allegiance to his king and native country, moved into East Florida, "...with all such parts of his moveable property as he should be able to take with him." East Florida was the sanctuary for displaced loyalists; with whatever they could carry and transport, they descended on the province as their last hope.

The villages were hastily built, some log cabins, some shanties, walled and thatched with palmetto leaves. The colonists along the seaboard were using prefabricated houses (manufactured in advance). "A new frame of a house purchased at 25 pounds to be erected" was George Tallack's order when he came to St. Johns Bluff. Naturally, all these prefabs had the same measure of spatial extent, especially width, height or length. "His dwelling house was about 18 by 24 feet, two rooms on a floor with a shingled roof, with a separate kitchen," was typical of these moveable dwellings. We know this from what they left behind on the beaches, since the only way to move these parts was by boat; they gave a fairly good picture of the dwelling. "That before his departure he took down the dwelling house and carried it down to St. Marys beach, where most of it was broken to pieces and stolen." Window and door frames, skeletons of the structure such as beams and joists, hardware, locks, plantation tools (all were portable and could be reused) are repeatedly referred to when the refugees had to move to another place.[8]

Another popular landing site for the refugees was along the St. Marys River. Two Bermudians, Ephraim and John Gilbert, obtained 40,000 acres on the St. Marys and Nassau rivers on which to settle 500 families from Bermuda. A town located on the river bluff, called New Bermuda, was planned but never settled. In London, 1770, Lord Hillsborough and the Treasury agreed to make St. Marys a port of entry, and appointed an officer for the port. In 1772, 60 people from the Isle of Skye, Scotland, part of 300 who had already landed in North Carolina, arrived in East Florida and were persuaded to settle on the St. Marys, in and about Hillsborough township, under their leader John Bethune. Plans for a fort at the mouth of the river came to nothing, but there was stage service from Cowford to Hillsborough Town on the St. Marys.[9]

The Seminoles, given to hunting deer, bear, wolves, and other wild animals, traded the skins of these creatures, besides honey, wax, and other products, for clothing, utensils, trinkets, and supplies offered by Spalding and Company or Spalding and Kelsall, who had no fewer than five trading posts in East Florida. The senior member of the company was James Spalding, who lived at Frederica on St. Simons Island. He had Spalding's Lower Store and Upper Store on the St. Johns River, and the company's stores on a bend of the St. Marys River, about 60 miles from the coast. The approximate location of this post is marked on certain maps by the place name "Traders Hill." The company's principal station was situated on the west bank of the St. Johns River a few miles north of Lake George.[10] As commerce in the colony increased, so did volume and profits at the trading posts — so much so that in 1780, 1,500 pounds sterling were spent for establishing the town of St. Marys, Georgia.[11]

Amelia Harbor, at the mouth of St. Marys River, led to the formation of the town of Arden on Amelia Island.[12] Lady Egmont was the widow of John Perceval, 2nd Earl of Egmont, and her Egmont estates included lands along the St. Johns River and a large plantation on Amelia Island, which was visited by the botanist William Bartram in the spring of 1773. Raids on the scattered plantations along the St. Marys River and Amelia Island began late in 1775. Lady Egmont's plantation and other settlements on the St. Marys River, in the midst of alarm about the aggressions from the Americans in Georgia, requested assistance in protecting their property. As we learned earlier, the patriots under Colonel Samuel Elbert landed on the north end of Amelia Island, burning and destroying houses and stock as they pleased. Because of the distance from St. Augustine the island was not properly defended, relegating it to banditti territory.

During these years Governor Tonyn said that many small and individual land grants were issued to settlements along the St. Johns and St. Marys rivers. The construction of roads had done a good deal to encourage settlement of the land, especially along the waterways. The rapid growth was prompted by a steady flow of refugees from the other colonies; and as the American Revolution was coming to an end, the exodus of the true-blue loyalists increased fivefold. Steps which led to this influx of displaced inhabitants were taken far away from the colony. In March 1782, the House of Commons forced King George III, much against his wishes, to accept the Marquis of Rockingham's government pledge to the making of peace and the recognition of American independence.

In New York, in April 1782, Sir Guy Carleton was ordered to withdraw the garrisons from New York, Charleston, and Savannah, and to use his own discretion regarding the garrison at St. Augustine. Captain Keith Elphinstone, who had been in East Florida waters in 1778, advised Carleton to postpone the evacuation of St. Augustine until Charleston and Savannah had been evacuated, partly because of a lack of shipping, partly because he felt if Tonyn informed the people that the evacuation would take place in the following winter or spring, they would take measures which would cause it to be accomplished more easily and speedily at that time.[13] Accordingly, Carleton informed General Leslie at Charleston of the plans; Leslie acknowledged Carleton's order, expressing gratification at the relief afforded the people of Charleston and Savannah, by having a refuge in the neighboring province of East Florida. This resulted in saving East Florida for the time being, but on condition that it opened its arms wide to receive the additional loyalist refugees from Charleston and Savannah. This comforting news reached St. Augustine in the latter part of July 1782. With no plan at hand to accommodate newcomers to East Florida, Governor Tonyn became excessively overburdened in the fall when loyalist refugees arrived by the hundreds. The wealthy South Carolina and Georgia planters and politicians had a choice of returning to England or taking their chance elsewhere. Most had enough money to pick up and leave with their possessions, servants, and families. Some sailed back to England, some to Canada, and very few to Florida. For the majority of the loyalists, the less affluent merchants, tradesmen, farmers, back woodsmen, Crackers, the indolent, and Negroes, their choice was East Florida, rather than stay and be intimidated by the victorious patriots.

Ostracized by friends and neighbors, they had to escape without having time to harvest their crops or sell their land; they had to abandon the homes, occupations, and everything they had worked for over the years, now sacrificed for their safety and welfare. Many loyalists at Savannah, having second thoughts about leaving home, aversely transferred their allegiance to the United States. The others, with their families and belongings, retired to Cockspur and Tybee Islands, encamping until time for embarkation. Chief Justice Anthony Stokes tells us, "We left Savannah on June 22, 1782, and reached the beach on the following day, that the season was extremely hot, the water on the barren island of Tybee unwholesome, and the other natural inconveniences there without remedy, and that many of the loyalists died on that island before the embarkation."[14]

Refugees escaped every which way, on land by paths and roadways, on rivers by rafts and canoes, and by sea in all sizes of sailing vessels. They invaded Florida at every entry point they could find. By November 1782, it was reported that 722 whites and 1,659 Negroes had come from Georgia; 1,383 whites and 1,681 Negroes from South Carolina. Tonyn settled them on granted but uncultivated lands and by procuring land among the settlements along the St. Johns River. The land was rented since there was no time to cultivate crops. By December additional refugees had arrived, numbering 911 whites and 1,786 Negroes from Georgia, 1,517 whites and 1,823 Negroes from South Carolina. Many of these Negroes of Georgia and South Carolina were country-bred who, it was said, dreaded being sent away to Florida. The Negroes did suffer on these moves; some were seized by bandits, others went missing rather than make the move, some were sold to give their owners ready cash to make the trip, many died from disease or lack of food and good water. The trek was relatively hard for them, yet they remained the primary wealth of their owners. Negroes outnumbered white inhabitants; a total of 3,060 whites to 4,519 blacks, with more to come in 1783.[15]

The plight of the whites and blacks at this time was pitiful; having already been forced to move two or three times from plantation to plantation, and from country to town, they were now herded together, surrounded by bundles of their salvaged personal effects (taking with them only provisions for six weeks' subsistence), crowding onto government transports that moved them out of harm's way for the present as they embarked for Florida. Many landed at the mouth of the St. Johns River because it was more easily reached by larger vessels; the bar at the mouth of the St. Johns lay twice as deep as that at St. Augustine.

It was common to see ships aground on the bar at St. Augustine. It was covered by a depth of not more than nine feet, was traversed by narrow tortuous channels, and was unprotected from the sweeping force of wind and wave. After the abandonment of Charleston, not fewer than 16 vessels bearing refugees and their effects went to pieces and many persons lost their lives.[16] Squadrons of British transports landed their throngs of refugees and their Negroes at St. Johns Bluff, and numerous ships unloaded great piles of barrels, boxes, parts of portable houses, and other receptacles filled with provisions of all kinds for the people who disembarked here and for those who wished to go to St. Augustine. With a quick glance, it seemed to the refugees that the whole country of East Florida was a waste of level grasslands and pine barren, compared to the low country and piedmont of their native colonies. There was no choice but to buy a town lot or take up a virgin tract of land in the colony, and begin pioneering all over again. It was winter and the planters of East Florida had little to offer in the way of provisions. The Georgians had brought scarcely a six weeks' supply for themselves, and the supply shipped along with the Carolinians from Charleston by General Leslie was so much less than he had intended to send that only half the allowance allotted to individuals could be issued.[17] John Winniett was appointed commissary agent for the refugees, and with the assistance of influential refugees, he received a six months' supply from General Carleton in New York.[18]

While some who had fled their homes settled in the capital or in the town of St. Johns Bluff, the greater number sought dwelling places in the country along the St. Johns River, the Matanzas River, or as far away as Doctors Lake, about 30 miles south from the bluff. Most of them squatted on vacant land. Others seeking shelter from the storm of woe unleashed upon them sailed south to Mosquito Inlet, where the massive infrastructure created at New Smyrna was abandoned and in deterioration. This was the last stop on the King's Highway for numerous refugees.

One of the notable Georgians who removed to East Florida was Lieutenant Governor John Graham. He had served as a lieutenant colonel of the royal militia, and since January 1783 had been superintendent of Indian affairs in the Western Division of the Southern District. He brought with him 200 slaves to clear land and make settlement of five tracts, 500 acres each at the head of the Matanzas River. Graham employed Lieutenant Colonel John Douglas as his superintendent and entrusted him with the task of clearing and planting the land. It is noted that parties of Choctaw and Creek Indians accompanied the Georgia refugees from Savannah to East Florida. When the refugees embarked, the Indians watched attentively without participating actively, and then the Choctaw began to return to their nation as did the Creeks, undoubtedly not impressed with their future prospects in East Florida.[19]

Upon the signing of a preliminary peace treaty between the Americans and England, the British evacuated Savannah on July 11, 1782, and then Charleston on December 14. General Leslie saw there was nothing the British army could do since both civil governments had been reactivated. Leslie embarked the collected British units from Gadsden's Wharf at Charleston. Accounted for were South Carolina Royalists, Carolina King's Rangers, and Royal North Carolina Regiment, all of which had been organized in Florida; the North Carolina Highlanders, who had not been, were nonetheless sent to Governor Tonyn at St. Augustine.[20]

Besides army units and citizen refugees, there were thousands of Negroes within British lines at Charleston who had to be taken out of the colony. These were chattels of the British forces, such as those who constructed fortifications, unloaded supply ships, and built government buildings. Mutual restitution of the Negroes was proposed: The first lot went to the government at St. Lucia island. The British West Indies had employment for several hundred Negroes. And 136 Negroes onboard were bound for Tonyn at St. Augustine. Officers were supplied Negroes as servants, cooks, and coachmen; those with long service in the South regarded these slaves as their own property. Negroes who were rented out were called in for the grand exodus. Colonel James Moncrief, former engineer from St. Augustine, is said to have taken with him 800 slaves under his charge. Transports were furnished to some of the loyalists to convey their plundered slaves to East Florida. There was little success in restoring the sequestered Negroes to their proper owners. Genealogically it was a nightmare for blacks and whites.[21]

By the end of 1782, Negroes, despite their majority, played an obscure role in the St. Augustine social structure. Free and slave Negroes sold fresh-caught fish, cakes, beer, and home-grown vegetables at stands in the public market downtown. There was a curfew established and those who ignored it after ten in the evening were subject to 39 lashes.

Because of the increase in the Negro population, it was difficult to know exactly which blacks were slaves. Those who had proof of freedom were to wear a silver armband engraved with "free," and slaves belonging to masters whose status was uncertain were to wear heart-shaped badges. Despite these regulations a number of blacks assumed that they were free; regardless of their pleas of guiltlessness, the provost escorted them to the jail at the plaza. As discussed earlier, a controversy at this time was the slave code for the colony, regarding condemned slaves. The solution was that local slave trials were permitted, but sentence of death was deferred until Tonyn and his advisors had a chance to review the proceedings at the capital. On a more practical level one must look at the provisions Governors Grant and Tonyn had made at an earlier time allowing Negroes in the military to carry muskets, bayonets, and knives as members of the East Florida Rangers. Without doubt the freedoms now available to plantation Negroes upset many whites from the slave colonies of Georgia and South Carolina. The controversy would not be decided until 1865.

The pace of life had quickened in the capital as the old city became a conglomerate of aged residents, soldiers, seamen, plantation owners, and now with newcomers made up of wealthy and poor whites, Negroes, farmers, and Jewish merchants. The large number of debarking refugees crowded into the narrow streets and the plaza in the center of town; others had to stay onboard the transports. Either way, they caused serious health problems for the authorities. Poor sanitation and overcrowding were deplorable, and soon became hopeless as an ill smell permeated the city and its harbor. The sufferers then moved outside the walled city seeking satisfactory arrangements by erecting huts, becoming squatters in the quest for some relief from their cursed plight, but all the time keeping control of their Negroes as best as possible under the circumstances. For the time being they had to depend on the provisions being distributed by the government as their food source.

As 1782 came to a close there was little to be celebrated by the refugees; it had been a terrible year for them. Little is known of Governor Tonyn's personal life during this period. His wife and children are never mentioned. Did they live in St. Augustine at the governor's house or did they prefer the plantation, which was located on the St. Johns River at Broclair Bluff? We do know one of his concerns was that the Americans or one of their allies, the French or Spanish, might strike St. Augustine by sea. This feeling of insecurity arose from the fact that a Spanish expeditionary force took the defenseless British garrison in the Bahamas in May 1782. Could such a sudden seizure be planned for St. Augustine by any of the enemy in 1783?

The headquarters of the Southern District was again located in St. Augustine. At the time of the evacuation of Savannah, Lieutenant General Leslie announced that Lieutenant Colonel Archibald McArthur was to assume command at St. Augustine. In the second week of October, the first fleet of transports sailing from Charleston to St. Augustine carried McArthur with four provincial regiments, on their way to replace Lieutenant Colonel Glazier as commandant. McArthur previously served with the 71st Regiment under Lord Cornwallis in South Carolina. At Camden he was head of a corps of cavalry made up of Hessians from Charleston. Arriving in Florida, Colonel Glazier departed with the 4th Battalion of the 60th Regiment for Halifax, Nova Scotia, Canada. At the beginning of 1783, General Carleton in New York wrote to McArthur, saying he should take the title of, and act as brigadier general.[23]

Generals McArthur and Tonyn would lead the colony into the new year of 1783. Early on in January they were greeted by a deputation of Indians from Detroit. St. Augustine and Indians were synonymous ever since Pedro Menéndez de Avilés came ashore in 1565, but they were Indians from local tribes, and their numbers of limited size. But on this day, 2,000 of them from a great distance were camped within the vicinity of the capital.

To regress, even after the Yorktown campaign in October 1781 and subsequent peace, the bloody war continued along the Ohio River Valley as Indian attacks on Americans increased with strength and ferocity. The tomahawk, the torch, and the scalping knife did their bloody and lurid work; and proud Indians brought to Detroit, from the lands across the beautiful river, scores of scalps, ghastly and pitiful evidence of slain men, women, and children. Detroit became a haven, a base, and a source of inspiration for the Ohio Valley tribes and Illinois country.[24]

But now without their British ally and supporter, in efforts to protect themselves from the daily push of patriots as the American tide of expansion would surely continue, the Indians sought guidance and explanation of current affairs. Without direction because the British had left the field of active military operations, they apparently decided as a force to travel south to Florida, the only remaining English colony of the Crown south of Canada.

The Indians came from the northern and southern nations, including chiefs of the Mohawk, Tuscarora, and Seneca from New York; Delaware Indians now in the Midwest; the Shawnee from the Missouri area; Mingo Indians, a detached band of Iroquois; plus other unnamed tribes. Traveling with their chief were 1,200 Cherokees from Virginia, North and South Carolina, and Georgia. In addition there were 600 braves from Florida, comprising Chickasaw, Seminole, and Creek tribes. Prior to this gathering, Superintendent of Indian Affairs Colonel Thomas Brown, who had returned from Savannah at the evacuation, recorded that since his arrival in St. Augustine, more than 3,000 Creeks had come down pleading their poverty and declaring friendship to him. But this meeting was different. These tribes came to learn the state of affairs in the South, to express their attachment to the British Crown, to confirm the southern tribes in that sentiment, and particularly to promote a confederation among all the tribes.

The Indians were not only left out of the peace conference, there was no consideration of them at all. They needed to evaluate their future under the hostile American pioneers and a new government. Lieutenant Colonel John Douglas, Deputy Secretary of Indian affairs, and Generals Tonyn and McArthur attended the council. Whether they smoked the pipe or not, it was important for the British to keep the Indians quiet and maintain their friendship. The commandant ordered that provisions be provided the visitors, causing a heavy drain on the stores for the refugees.[25] While this visitation was notable for its large numbers in attendance, it was not documented very well as to where the Indians were located, in St. Augustine, or the roads and rivers they had to travel to and from the colony. They departed on January 12, 1783, disappearing back into the woods, their future in the hands of the Americans, Spanish, and French. In the end, the efforts of the American Indians to protect themselves and to push back the patriots below the Ohio, supported though they were by the British, became fruitless, as Americans increased their grip south of the Ohio and the British had to say adieu.

Commander in Chief Carleton, in New York, advised General McArthur to continue to pay attention to the defenses of East Florida. McArthur regarded Fort Matanzas at the mouth of the river as the key to St. Augustine, manning it with a captain and 30 men. He stationed a large and a small galley in that harbor south of town. McArthur also ordered three galleys in the harbor of St. Augustine and in that of the

St. Johns River, while he sent an 18-pounder cannon to the blockhouse near the bar of the river. The commandant also urged Governor Tonyn to assemble the militia companies, at least on Sundays.[26] John Winniett, Commissioner of Refugees, had his title changed to Inspector of Refugees, besides forming a committee of four of the principal refugees, namely Colonels Elias Ball and James Cassels from South Carolina, and Colonels John Douglas and Josiah Tattnall from Georgia, to take a census of the newcomers and their Negroes, and supply them with provisions.

The committee's final count on April 20, 1783, was 6,090 white refugees and 11,285 Negroes, for a sum of 17,375 refugees.[27] When adding these totals to the East Florida population, 1,000 whites and 3,000 Negroes, the population of East Florida at this time was approximately 21,000 inhabitants.

In February of this year, the last Florida episode in the American Revolution had begun, led by Major Andrew Deveaux, a refugee of the royal militia of Beaufort, South Carolina. On the evacuation of Savannah, Deveaux came to East Florida where he began recruiting volunteers for an expedition against New Providence in the Bahama Islands, which was recently captured by the Spanish. Under his articles of agreement, Deveaux was to furnish arms, ammunition, and provisions for the expedition; all prizes taken on sea or land were to be divided among the officers and men according to rank, after deducting the expenses of the expedition. Those who wished to settle in the Bahamas would be provided with land. The recruits rendezvoused in St. Augustine on March 15, embarked on April 1 with 65 men in two armed brigantines, and sailed to Harbor Island, where Deveaux recruited for a few days, principally securing Negroes. This polyglot army was named the Royal Foresters. They landed on New Providence Island near the eastern fort that guarded the harbor of Nassau. With 150 men, Deveaux captured this fort while the garrison slept, and a detachment of 70 Royal Foresters captured three galleys lying abreast at the fort. The invaders then climbed the heights in the upper part of Nassau, and Deveaux summoned the grand fortress to surrender. On April 18, Deveaux erected a battery of 12-pounders on each of two commanding hills and hoisted the English colors, again summoning the Spanish to surrender. A well-directed shot at the governor's house from a fieldpiece brought the governor to terms. He signed the articles of capitulation by which he and his garrison marched out with all honors of war, surrendering 700 Spanish regular troops, 70 cannon, and four large galleys, all of which Deveaux sent to Havana with the troops.[28] However, there was a downside to Deveaux's victory. When the news reached St. Augustine, General McArthur sent the news to Sir Guy Carleton with a brief message: "...a very splendid action lately performed by Major Deveaux of the Beaufort militia," but added, "...unluckily he was nine days too late." On April 9, England already had signed a treaty with Spain by which the Bahamas were restored to England.[29]

As St. Augustine became more prosperous with the arrival of refugees, so did the established businesses, especially taverns and gaming places; the skittle-alley, shuffleboard, and billiard table were always in demand. But without a shadow of doubt the most appreciated item was the *East-Florida Gazette*, edited and published by Dr. William Charles Wells. At the evacuation of Charleston in December 1782, he sailed for St. Augustine, taking his printing press and pressman with him. In the latter part of January 1783, he issued the first newspaper ever published in East Florida. On April 21, 1783, he issued a special number of his paper as the *East-Florida Gazette Extraordinary*, which contained the news of the peace. Mrs. Elizabeth Lichtenstein Johnston, a refugee from Georgia, mentions after reading the accounts of a peace being made, with terms most shameful to Britain, adds, "The war never occasioned half the distress which this peace has done, to the unfortunate loyalist."[30]

Nearly as confusing as the present events, with no two days being the same, were the financial aspects confronting East Florida. Refugees from surrounding states began pouring into Florida while various state military units, officials, merchants, and prisoners followed suit. They brought a hodgepodge of coin and paper money with them; coins from England, Spain, France, Portugal, and Holland were all legal tender. The Spanish-milled dollar, or piece of eight, and English pounds, shillings, and pence predominated the hard money; the English pound and Spanish dollar had the same relative value.

A year before the Revolution, the Continental Congress resolved to finance the coming war with paper money, i.e., Continental currency, which quickly depreciated. Added to this paper float was printed money of each colony, which had established its own currency laws. Counterfeiting by the British as well as by Americans helped cheapen all paper currency. East Florida had been isolated from the fiscal scheming to the north of them by maintaining the English pound and Spanish dollar for daily living. Yet there was an extraordinary amount of credit being extended on the books because there was a chronic shortage of currency.

These account books of debt were used widespread at trading posts and trading houses along the rivers and trails with the Indians. Storekeepers had to excel in the debt and credit system to keep track of trades. Because there was no banking system in place, no clearing-houses for the exchange of paper money, scrip, plantation coins, or money of lesser countries, the refugees had no recourse but to pay for their land purchases, dwellings, and supplies by entering into debt.[31]

As for as the Americans, by May 1781, they were financially collapsed with their money schemes. However, by now the war was effectively over so it would seem the ideas of financing carried them through the difficult times. Nevertheless, they had to go the road where it became necessary to resort to loans from their allies. The French and Spanish governments and private Dutch bankers loaned the new democracy $7,830,000. Robert Morris, a major financier of the American Revolution, undertook the establishment of the Bank of North America in 1782 and secured a loan of specie from France; after a French fleet brought over $200,000 in specie, the Bank of North America opened its doors for business.[32]

10

The Defining Peace Negotiation

By 1782–83, Great Britain was hard pressed in the world with its numerous enemies. France, Holland, Spain, and the American colonies would have to be dealt with in a series of steps to a long, uneasy summit. Richard Oswald and Henry Strachey served as British peacemakers, while Benjamin Franklin, John Adams, John Jay, and Henry Laurens (recently released from the Tower of London) would represent the United States. From the beginning the British wanted to deal with the Americans separately from France, Holland, and Spain. John Adams went to The Hague to secure Dutch recognition of the United States, arrange a loan, and bring about a treaty of amity and commerce. Richard Oswald reached Paris and started talks with Franklin, the only American on the scene, as John Jay was named minister to Spain to draw up the peace treaty with that country at Madrid. When both diplomats, Adams and Jay, concluded their treaties, all parties met in Paris to draft and approve the treaty, signed by Franklin, Adams, Jay, and Laurens.

The Peace Treaty signed in Paris, on September 3, 1783, contained nine articles: (1) United States independence was recognized by Great Britain; (2) various boundaries in Maine, Nova Scotia, and the Great Lakes were established; (3) fishing rights off Newfoundland and Nova Scotia were defined; (4) creditors of each country were to be paid by citizens of the other; (5) the U.S. Congress would recommend that states fully restore the rights and property of loyalists; (6) no future action would be taken against any person for his actions during the war just ended; (7) hostilities were to end and all British forces were to be evacuated; (8) navigation of the Mississippi, from its source to the ocean, shall forever remain free; and (9) conquests made by either country from the other before the arrival of the peace terms would be restored.[1] This agreement would become effective after Britain had reached terms with its other enemies.

By the Treaty of Paris of 1783, which acknowledged the independence of the American colonies of Great Britain, East Florida, not having joined the American Revolutionists, was exempt from the agreement's articles. Nevertheless it became part of the Anglo-French-Spanish diplomatics. John Jay, America's diplomat at Madrid, early on found that the Spanish king and his advisers were by no means friends of the United States even though they had secretly supported their cause with loans and materials of war. They refused to recognize American independence, at least until Britain had done so. They disliked and feared the possibility that a republican regime in the United States would encourage revolution in Spain's colonies in the New World. After General de Galvez's campaigns and victory in West Florida, they claimed the Floridas by right of past conquest.

John Jay was not recognized by the Spanish government; in fact he was treated as a nuisance in Spain. In Paris, Jay ardently supported Franklin in asserting American claims against both Britain and Spain. Jay even turned against France because he suspected that the ruling French Bourbon secretly supported Spanish interests when it came to negotiations with America.[2] He was right; but to hasten the pacification, William P. F. Shelburne, a British statesman, suggested Britain should keep Gibraltar and offer the Floridas and Island of Minorca to Spain in compensation. To this, the Spanish diplomatic agent, Count Florida Blanca, listened with distrust and misgiving yet, after a long hesitation, yielded. It should be noted that the negotiations in Paris, from which the treaty between Great Britain and the United States resulted, were performed at the same time the disputes between Great Britain, France, and Spain were far advanced in coming to terms. The preliminaries of peace between Great Britain, France, and Spain, the second treaty, were signed on January 20, 1783, and ratified September 19, 1783.

By the fifth article of the Anglo-Spanish Treaty, East Florida was ceded to Spain, a term of 18 months being allowed for British subjects to sell their estates, recover their debts, and remove their families and effects without being restrained under any pretense whatever, except that of debts and criminal prosecutions. The British were also entitled to remove artillery and other government property.[3]

For the sake of Gibraltar, Great Britain could well afford to yield the Floridas, reasoned Lord Shelburne. West Florida had been conquered by the Spanish, and East Florida had been in British possession for only 20 years, and was scarcely settled. Shelburne also observed that the trade of the Floridas was valued at only 100,000 pounds sterling in imports, 120,000 pounds sterling in export, and that this was not an object worth contending for at the hazard of losing the peace. William Knox, who had considerable influence in the development of East Florida, pointed out that the British government had in ignorance given to Spain more of Florida than had been received from Spain 20 years earlier, namely Mobile and parts of West Florida ceded by France in 1763. Another Lord questioned whether East Florida's cession was either legal or political, particularly since no guarantees had been obtained for the inhabitants' religious freedom as the Anglican and Catholic Churches did not mix well. Ex-Governor Johnston of West Florida deplored the loss of the Bay of Tampa, one of the finest harbors in the world, he declared. Lord North argued that the loss of West Florida made it less valuable as a protection against privateers preying on the Jamaica trade. In reality, the heavy cost of maintaining and defending the government of East Florida was out of all proportion to the value of its trade.

The news of the unwelcome treaty came as a shock to the people of East Florida. Nothing could exceed the distress to which the loyalists were then reduced. They had little choice: They could either leave America, abandoning their property forever; remain behind to risk the harshest treatment from the victors; sail for England and disappear into English life without leaving any trace of their presence in America; or sail for Canada or to the West Indies, where they could begin their lives anew within the remaining British colonies.[4] The heartbreak of the Acadians pictured so poignantly by Longfellow's *Evangeline* was not greater than that of the Floridians. They pleaded and remonstrated with the British government in the most piteous terms, but to no avail.[5] On receiving the news, Governor Tonyn published a proclamation requesting the inhabitants to lose no time in settling their affairs, and that Admiral Robert Digby had promised assistance and shipping in removing the population to England, the West Indies, and any other of the king's dominions. General McArthur was ordered to conduct the evacuation.

John Moultrie wrote to his friend, former governor James Grant, now a lieutenant general living in England: "I may probably once more join company with you. We have often parted without a prospect of meeting again, but the chapter of accidents has brought us together; 'tis the only good chapter." After finally achieving a life of real plenty, ease and elegance, in a province that had recently shown an astonishing productivity in agriculture, lumber, and naval stores, Moultrie was about to be turned adrift, to again seek a resting place. Moultrie was disturbed about the fate of his Negroes, especially a number of faithful servants brought up for several generations in his family. Moultrie contemplated freeing them all, burning his houses, and becoming a real philosopher. "For the future England, I think, will bring me up. My feelings, principles, everything prevents me having any idea of remaining in America."[6] In July 1784, he sailed to England, leaving behind three brothers, Thomas, Alexander, and William, all patriot soldiers.

Not everyone had or wanted to sell their Negroes to raise money, so they had to make their purchases with a credit line. This was done between merchants, landowners, real estate transfers, and captains of ships. Drawn-on account ledgers flourished since no party to these agreements ever thought the line of credit would be short-lived — until England announced that by treaty, Florida was being returned to Spain. Now the squeeze was on for both debtor and creditor. Would there be any relief? Hard money was king and had better be saved, as there was no telling where the Floridians' next home might be, either in Canada, the West Indies, or back to the States. Regardless, creditors now renamed their ledgers as books of recoverables, in hopes of receiving some value from the assets, or future compensation from the Crown.

There were others who stood to lose money from this turn of events; the absentee merchants, planters, and proprietors of land in Florida living in England, experienced losses to the amount of 300,000 pounds sterling. They rallied, claiming their property had been given up as the price of peace and for the recovery of the Bahama Islands; they hoped for compensation from the government. Although all parties were angry at heart for being abandoned by their government, eternal hope persisted that in some fashion Britain might retain East Florida if the right deal came along.

The record of the evacuation and embarkment for the next year and a half tells the tale of what became of the loyalists, the armed forces, the Indians, the property, and the shattered dreams. In April, General Carleton issued instructions for the recall of all officers and traders from the Creek and Cherokee Indian tribes. In May, General McArthur wrote his commander in chief that the minds of the Indians appeared to be as much agitated as those of the unhappy loyalists, and that the Indians had proposed to abandon their country and accompany their friends. Superintendent Thomas Brown gave further proof of their loyalty by writing for vessels to remove the Creeks, who were determined to follow the fate of their English friends. The Cherokees felt the same, as Cowdriver, an old warrior, assured Governor Tonyn that if the great man over the water would give them large canoes and land for hunting, most of the Cherokee would be willing to withdraw with the governor. General Carleton was opposed to the idea, believing the Bahamas were poorly adapted to their mode of life, the West Indies islands were already populated and subject to unremitting heat, and Nova Scotia was too cold for those accustomed to a southern clime. He urged that they be dissuaded from going, although he agreed to furnish conveyance for those who persevered in their demand. General McArthur hoped to convince the Creeks and Cherokees that their emigration with the loyalists would be the greatest evil that could befall them. In fact, they and the other Indians accepted the advice given them.

When the Georgia and South Carolina newspapers announced the Anglo-Spanish Treaty, a considerable influx of transient people, the bounty hunters, came to East Florida to recover their plundered Negroes. This was a touch-and-go situation with over 10,000 Negroes scattered about living in cabins and shanties outside of town; but in the end the bounty hunters did find sellers who could no longer support Negroes where they planned to settle.

Fortunately for everyone, the systematic British had ordered and delivered a number of victualing (cargo) ships that arrived at St. Augustine and St. Johns Bluff in May, carrying provisions for the refugees. These huge ships carried as much as a thousand barrels of flour, beef, pork, oatmeal, peas, and casks of rice. The safe arrival of these seven victualers now made it possible to subsist the loyalists until the end of September. This encouraged Governor Tonyn to try to keep the refugees in the province, allowing those with crops time to harvest them, and sufficient food until they should find some suitable retreat.

The arrival of provisions seemed to attract the Indians. Cowdriver and other chiefs returned to St. Augustine swearing vengeance against the king for giving away their country, and declaring that on the departure of the English they would claim their own and kill every Spaniard who should thrust his head beyond the lines of St. Augustine. The Indians, now grandfathered as part of the colony, shared in the public stores as per past practice.⁷ The news of Florida's cession did not incite the Indians; instead they remained loyal to the British. But there were lawless banditti left over from the war, a mixed group of Georgia refugees and Florida residents, veterans of the cattle and slave raids that had traumatized both sides of the Florida-Georgia border during the war. Led by Daniel McGirth, a former East Florida Ranger, and Roger Moore and his gang of thieves, the banditti raided plantations and stole horses and cattle. They committed robberies on the roads, plundered houses, and carried away Negroes; a state of lawlessness was practiced from their lurking places between the St. Marys River and the St. Johns River.⁸ For a short time the escapades of these banditti, who owed allegiance to no government, went unchecked by Tonyn.

By May 20, 90 refugees had chosen the island of New Providence in the Bahamas, 85 Jamaica, and 47 England, as their destination. General McArthur promised to furnish an eight weeks' supply of provisions for going across the Atlantic, a six weeks' supply for those leaving for Jamaica, and a three weeks' supply for those going to New Providence.

In the meantime, committees were busy appraising the land, houses, and other property. Governor Tonyn appointed William Slater and John Champneys to conduct public sales; selling prices immediately plummeted to approximately ten percent of construction costs in the town, and the market for plantations was even more depressed. A handful of refugees disassembled their wooden houses, transferring the framing, windows, and hardware to St. Marys Harbor to be shipped on a transport to their destination. The ships for Jamaica and New Providence sailed around June 25 and two transports for England did not leave until July 9. This was the first contingent of refugees who took advantage of free government transports and land grants offered by the British. These early birds sailed with heavy hearts, having to abandon everything they had worked for. Now, with limited knowledge they had to start all over in another land. The majority were extremely anxious to know what lands or gratuities would be allowed to those who chose another British settlement, Halifax in Nova Scotia, or one of the Bahamas bank of islands.

The Bahamas stretch about 800 miles southeast of Florida to northeast of Cuba, and are covered with rock, coral keys, and reefs.

Nassau, on New Providence Island, is the chief port. The Treaty of 1783 restored the Bahamas to the British. The acquisition of the Bahamas and the prospect that the habitable islands among them could be occupied by loyalist refugees appealed to many ... if only they knew more about them, they could make a decision on moving to one of the islands. Also facing the same determination were the loyalist refugees at New York City: get out of the country or face the terms imposed. Sir Guy Carleton was privy to all inhabitants' desires, so he sent Lieutenant John Wilson, the acting engineer at St. Augustine, to examine into the military state of New Providence. Carleton earlier recommended to the British government that the lands ungranted, or escheated, in the Bahamas be given free of all expense to those loyalists who had lost their estates. Wilson returned to St. Augustine with an unfavorable report; the soil was rocky and there were no tracts of land contiguous where any considerable number of Negroes could be employed.[9] The latter news dissuaded the plantation owners and overseers, who continued weighing the options to continue their way of life.

In the months following the signing of the peace treaty, more than 28,000 loyalists left New York City to settle in Canada, which Jonathan Sewall termed "the American New Jerusalem."[10] Likewise, many exiles who had been living in England also sailed for Canada. It was also revealed that a number of New York refugees had decided on settling the Great Abaco Island, the largest of the Bahamas group; furthermore they expected some refugees from St. Augustine would be joining them, which was true. Upwards of 1,500 loyalists from East Florida and about the same number from New York emigrated to Abaco Island.

Sir Guy Carleton decided to include the Bahamas as a part of the Southern District, and instructed McArthur to consider them under his command. Eight companies of militia were also going to the Bahama Islands for General McArthur's use on New Providence Island, in sufficient numbers to support the refugees for six months. In part the prayers of these petitioners were answered, for on September 12, a fleet of transports and victualers arrived at St. Augustine. It was time to muster out the armed forces; Superintendent Brown and a large proportion of his Carolina King's Rangers decided to embark for Nova Scotia; nearly two-thirds of the South Carolina Royalists wished their discharge at St. Augustine; more than half of the Royal North Carolina Regiment chose to go to Nova Scotia; and about 40 emigrants went to Great Britain.[11] The disbanding of the provincial troops left the governor with few options for defending the remaining inhabitants, especially from the banditti. It was decided that the Royal Artillery, under the command of Captain Henry Abbott, should remain on duty and in possession of the fort until the Spaniards should arrive.

A few days after the embarkation of the provincial forces, three companies of the 37th Regiment, comprising 150 men, arrived from New York City to assist the governor in keeping the peace and order.

Horses and Negroes seemed to have been the favorite booty of the banditti. In the face of continuing widespread banditry and disorder, Tonyn authorized the formation of two troops of horse (cavalry) to check banditry. He commissioned Colonel William Young of Georgia, and Captain Alexander Stewart of South Carolina, to command the horse cavalry to protect the persons and property of their fellow provincials. Later, Colonel Young testified he apprehended Daniel McGirth and Daniel Cargill for stealing Francis Levett's horses. Captain Stewart stated that he succeeded in dispensing the banditti who infested the frontier of East Florida, and received the thanks of Governor Tonyn for his services.

Although the banditti committed all of the dastardly offenses known to man, the white Whigs, British officers, and other upstanding citizens were equal in their crimes. The citizens in Georgia and South Carolina were trying to prevent the plundering of their slaves by the departing British officers and loyalist inhabitants, who brought rebel property with them and were then shipping them to the West Indies. This was kidnapping. Even Governor Tonyn refused to surrender those Negroes who were without owners; all this was being done under the cloak of friendship for the suffering loyalists and in ignorance of the confiscation acts of the new states. No opportunity was being missed to carry off Negroes by persons who did not own them. It was only natural that out-of-state victims charged Governor Tonyn with concealing sequestered property for his own profit.[12]

Regardless, he was asked to remain, regulate the embarkations, and prevent confusion as far as possible, which he did. His governorship would terminate with the actual cession.

The United States and Great Britain signed the final peace treaty in Paris, on September 3, 1783. This month Governor Tonyn wrote to Rear Admiral Robert Digby about the tonnage necessary for final evacuation. He imagined nearly 10,000 refugees would emigrate, but was not sure. Some people with Negroes preferred Jamaica and the Windward Islands; many the Bahamas; the officers of the civil government, with their families, were going to England. William Brown, Speaker of the Commons House of Assembly, was appointed Commissioner of Evacuation, and kept the books in his office in which emigrants' names were entered, the number of their slaves, and destinations where they were bound. Robert Leaver gave orders to the masters of the vessels, while regulation of small craft that carried much of the personal effects was in the hands of John Mowbray. The record of all expenses connected with the evacuation was kept by Peter Edwards.

British redcoats evacuated New York City on November 25, 1783, and American patriots marched in jubilation as they reentered New York City, which they had lost seven years before. Of course, gone were the loyalist refugees who had shipped out earlier. Test laws confiscating Tory property had been passed by the new states. New York state made $3,600,000 from the sale of confiscated loyalist property, and Maryland collected over $2,000,000. An estimated total of those who left America during the Revolution is almost 100,000.[13]

Back in Florida at this time, General McArthur, with a detachment of the 37th Regiment, sailed to assume command of the Bahamas, where he rendered material aid to large numbers of exiles recently settled there. The stream of refugees continued to flow out of Florida, most of them embarking onboard government transports in Amelia Harbor at the mouth of the St. Marys River, where seven transports had recently arrived from New York. Such government sailing vessels carried passengers without charge, thus saving them a great expense.

One passenger, Johann David Schoepf, on a sloop for New Providence, gives an account of life on these transports. "It was crammed with people and cattle, luggage and household furniture, and carried a number of black women and children who were being sent to the island for sale. Along the coast Schoepf noticed at frequent intervals the skeleton, or wreckage, of a foundered ship. Onboard, one of the Africans entertained his fellows by playing on a rude 'gambee' and singing in the Guinea tongue. The Negro's viol de gamba was only a notched bar of wood with one end resting against an empty cask and the other against his breast. Over the notches he rubbed, in time with his rhythmic song, a stick, while shaking the clappers of another stick split lengthwise."[14] After entering the harbor of New Providence the passengers landed at Nassau, the small capital of the Bahamas, whose single street with row houses hugged the hilly shore.

Not everyone wanted to start life over in the Out Islands, which had neither churches, courts of justice nor adequate jails, especially those planters who had a fair count of Negroes accustomed to the plantation system. Most were Southerners who had settled in Florida after the evacuation of Charleston, in the mistaken belief that the area would remain in British hands. Consequently, many of them had endured two confiscations, first in the Carolinas or Georgia, then in Florida.[15] William Brown, Commissioner of Evacuation, said on the news of the peace treaty's being signed, he supposed over 3,000 people, 462 whites, and 2,561 blacks, mostly from the backcountry, returned to their home state. It was very difficult to keep records of the people scattered over East Florida. Some inhabitants started overland for settlements on the lower Mississippi around Natchez; others crossed over the St. Marys River and returned to their own state, hoping to pick up the pieces of their lives, and were forgiven for past transgressions. They skedaddled out of Florida with empty hands, no free transportation, no British provisions, and no land grants. At the same time, the new states relaxed their laws of confiscation and banishment under the treaty, encouraging the wayward to return. Most who took advantage of these modifications and attitudes owned considerable numbers of slaves who, like their masters, much preferred going back to the old plantation than venture abroad into some unknown British colony.

Almost as many whites remained in East Florida as returned to the states, while only 200 Negroes stayed, most likely former slaves who had been with the Minorcans in Dr. Turnbull's colony at New Smyrna. Of those who remained, most were undoubtedly Minorcans who lived in and around St. Augustine, although a few preferred settling in Jamaica or Dominica. By reason of their Catholic religious affiliation with the Spaniards, 500 Minorcans, Greeks, and Italians remained. Assorted artisans, shopkeepers, tavern owners, and Jewish merchants stayed in the town, and outside the walled city there were still the Indians and the Crackers.[16]

When the tidal wave of evacuation was completed, East Florida was swept nearly clean of its 17,000 British subjects, who fled in many directions, especially southward to the Bahama Islands. In actuality loyalists and their slaves from other colonies were on the move after peace terms were published. The island of Jamaica received refugees from Connecticut, Massachusetts, New York, Philadelphia, Maryland, Virginia, the Carolinas, and Georgia in 1782. They came in large numbers, especially from Georgia and South Carolina. After the evacuation of Savannah, 400 families with nearly 5,000 slaves went to Jamaica; the great convoy from Charleston arrived at Kingston in January of 1783, with 1,278 white people and 2,600 Negroes. East Florida did not furnish more than one-fifth of this total to the population of Jamaica. The following month, a convoy arrived from Charleston with 1,600 troops, including the 63rd, 64th, and 71st regiments, together with a detachment of the 84th. With this fleet were 400 white families who brought with them 4,500 Negroes.[17]

Later in the spring, in Dominica there was not a house or shed for the refugees' shelter. Governor J. Orde was at a loss as to what to do with them; everyplace was full. His only resource seemed to be the transports in which they came, so he detained the passengers until the rainy season was over. There was complete cooperation, with the colonial officials, military and navy sometimes having to perform more than one order. Brigadier General Alured Clarke, who conducted the evacuation of Savannah after sending out the Georgia refugees, later served as muster master general of the Hessian prisoners. During May 1783, he had been at Philadelphia, arranging for the march of the prisoners of war to Elizabethtown, New Jersey. The Hessians at the end of the war were permitted to remain in America, entering the American melting pot.

11

The Spaniards Return

Preparations were being made to transfer the possession of East Florida to Spain. In conformity with Governor Tonyn's orders a printed proclamation on May 6, 1784, ordered inhabitants to make application before May 29 to Lieutenant Colonel William Brown, Commissioner of Embarkation at St. Augustine, to receive directions to embark on the last vessels allotted to them. Many had tarried in hopes of finding purchasers for houses and land, but few Spaniards arrived beforehand; thus the market remained depressed at a quarter of its value. At last, on June 26, the lookout's cannon on Anastasia Island boomed, announcing the approach of many ships from the south. Aboard were Vizente Manuel de Zespedes, the new Spanish governor, with 500 troops and civilians from Havana, Cuba.

The new governor expected to sail into Matanzas Bay and take possession of St. Augustine, but his pilot said the channel was almost closed and that artillery must be landed at St. Marys River and brought overland to the city. Tonyn stationed detachments in the town of St. Johns Bluff, while Governor Zespedes arrived at St. Augustine on June 27, 1784. He was received by General Tonyn in the plaza, and then conducted to the Government House, where he exchanged compliments and produced his dispatches for Tonyn. It was agreed that delivery of the fort should mark the end of the British regime and the beginning of Spanish rule. Because of delay in the removal of stores, this did not take place until July 12, 1784. Consequently, an awkward interregnum ensued, when it was doubtful whether English or Spanish law was in effect.[1]

On July 14, Zespedes issued his first proclamation, in which he announced his assumption of the government in the name of His Catholic Majesty; he assured the population of his protection and declared that the banditti must retire from the province. In early 1784, McGirth's party took two coach horses belonging to Chief Justice James Hume from his servants on St. Johns Road, about 25 miles from St. Augustine. At the same time Captain Peter Edwards, Clerk of Public Accounts, lost a horse to these land pirates. Francis Levett, a rice planter from Georgia, had two horses stolen by McGirth. Tonyn assigned Colonel William Young to secure the country from the depredations of these thieves; it was Colonel Young who seized McGirth and Daniel Cargill for stealing Levett's horses. Tonyn called Zespedes's attention to the plundering operations of the banditti that had been adding to the misery of the inhabitants. The new governor appointed justices of the peace to decide disputes among the adherents to the British Crown, appointing John Leslie and Francis Philip Fatio judges.

One of the first disputes to be heard involved the activities and punishment of Daniel McGirth and his gang of banditti, and countermeasures by the Spaniards of the troop of light horse cavalry previously raised by Tonyn. Once the dispute was heard and resolved, the notorious Daniel McGirth, Major William Cunningham, and others were finally confined to the dark, filthy dungeons of Morro Castle at Havana, Cuba. After an imprisonment for five years McGirth went to South Carolina, "ruined in health, reputation, and estate."[2]

Also of this clan was John Cruden, a member of the firm John Cruden & Co., merchants in Wilmington, North Carolina. Cruden vowed never to leave the land his family had settled. His personal scheme was a little more political. Cruden plotted to establish an independent government on the land between the St. Johns and St. Marys rivers, an area of 650 square miles. He named it "United Loyalist" to gain support from his friends in Georgia and the Carolinas. Over time Cruden lost faith in his own private rebellion when he discovered that he could not control the banditti who professed to support his idea.[3] Cruden and his family soon left the states and sailed to Nassau on the island of New Providence, joining his uncle John Cruden, the elder of the house of John Cruden & Co., who had taken refuge there.[4]

Zespedes's second dispute was the proclamation dealing with the Negro situation, and proved most damaging to the Anglo-Spanish disposition. Disguised in settling personal estates was language which, in Tonyn's appointed Justice Hume's opinion, meant that every person, white or black, slave or freeman, who had enjoyed British protection at the time of the Spanish governor's arrival, had the full right to withdraw from the colony. Justice Hume therefore objected to the clause ordering that every Negro who could not produce a certificate of manumission proving his freedom, would be required to take out a written permit within 20 days to work for the public, or hire himself to private persons, under the penalty of becoming the property of His Catholic Majesty.[5] This article worked against the Negroes who had joined the British standard by invitation of generals and commanders, and others who promised them their freedom; now these Negroes could not produce a certificate of manumission, and thus the solemn promise became meaningless and void. On the other hand it would also operate against those who plundered Negroes, such as the American banditti. Hume asserted that five out of every six slaves in the province were held without title deeds.

Governor Zespedes insisted that the Spanish government had no wish to meddle with Negroes having proper masters, but his administration would look after those having no master, or no right to freedom, since they were a pest to the public tranquility. He denied that simple possession was sufficient proof of ownership; his policy was to restore slaves to their proper owners, and to give liberty to those who were the slaves of uncertain owners. Zespedes appointed Francis Philip Fatio as justice of the peace. He was a foreigner who was not acquainted with the laws and constitution of Great Britain. Tonyn called him an obnoxious character; hence, various disputes over property, which caused complaints against decisions made by Fatio, whom Zespedes had appointed "Judge over His Britannic Majesty's Subjects."[6] He prevailed for the next year.

The slow sales of houses in St. Augustine continued to depress the market; the outlook was poor since early arrivals were only military and civil departments. Settlers from other parts of the Spanish dominions were not to be admitted until the British subjects left. There was little market for the houses and land, as well as the mountain of personal effects of the departing loyalists.[7] No property was sold at public vendue after July 18, 1785, which had been named as the last day for that purpose. In the intervening time Zespedes's weighty problem was finding new settlers for the walled city, which he complained was in a state of disrepair that he attributed to British neglect and the surge of refugees.

The governor wrote a letter describing the problems encountered so far. "Outside St. Augustine the population is almost all composed of foreigners, most British subjects who had remained and troublesome Americans who had crossed over the border." He saw American immigrants as a threat to the security of the colony. "The most troublesome of these invaders, the 'Crackers.' These white Crackers are nomadic like Arabs, and are distinguished from savages only in their color, language, and the superiority of their depraved cunning and untrustworthiness. They erect Indian-style huts in the first unpopulated space fit to grow corn. Once done, they move again, always keeping themselves beyond reach of all civilized law."[8]

The Spanish continued the British policy of reserving lands west of the St. Johns River for the Indians. Success of the Spanish colony depended on trade, so they capitalized on British relations with the tribes, careful not to interrupt the fur and hide export trade. In an unprecedented move they continued the arrangement with the British Panton, Leslie and Company, and their trading posts at St. Marks and elsewhere along the St. Johns River, precluding trade with Americans.

Various causes delayed the completion of this huge evacuation, even though Tonyn published an advertisement that the last transports would leave on February 20, 1785. Governor Tonyn and David Yeats, Deputy Clerk of the Council under Governor Grant, and now secretary of the province under Tonyn, moved to the St. Marys River on June 1, 1785, to help supervise the final departures. A tent city had sprung up there, with planters living alongside their Negroes. They were threatened by plunderers as they awaited transports out of East Florida. It was a hot and humid wait living on the beach, but necessary. Poor Tom Williamson at St. Johns Bluff found that the sales of his lots vanished in the spring of 1784 when news of the cession was announced. St. Johns Bluff had trebled in size and reached a population of 1,500 or more. Almost overnight the flourishing village stopped growing; he was left with 198 pristine lots, but no takers. Inhabitants began to dismember their houses and transport them more than 20 miles to St. Marys beach, with a view of sending them to the destination they would select. Sometimes property was lost by theft or through failure to secure space on the crowded transports for their bulky lumber. At length, Williamson also dismembered his own dwelling house and shipped it to Jamaica; by 1785 the village of St. Johns Bluff was a deserted place; on St. Marys beach there was left only a medley of discarded flatboats, frames of dismantled houses, and other personal property discarded by refugees.[9] Whatever real property was not sold was to become the property of the Spanish Crown.

Much to the surprise of everyone, the Minorcans were not a sure bet to stay on under the Spanish. They intended to emigrate along with other British subjects, and consulted Tonyn about it. They solicited him to send most of them to Gibraltar and others to Dominica and the Bahamas. Father Pedro Camps, the Minorcan priest, decided to leave the country along with the governor, but Governor Zespedes brought with him a promotion in the church of Minorca and detained him for another year, besides bringing three other priests, two of whom were Irishmen. Father Campo exerted himself to induce persons of the Catholic faith to become Spanish subjects and remain in St. Augustine, which they did.[10]

Tonyn expected the evacuation would be completed in a few weeks, and wrote that he would sail for Britain in the armed ship *Cyrus* with other civil officers. Tonyn did not make any reference to his family, though undoubtedly they had returned to England at an earlier date. As for his Negroes, he failed to find a buyer in Florida and sent them to Dominica where he found a market for them.[11] Tonyn had already informed Lieutenant Governor James Edward Powell in the Bahamas: "I have sent the boards that were the frames of the pews of the church of St. Augustine to be erected in the church intended to be built by the loyalists in the Island of Providence. I shall likewise send the bells of this city, and the fire engine for the use of the above-cited town intended to be raised by the loyal emigrants."[12]

In September 1785, the last division of transports sailed from East Florida for the Bahamas with the last refugees. Governor Tonyn wrote to Lord Sydney, the secretary of state in London, and said the evacuation was now completed. Tonyn asserted that no country was ever left in a more deplorable state of desolation than Florida was then. The governor, now aboard the *Cyrus* with his entourage, was awaiting a fair wind to carry them out of the port of St. Marys over the first bar. On September 11 they set sail and got over the first bar. Then the wind shifted, forcing the ship back. The *Cyrus* struck a lost anchor, and was perforated with a hole that let in six inches of water an hour. Tonyn and the passengers would not sail in a leaky ship, and so returned to Amelia Harbor while another transport had to be brought up from the Bahamas. The second ship, *Two Sisters*, made the crossing in 53 days, arriving at Portsmouth, England, on January 11, 1786; thus was completed the evacuation of East Florida.[13]

During 1785 and 1787 the British Parliament passed acts providing compensation for the American Sufferers who had undergone financial losses because of the American Revolution. A close examination of this evidence by the claims commissioners would be lengthy. Unfortunately, from the very beginning the commissioners seemed to work hard to limit the number of persons who could claim a right to a government allowance.

In the interim the loyalists found their lot damnably hard wherever they were located. Joshua Weeks, a refugee, revealed, "...every object around me fills me with melancholy. Even the beams of the sun do not shine with their wonted cheerfulness, places of amusement seem to wear a dismal gloom, and even the house of God does not afford me that pleasure it used to."[14]

Time heals. As weeks and months passed, memories of hardship and persecution faded. The loyalists became accustomed to their exile, still believing that Britain did not fully appreciate their sacrifices. Accordingly the British province of East Florida ceased to exist as the streets of St. Augustine were once again nearly deserted. For a brief time John Wells continued the publication of the *East-Florida Gazette*, but he, too, packed up and moved the printing press from St. Augustine to the Bahamas, establishing the *Royal Bahama Gazette*.[15]

It took over three years for the commissioners to examine and rule on 4,118 claims, distributing British pounds sterling in compensation to American loyalists. The claims for East Florida were filed from the Bahamas, Jamaica, and elsewhere, totaling 372 claims. The claimants went to utmost lengths in describing every detail of their claims. They naively believed that the estimates would be accepted more or less as submitted, assuming that the more one claimed, the more he would receive. Demanding precision in written and oral evidence, the commissioners exhibited no qualms whatsoever about striking unsupported items from exiles' accounts. It was more like, "Blessed are ye who expect nothing, for ye then shall not be disappointed."[16] Most living landowners or their heirs applied for compensation, including Governors Grant and Tonyn.

A typical example was the general state of the settlement for the memorialist Denys Rolle of East Florida. Detailed claims were submitted. An excerpt:

11. The Spaniards Return

- He chartered a vessel from England and carried with him to East Florida 49 white persons, in 1779, and in another charter vessel 89 persons, which all were settled by him on his said estate.
- Cleaning and cultivating said lands, upwards the sum of 23,000 pounds.
- Interest expense on settlement amounting annually, the sum of 2,000 pounds.
- Tract of land containing more than 76,000 acres extending nearly 23 miles in length and 8–9 miles in breadth, Chichester Plantation.
- Had more than 1,000 head of cattle, which were stolen, and had to restock, which were destroyed by indigent refugees.
- Loss by sickness and death of 42 Negroes on their removal to the Bahama Islands.
- Expense of chartering the scow *Peace and Plenty*, bound from the Thames to Savannah, to make as many trips as necessary to remove slaves, livestock, and effects to the Bahamas; taking down the buildings on the said estates in order of their removal, which suffered a great diminution in value.
- Descriptions of his personal possessions lost on the removal from the province.
- Relevant documents supported the claims, by

       Denys Rolle at Stevenstone, Devon
         December 23, 1786

According to his figures his own investment was 24,000 pounds. His claim for compensation as finally made was reduced to 19,886 pounds. His award was 6,597 pounds, (only 33 percent of what he claimed.[17]

The East Florida Claims Office, which was established in London, heard 372 claims. A total of £647,405/6/9 was claimed, and £170,351/11/0 was awarded. The awards were about 26 percent of what was claimed, sums which hardly compensated the explorers who took their chance in the "Garden of Eden," Florida. It was tardy justice to the people of East Florida, whom the British government had unceremoniously consigned to such an uncertain fate.[18]

For John Moultrie, in retirement in London, there were reminiscences of the comfort and prosperity of Bella Vista. Altogether the lieutenant governor spent 17 years in East Florida. He declared that he was entirely dependent upon an annuity of 500 pounds for the life of his wife. His Negroes were then in the Bahama Islands. His claim for losses was 9,432 pounds, his award 4,479 pounds.[19] He died in London in 1798.

Governor Tonyn was promoted from the rank of major general to that of general, but was disappointed in his hopes of another governorship. Governor Tonyn's claim for losses amounted to 18,347 pounds, of which he was allowed 5,919 pounds. (Miss Jane Lydia Tonyn, presumably his daughter, was mentioned in the list of claimants, but no award was given). He died in London, age 79, on December 30, 1804.[20]

Governor James Grant, a corpulent general, had returned from service in America and the Bahamas. He was transferred from the 55th Foot, and appointed governor of Stirling Castle in Scotland. During this period he was returned several times to Parliament. He submitted claims amounting to 7,875 pounds, and was allowed 3,327 pounds.[21] He outlived Tonyn by more than a year, and died on April 13, 1806.

James Moncrief, British engineer officer, distinguished himself in the South in the American Revolution. During the Charleston evacuation he remained in charge of the defenses; his removal of 800 slaves from Charleston to the West Indies raised suspicious, that he was war profiteering. Returning to England, he directed the Duke of York's siege at Dunkirk in Holland, and was mortally wounded. He had never married and his estate was willed to his sisters. The estate's claim was for 7,162 pounds; they were awarded 2,679 pounds.[22]

Dr. Andrew Turnbull and his wife, fearing imprisonment at the hands of Governor Tonyn, fled East Florida in 1781, to take up residence in Charleston. They became two of the earliest members of the South Carolina Medical Society. In 1786, through a power of attorney held by James Penman, Turnbull sought compensation for the losses to himself and his four children due to the cession of East Florida to Spain. His first claim of 6,462 British pounds sterling for loss of real property, awarded nothing. Second claim for self and children, 15,057 pounds, awarded 916 pounds. Dr. Turnbull died in Charleston in 1792; his Greek wife, Marcia Gracia Turnbull, for whom New Smyrna was named, died in 1798.[23] Turnbull held but a few shares of New Smyrna, having distributed the additional shares to other claimants, his partners who fared no better.

The group of claimants that suffered the most in relative terms were the merchants. Since much of their business was conducted on credit, the commission's decision to exclude claims for uncollectible debts hit them particularly hard. A majority of refugee merchants received less than 30 percent return on their loss estimates. As George Erving, a Bostonian allotted only 500 pounds to a claim of approximately 20,000 pounds, accurately declared, "Those who have lost dirt are paid in gold, and those who have lost gold are paid in dirt."[24] And to beat all, the claimants were not paid in a lump sum; in lieu they were provided with annuities, a fine financial security and certainly decent for their later years, but which would cause significant adjustments in the meantime.

One person who stayed on in St. Augustine for a year or two was Jesse Fish. The bilingual Fish had sold property to the British. Now, as the Spanish returned he reversed the procedure. Fish married a young wife, had two children, but eventually separated from her and the children. He was allowed to keep 10,000 acres on Anastasia Island, out of all the land he and Gordon claimed to have purchased from the Spaniards on their first departure. He cultivated groves of orange and lemon trees; in addition he owned over 1,850 acres in different tracts, most of which were on Mousa Creek. Fish died around the time of the evacuation of East Florida. The remaining family members took refuge in the Bahamas. Jesse Fish Jr. presented a claim of 1,175 pounds and was awarded 735 pounds. Sarah Fish filed a claim of 375 pounds for loss of house and lot, on behalf of Phoebe and Furman Fish, who were granted the full amount.[25]

Luciano de Herrera, the Spanish spy, returned to St. Augustine in the summer of 1784. Rewarded for the years he reported to Spanish Cuba on events in British East Florida, he became Governor Zespedes's overseer of public works, plus an intermediary for the Spanish governor in his relations with the Seminole and Creek Indians.[26]

During what is called the Second Spanish Period (1784–1821), Spain suffered the Napoleonic invasions at home and struggled to retain its colonies in the Western Hemisphere. The ever-expanding United States soon regarded the Florida peninsula as vital to its interests. It was only a matter of time before the Americans devised a way to acquire Spanish Florida. The Adams-Onis Treaty, in 1819, peacefully turned over Spanish West Florida and East Florida, including St. Augustine of course, to the United States of America for $5,000,000.

Throughout the interim of Spain's control, the traces of 20 years of British heritage disappeared rather quickly. The deserted plantations became overgrown and their structures doomed to termites and weather; the new towns and villages soon were impossible to locate. As a matter of fact, the British legacy was limited to the St. Marys River which became the boundary between the states of Georgia and Florida, and a town south of St. Augustine named New Smyrna. St. Augustine survived as it always did. As to the principals of this history, the good, the bad, and the evil, they shall be remembered forever.

II. Florida in the American Revolution, 1776–1783

> All things to nothingness descend,
> Grow old and die and meet their end,
> Man dies, iron rusts, wood goes decayed,
> Flowers fall, walls crumble, roses fade....
> Nor long shall any name resound
> Beyond the grave, unless't be found
> In some clerk's book, it is the pen
> Gives immortality to men.
>
> > Master Wace
> > from his *Chronicles of the Norman Dukes*

Appendix

Certain buildings and streets identified with the Spanish and British periods have survived into the 21st century, helping to make St. Augustine, Florida, one of the most interesting towns in the United States to visit. The fort that has never been captured, the Castillo de San Marcos, now a U.S. National Historic Landmark, continues to dominate the town as it guards the harbor entrance to the Oldest City. Within easy walking distance is the old Spanish Plaza de la Constitucion. Government House at the plaza is where Governors Grant and Tonyn lived and, more recently, King Juan Carlos I of Spain and Queen Sophia visited in 2001. Across the street the modern Episcopal church on the plaza occupies the site of the Spanish bishops' house first transformed by the British into an Anglican church and later into a statehouse.

A few steps to the east takes you to Aviles Street, the location of a Spanish military hospital and the Ximinez-Fatio House (built around 1797). Across the plaza on Cathedral Street is the Cathedral Basilica of St. Augustine, seat of the oldest Catholic parish in the United States, from August 28, 1565. At the northwest corner is St. George Street, which marks the beginning of the Historic District. Merchant shops carry on the trade amidst wooden houses and artisans' crafts. The redcoats had marched to and from the fort on this street. Along the way is the Peck House, the town house of Lieutenant Governor Moultrie; then glance down Treasury Street, one of the narrowest streets in the Old City. Proceed north along St. George Street, enjoying the ancient coquina stonework and glimpses of courtyards between buildings. St. Photios Shrine, the first national shrine of the Greek Orthodox Church of North America, is located along the way. As you approach the City Gate, which is always open, you can visit the Oldest Wooden School House, built during the first Spanish occupation. In addition there are numerous restored houses such as Casa de Gallegos and Casa de Gomez, De Mesa-Sanchez site, and the Colonial Spanish Quarter Museum, with its authentically costumed guides depicting how people lived on the Florida frontier in the mid–1700s.

The downtown area is surrounded by other chronicled historical areas and easily visited. Traveling south of the Bridge of Lions along the bay front you will reach the Oldest House, a U.S. National Historic Landmark occupied continuously since 1727. Continuing along the bay front you will find the location of the old Spanish monastery which the British turned into a barracks, now the modern St. Francis Barracks, headquarters of the Florida National Guard. Immediately south of the barracks is the old St. Augustine National Cemetery. Reversing your direction, travel north along the bay front, past the Castillo de San Marcos fortress on San Marco Avenue and you will find the Fountain of Youth, a 21-acre archaeological park, the site of the landing place of Ponce de León in 1513. Close by is the Mission of Nombre de Dios and the Shrine of Our Lady of La Leche, America's first mission where the first Catholic Mass was celebrated in 1565. A 280-foot-high stainless steel cross marks the site of the city's founding. Close by is the site of Fort Mose, another U.S. National Historic Landmark.

Take a drive over the Bridge of Lions, south on A1A, to tour the St. Augustine Lighthouse, then a trip of about 15 miles to the end of Anastasia Island, and south of Crescent Beach you will find Fort Matanzas. It was constructed between 1740–42 of coquina, quarried on Anastasia Island, by the Spaniards, to guard the southern approach of St. Augustine. This U.S. National Park monument can be viewed from the shore or visited by a short ferry ride. Also, miles of wide, hard-packed sand beaches north of the fort afford beach driving, just about the last in the United States.

Notes

Preface

1. John Grafton, *The American Revolution: A Picture Sourcebook* (New York: Dover Publications, 1975), Introduction page.

Part I Prologue

1. *Reading Eagle* (newspaper), June 8, 2005, p. 10.
2. Louis B. Wright, *The Colonial Search for a Southern Eden* (Tuscaloosa: University of Alabama Press, 1953. Reprint by Haskell House, 1973), pp. 4, 5.
3. *Ibid.*, p. 17.
4. *Ibid.*, p. 59.
5. *Ibid.*, pp. 25, 35.

Chapter 1

1. Susan Parker, "The Exception of Fort Mose," *St. Augustine Record*, February 13, 2005.
2. Amy Bushnell, "The Noble and Loyal City, 1565–1668," ch. 2 in *The Oldest City, St. Augustine: Saga of Survival*, ed. Jean Parker Waterbury (St. Augustine: St Augustine Historical Society, 1983), p. 33.
3. *Ibid.*, p. 35.
4. Michael Gannon, PhD, "Churches in the Wilderness," *St. Augustine Catholic Magazine* (July–August 2006): p. 7.
5. Bushnell, p. 54.
6. *Ibid.*
7. Luis Rafael Arana, "Defenses and Defenders at St. Augustine (A Collection of Writings)," *El Escribano* 36 (St. Augustine Historical Society, 1999): p. l68.
8. Louis B. Wright, p. 4.
9. Arana, pp. 78, 82.
10. Parker, "The Exception of Fort Mose."
11. Mark M. Boatner III, *Encyclopedia of the American Revolution* (Mechanicsburg, PA: Stackpole Books, 1966), p. 252.
12. *Ibid.*
13. Arana, p. 90.
14. *Ibid.* p. 98.
15. Boatner, *Encyclopedia of the American Revolution*, p. 402.
16. Parke Rouse Jr., *The Great Wagon Road* (Richmond: Dietz Press, 1995), pp. 83, 88, 89.
17. Robin F.A. Fabel, "British Rule in Florida," in *The New History of Florida,* ed. Michael Gannon (Gainesville: University Press of Florida, 1996), p. 135.
18. Burton Barrs, A.B., L.L.B., *East Florida in the American Revolution* (Jacksonville: Guild Press, 1932), p. 3.
19. Fabel, "British Rule in Florida," p. 135.
20. *Ibid.*, p. 136.
21. Daniel L. Schafer, PhD, "St. Augustine's British Years, 1763–1784," *El Escribano* 38 (St. Augustine Historical Society, 2001): pp. 4, 5.
22. Wilbur Henry Siebert, ed., *Loyalists in East Florida, 1774–1785*, Vol. 2 (Boston:

Gregg Press. Reprint, Deland, FL: American Revolutionary series, Florida State Historical Society, 1929), p. 277.
23. *Ibid.*
24. Schafer, "St. Augustine's British Years, 1763-1784," p. 9.
25. *Ibid.*, pp. 6, 7.
26. *Ibid.*, p. 7.
27. *Ibid.*
28. Schafer, "St. Augustine's British Years, 1763-1784," pp. 5, 8, 9.
29. *Ibid.*, p. 12.
30. J. Leitch Wright, Jr., *British St. Augustine* (St. Augustine: Historic St. Augustine Preservation Board, Florida Department of State, 1975), p. 2.
31. Charles L. Mowat, *History of East Florida: East Florida as a British Province, 1763-1784* (Berkeley: University of California Press, 1943), p. 53.
32. Schafer, "St. Augustine's British Years, 1763-1784," p. 6.
33. Siebert, Vol. 2, p. 277.
34. *Ibid.*, p. 365.

Chapter 2

1. Boatner, *Encyclopedia of the American Revolution*, pp. 220, 876.
2. *Ibid.*, p. 433.
3. John Richard Alden, *The South in the Revolution, 1763-1789* (Baton Rouge: Louisiana State University Press, 1957), p. 122.
4. Boatner, *Encyclopedia of the American Revolution*, p. 444.
5. Daniel L. Schafer, PhD, "Governor James Grant's Villa, a British East Florida Indigo Plantation," *El Escribano* 37 (St. Augustine Historical Society, 2000): p. 3.
6. Clinton N. Howard, *History of Florida: The British Development of West Florida, 1763-1769* (Berkeley: University of California Press, 1947), p. 29.
7. Louis B. Wright, p. 7.
8. Boatner, *Encyclopedia of the American Revolution*, pp. 749, 750.
9. Siebert, Vol. 2, pp. 237, 240.
10. Schafer, "Governor James Grant's Villa," p. 4.
11. Siebert, Vol. 2, p. 379.
12. Wright Jr., *British St. Augustine*, p. 12.
13. Siebert, Vol. 2, p. 24 footnote.
14. Wright Jr., p. 12.
15. Schafer, "St. Augustine's British Years, 1763-1784," p. 100.
16. Schafer, "Governor James Grant's Villa," pp. 9, 13.
17. *Ibid.*, pp. 5, 6.
18. Louis B. Wright, pp. 48, 49.
19. Siebert, Vol. 2, p. 149 footnote.
20. Barrs, p. 3.
21. Fabel, "British Rule in Florida," p. 143.
22. Alden, p. 124.
23. Fabel, "British Rule in Florida," p. 143.
24. Louis B. Wright, p. 12.
25. Cecile-Marie Sastre, "Picolata on the St. Johns: A Preliminary Study," *El Escribano* 32 (St. Augustine Historical Society, 1995), p. 25.
26. Siebert, Vol. 2, p. 360.
27. Mowat, pp. 58, 59, 64.
28. Bushnell, p. 100.
29. Daniel L. Schafer, PhD, "...not so gay a Town in America as this..., 1763-1784," ch. 4 in *The Oldest City, St. Augustine: Saga of Survival*, ed. Jean Parker Waterbury (St. Augustine: St. Augustine Historical Society, 1983), pp. 101, 102, 106.
30. Mowat, p. 6.
31. Howard, p. 7.
32. Boatner, *Encyclopedia of the American Revolution*, p. 1218.
33. Howard, p. 11.
34. Fabel, "British Rule in Florida," p. 136.
35. Boatner, *Encyclopedia of the American Revolution*, p. 563.
36. Howard, pp. 8, 9, 11, 12, 15.
37. Siebert, Vol. 2, p. 121 footnote.
38. Howard, pp. 14, 17-19, 113, 117.
39. Mowat, p. 12.
40. Fabel, "British Rule in Florida," p. 136.
41. Howard, p. 21.
42. R.C. Simmons, *The American Colonies: From Settlement to Independence* (New York: W.W. Norton, 1976), p. 332.
43. Howard, p. 22.
44. Alden, p. 283.
45. Howard, pp. 23, 27-29.

46. Fabel, "British Rule in Florida," p. 141.
47. Howard, p. 22.
48. Boatner, *Encyclopedia of the American Revolution*, p. 564.
49. Howard, pp. 29, 38, 39.
50. *Ibid.*, p. 128.
51. *Ibid.*, p. 36.
52. Fabel, "British Rule in Florida," p. 145.
53. Mark Van Dorn, *Travels of William Bartram* (New York: Dover Publications, 1955), p. 197.
54. *Ibid.*, p. 180.
55. Siebert, Vol. 1, p. 11.
56. Mowat, p. 10.
57. Daniel L. Schafer, PhD, "The Forlorn State of Poor Bill Bartram," *El Escribano* 32 (St. Augustine Historical Society, 1995): pp. 2–4.
58. Van Dorn, pp. 185, 305.
59. *Ibid.*, pp. 355, 356.
60. Schafer, "Governor James Grant's Villa," p. 22.
61. Boatner, *Encyclopedia of the American Revolution*, pp. 443, 683.

Chapter 3

1. Schafer, "St. Augustine's British Years, 1763–1784," p. 127.
2. *Ibid.*, p. 124.
3. *Ibid.*, p. 130.
4. Rouse, *The Great Wagon Road*, pp. 30, 31.
5. Siebert, Vol. 2, p. 325.
6. Schafer, "Governor James Grant's Villa," p. 25.
7. Siebert, Vol. 1, pp. 37, 173.
8. Schafer, "St. Augustine's British Years, 1763–1784," p. 124, 142.
9. Siebert, Vol. 2, pp. 55, 330.
10. Boatner, *Encyclopedia of the American Revolution*, p. 821.
11. William Garrott Brown, *The Lower South in American History* (New York: Haskell House, 1968), p. 12.
12. *Ibid.*, pp. 14, 15.
13. Brown, p. 13.
14. Siebert, Vol. 2, p. 359.
15. *Ibid.*, p. 379.
16. *Ibid.*, p. 256.

17. Schafer, "St. Augustine's British Years, 1763–1784," pp. 164, 165.
18. *Ibid.*, p. 163.
19. Schafer, "St. Augustine's British Years, 1763–1784," p. 166.
20. Siebert, Vol. 2, pp. 276, 365.
21. Rouse Jr., p. 11.
22. Boatner, *Encyclopedia of the American Revolution*, p. 357.
23. Rouse Jr., p. 22.
24. Boatner, *Encyclopedia of the American Revolution*, p. 358.
25. Sastre, "Picolata on the St. Johns," p. 50.
26. Walter Edgar, *Partisans and Redcoats: The Southern Conflict That Turned the Tide of the American Revolution* (New York: Perennial, HarperCollins, 2001), p. 3.
27. Rouse Jr., p. 35.
28. Louis B. Wright, p. 57.

Chapter 4

1. Schafer, "Governor James Grant's Villa," p. 63.
2. Boatner, *Encyclopedia of the American Revolution*, p. 1109.
3. Schafer, "...not so gay a Town in America as this," p. 110.
4. Schafer, "St. Augustine's British Years, 1763–1784," pp. 178–180.
5. Wright Jr., *British St. Augustine*, p. 19.
6. *Ibid.*, p. 17.
7. Brown, *The Lower South in American History*, p. 125.
8. Boatner, *Encyclopedia of the American Revolution*, pp. 472, 810, 811.
9. *Ibid.*, pp. 17, 512, 768, 770.
10. Brown, p. 91.
11. Boatner, *Encyclopedia of the American Revolution*, pp. 421, 422, 474, 475.
12. Siebert, Vol. 2, p. 318.
13. Henry Davenport Northrop, *Pictorial History of the United States* (n.p., J.R. Jones, 1893), p. 376; Boatner, *Encyclopedia of the American Revolution*, pp. 424–426.
14. Boatner, *Encyclopedia of the American Revolution*, p. 827.
15. *Ibid.*, p. 895.
16. Wright Jr., p. 25.

17. Schafer, "St. Augustine's British Years, 1763–1784," pp. 102–104.

Chapter 5

1. Wright Jr., *British St. Augustine*, p. 20.
2. Schafer, "St. Augustine's British Years, 1763–1784," p. 189.
3. Mowat, p. 109.
4. Boatner, *Encyclopedia of the American Revolution*, p. 1017.
5. Edgar, p. 13.
6. Mowat, pp. 111, 115.
7. Siebert, Vol. 2, p. 324; Edgar, p. 31.
8. Siebert, Vol. 2, p. 329.
9. Susan R. Parker and Jacqueline K. Fretwell, *Clash Between Cultures* (St. Augustine: St. Augustine Historical Society, 1988), p. 27.
10. Schafer, "St. Augustine's British Years, 1763–1784," pp. 196, 198.
11. Alden, p. 317.
12. Boatner, *Encyclopedia of the American Revolution*, p. 1220.
13. Edgar, pp. 1–47 source material.
14. S.G. Goodrich, *Goodrich's Pictorial History of the United States* (Philadelphia: J.H. Butler and Co., 1874), p. 206.
15. Boatner, *Encyclopedia of the American Revolution*, p. 202.
16. Edgar, p. 35.
17. Goodrich, p. 207.
18. Barrs, p. 14.
19. Siebert, Vol. 2, p. 348.
20. Barrs, p. 15.
21. Boatner, *Encyclopedia of the American Revolution*, p. 443.
22. Wright Jr., pp. 25, 28.

Part II Prologue

1. Mary Beth Norton, *The British-Americans: The Loyalist Exiles in England, 1774–1789* (Boston: Little, Brown, 1972), p. 6.
2. *Ibid.*, p. 15.
3. Alden, p. 266.
4. Mark M. Boatner III, *Landmarks of the American Revolution* (Harrisburg, PA: Stackpole Books, 1992), pp. 775–777.

Chapter 6

1. Boatner, *Encyclopedia of the American Revolution*, p. 594.
2. *Ibid.*, p. 1041.
3. Siebert, Vol. 2, p. 253.
4. Barrs, p. 13 footnote.
5. *Ibid.*, pp. 18, 20.
6. Mowat, p. 120.
7. Barrs, pp. 21, 22.
8. Mowat, p. 120.
9. Barrs, p. 23.
10. Boatner, *Encyclopedia of the American Revolution*, p. 262.
11. Mowat, p. 120.
12. Barrs, p. 24.
13. Boatner, *Landmarks of the American Revolution*, pp. 68, 73.
14. Mowat, p. 70.
15. Barrs, p. 25.
16. Siebert, Vol. 2, pp. 215, 216.
17. Siebert, Vol. 1, p. 52.
18. Siebert, Vol. 1, pp. 54, 55.
19. Rouse, p. 147.
20. Siebert, Vol. 1, pp. 47, 51.
21. Mowat, p. 121.
22. Boatner, *Encyclopedia of the American Revolution*, p. 894.
23. Siebert, Vol. 1, p. 56.
24. Wright Jr., p. 32; Mowat, p. 121; Barrs, p. 29.
25. Barrs, p. 32.
26. Mowat, p. 122.
27. Barrs, p. 33.
28. Boatner, *Landmarks of the American Revolution*, p. 68.
29. Barrs, p. 37.
30. Siebert, Vol. 1, p. 59.
31. Mowat, p. 101.
32. Siebert, Vol. 1, p. 62.
33. Mowat, p. 111.
34. Siebert, Vol. 1, p. 66.
35. Mowat, pp. 111, 113.
36. Siebert, Vol. 1, p. 66.

Chapter 7

1. Siebert, Vol. 1, p. 52; Siebert, Vol. 2, pp. 322, 323.
2. Barrs, p. 38.
3. Barrs, p. 36; Boatner, *Landmarks of the American Revolution*, pp. 85, 86.

4. Siebert, Vol. 1, pp. 72, 73.
5. *Ibid.*, p. 60.
6. Boatner, *Encyclopedia of the American Revolution*, p. 980.
7. *Ibid.*, pp. 170, 172, 980–982.
8. Siebert, Vol. 1, p. 74.
9. *Ibid.*
10. Boatner, *Encyclopedia of the American Revolution*, p.113.
11. Barrs, p. 38.
12. Boatner, *Encyclopedia of the American Revolution*, p. 1062.
13. Siebert, Vol. 1, pp. 76–79; Boatner, *Encyclopedia of the American Revolution*, pp. 670, 776, 889, 1062; Edgar, pp. 45, 46.
14. Siebert, Vol. 1, p. 80.
15. Boatner, *Landmarks of the American Revolution*, p. 462.
16. Norton, p. 35.
17. Boatner, *Encyclopedia of the American Revolution*, p. 883; pp. 159–170, 550 (Camden Campaign).
18. Alden, p. 242.
19. Mowat, p. 77.
20. Mowat, p. 124; Boatner, *Encyclopedia of the American Revolution*, p. 895; Wright Jr., pp. 32, 35.
21. Wright Jr., p. 30.
22. *Ibid.*, p. 31.
23. Siebert, Vol. 2, pp. 253, 254, 309.
24. Siebert, Vol. 2, p. 158.
25. Siebert, Vol. 1, p. 60.
26. Schafer, "...not so gay a Town in America as this," p. 119.

Chapter 8

1. George Otto Trevelyan, *The American Revolution* (New York: Columbia University, David McKay Company, 1964), p. 336.
2. Boatner, *Encyclopedia of the American Revolution*, p. 171.
3. Alden, p. 276.
4. Alden, pp. 276, 277; Fabel, "British Rule in Florida," p. 144.
5. Alden, pp. 230, 303.
6. Boatner, *Encyclopedia of the American Revolution*, pp. 410, 444, 788, 875, 965, 1042, 1182.
7. Fabel, "British Rule in Florida," p. 145.

8. Boatner, *Encyclopedia of the American Revolution*, pp. 549, 711; Fabel, "British Rule in Florida," p. 146; Alden, p. 277; Arana, p. 117.
9. Boatner, *Encyclopedia of the American Revolution*, pp. 854, 948.
10. *Ibid.*, pp. 854, 864.
11. Fabel, "British Rule in Florida," p. 146.
12. Siebert, Vol. 2, pp. 365, 366.
13. Alden, p. 278.
14. Siebert, Vol. 1, pp. 81, 89, 91, 93.
15. Wright Jr., p. 41.
16. Siebert, Vol. 1, pp. 95, 98, 187.
17. Boatner, *Encyclopedia of the American Revolution*, pp. 298, 356.
18. Alden, p. 266.
19. Rouse, p. 159.
20. Grafton, pp. 101–107.
21. Barrs, p. 40.
22. Trevelyan, p. 552–559.
23. *Ibid.*, p. 554.
24. Boatner, *Encyclopedia of the American Revolution*, p. 600.

Chapter 9

1. Patricia C. Griffin, PhD, "The Spanish Return: The People-Mix Period, 1784–1821," ch. 5 in *The Oldest City, St. Augustine: Saga of Survival*, ed. Jean Parker Waterbury (St. Augustine: St. Augustine Historical Society, 1983), p. 108.
2. Boatner, *Encyclopedia of the American Revolution*, p. 663.
3. Siebert, Vol. 2, pp. 289–291, 368, 369.
4. *Ibid.*, pp. 295, 370.
5. Siebert, Vol. 1, p. 117.
6. Siebert, Vol. 2, pp. 33, 101, 109.
7. *Ibid.*, pp. 104, 108, 220.
8. *Ibid.*, pp. 33, 107, 223.
9. Mowat, pp. 64, 68, 75, 117.
10. Siebert, Vol. 1, p. 9.
11. Mowat, p. 126.
12. *Ibid.*, p. 68.
13. Mowat, p. 136.
14. Siebert, Vol. 1, p. 106.
15. Mowat, pp. 136, 137.
16. Siebert, Vol. 1, pp. 117, 119.
17. *Ibid.*, pp. 119, 120.
18. Mowat, p. 137.

19. Siebert, Vol. 1, pp. 109–111.
20. Barrs, p. 40.
21. Siebert, Vol. 1, pp. 115, 116.
22. Wright Jr., pp. 39–41.
23. Siebert, Vol. 2, p. 335.
24. Alden, pp. 280–289.
25. Siebert, Vol. 1, pp. 120, 121.
26. *Ibid.*, p. 121.
27. *Ibid.*, p. 131.
28. *Ibid.*, pp. 145–147.
29. *Ibid.*, p. 147.
30. *Ibid.*, p. 134.
31. Siebert, Vol. 2, p. 43.
32. Boatner, *Encyclopedia of the American Revolution*, pp. 367, 744.

Chapter 10

1. Boatner, *Encyclopedia of the American Revolution*, pp. 848, 849.
2. Alden, p. 305.
3. Mowat, p.141.
4. Norton, p. 36.
5. Barrs, p. 41.
6. Schafer, "...not so gay a Town in America as this," p. 120.
7. Siebert, pp. 139–148.
8. Schafer, "...not so gay a Town in America as this," pp. 120, 121; Siebert, Vol. 1, pp. 140, 141.
9. Siebert, Vol. 1, pp. 143, 149.
10. Norton, p. 236.
11. Siebert, Vol. 1, pp. 149, 150, 153.
12. *Ibid.*, pp. 123, 124.
13. Boatner, *Encyclopedia of the American Revolution*, p. 663.
14. Siebert, Vol. 1, p. 188.
15. Norton, p. 224.
16. Siebert, Vol. 1, pp. 158, 210.

17. *Ibid.*, pp. 200, 201, 203.

Chapter 11

1. Wright Jr., pp. 49, 50; Mowat, p. 145
2. Siebert, Vol. 2, p. 329.
3. Mowat, p. 146; Siebert, Vol. 1, pp. 164, 165, 167.
4. Siebert, Vol. 1, p. 170.
5. *Ibid.*, p. 163.
6. Mowat, p. 146.
7. Siebert, Vol. 1, p. 171.
8. James A. Lewis, "Cracker—Spanish Florida Style," *Florida Historical Quarterly*, p. 191.
9. Siebert, Vol. 1, pp. 172, 177.
10. *Ibid.*, p. 173.
11. *Ibid.*, p. 208.
12. Schafer, "...not so gay a Town in America as this," p. 122.
13. Mowat, p. 147; Siebert, Vol. 1, p. 176.
14. Norton, pp. 125, 229.
15. Siebert, Vol. 1, p. 189.
16. Norton, pp. 60, 200, 201.
17. Siebert, Vol. 2, pp. 296, 371.
18. Mowat, p. 148.
19. Siebert, Vol. 2, p. 332.
20. *Ibid.*, p. 313.
21. *Ibid.*, p. 310.
22. Boatner, *Encyclopedia of the American Revolution*, p. 712; Siebert, Vol. 2, p. 342.
23. Siebert, Vol. 2, p. 327.
24. Norton, pp. 219, 220.
25. Siebert, Vol. 1, p. 365.
26. Griffin, p. 133.

Bibliography

Alden, John Richard. *The South in the Revolution, 1763–1789.* Baton Rouge: Louisiana State University Press, 1957.

American Heritage Dictionary of the English Language. William Morris, ed. Boston: American Heritage Publishing Co., Houghton Mifflin, 1969.

Arana, Luis Rafael. "Defenses and Defenders at St. Augustine (A Collection of Writings)." *El Escribano* 36 (St. Augustine Historical Society, 1999).

Barrs, Burton, A.B., L.L.B. *East Florida in the American Revolution.* Jacksonville: Guild Press, 1932.

Benjey, Tom. *Keep A-Goin': The Life of Lone Star Dietz.* Carlisle, PA: Tuxedo Press, 2006.

Boatner, Mark M. III. *Encyclopedia of the American Revolution.* Mechanicsburg, PA: Stackpole Books, 1966.

_____. *Landmarks of the American Revolution.* Revised. Harrisburg, PA: Stackpole Books, 1992.

Brown, William Garrott. *The Lower South in American History.* New York: Haskell House, 1968.

Bushnell, Amy. "The Noble and Loyal City, 1565–1668." Ch. 2 in *The Oldest City, St. Augustine: Saga of Survival.* Edited by Jean Parker Waterbury. St. Augustine: St. Augustine Historical Society, 1983.

Dewhurst, William W. *The History of Saint Augustine, Florida.* New York: G.P. Putnam's Sons, 1885. Facsimile reprint, Bowie, MD: Heritage Books, 1990.

Edgar, Walter. *Partisans and Redcoats: The Southern Conflict That Turned the Tide of the American Revolution.* New York: Perennial, HarperCollins, 2001.

Fabel, Robin F.A. "British Rule in Florida." In *The New History of Florida.* Edited by Michael Gannon. Gainesville: University Press of Florida, 1996.

Gannon, Michael, PhD. "Churches in the Wilderness." *St. Augustine Catholic Magazine*, July–August 2006.

_____, ed. *The New History of Florida.* Gainesville: University Press of Florida, 1996.

Gately, M.R., and Charles E. Beale. *Gately's Universal Educator.* Boston: M.R. Gately, 1883.

Goodrich, S.G. *Goodrich's Pictorial History of the United States.* Philadelphia: J.H. Butler and Co., 1874.

Grafton, John. *The American Revolution: A Picture Sourcebook.* New York: Dover Publications, 1975.

Griffin, Patricia C., PhD. "The Spanish Return: The People-Mix Period, 1784–1821." Ch. 5 in *The Oldest City, St. Augustine: Saga of Survival.* Edited by Jean Parker Waterbury. St. Augustine, FL: The St. Augustine Historical Society, 1983.

Harman, Joyce Elizabeth. *Trade and Pri-*

vateering in Spanish Florida, 1732–1763. St. Augustine: St. Augustine Historical Society, 1969.

Howard, Clinton N. *History of Florida: The British Development of West Florida, 1763–1769.* Berkeley: University of California Press, 1947.

Landers, Jane. "Slave Resistance on the Southeastern Frontier. Fugitives, Maroons, and Banditti in the Age of Revolutions." *El Escribano* 32 (St. Augustine Historical Society, 1995).

Lewis, James A. "Cracker—Spanish Florida Style." *Florida Historical Quarterly* (1984): p. 191.

Mowat, Charles L. *History of East Florida: East Florida as a British Province, 1763–1784.* Berkeley: University of California Press, 1943.

Northrop, Henry Davenport. *Pictorial History of the United States.* N.p., J.R. Jones, 1893.

Norton, Mary Beth. *The British-Americans: The Loyalist Exiles in England, 1774–1789.* Boston: Little, Brown, 1972.

Page, Dave. *Ships Versus Shore.* Nashville: Rutledge Hill Press, 1994.

Parker, Susan R., and Jacqueline K. Fretwell. *Clash Between Cultures.* St. Augustine: St. Augustine Historical Society, 1988.

Reading Eagle (newspaper), Reading, PA: June 8, 2005.

Rouse, Parke, Jr. *The Great Wagon Road.* Richmond: Dietz Press, 1995.

Sastre, Cecile-Marie. "Picolata on the St. Johns: A Preliminary Study." *El Escribano* 32 (St. Augustine Historical Society, 1995).

Schafer, Daniel L., PhD. "The Forlorn State of Poor Bill Bartram."*El Escribano* 32 (St. Augustine Historical Society, 1995).

_____. "Governor James Grant's Villa, a British East Florida Indigo Plantation." *El Escribano* 37 (St. Augustine Historical Society, 2000).

_____. "...not so gay a Town in America as this..., 1763–1784." Ch. 4 in *The Oldest City, St. Augustine: Saga of Survival.* Edited by Jean Parker Waterbury. St. Augustine: St. Augustine Historical Society, 1983.

_____. "St. Augustine's British Years, 1763–1784." *El Escribano* 38 (St. Augustine Historical Society, 2001).

Siebert, Wilbur Henry, ed. *Loyalists in East Florida, 1774–1785.* Vols. 1 and 2. Boston: Gregg Press. Reprint, Deland, FL: American Revolutionary series, the Florida State Historical Society, 1929.

Simmons, R.C. *The American Colonies: From Settlement to Independence.* New York: W.W. Norton, 1976.

Stoutenburgh, John, Jr. *Dictionary of the American Indian.* New York: Bonanza Books by Philosophical Library, 1960.

Trevelyan, George Otto. *The American Revolution.* Reissue. Notes by Richard B. Morris. New York: Columbia University, David McKay Company, 1964.

United States National Park Service. "Fort Necessity hosts events commemorating its place in history." Reading, PA: *Reading Eagle*, the Associated Press, July 2005.

Van Dorn, Mark. *Travels of William Bartram.* New York: Dover Publications, 1955.

Waterbury, Jean Parker, ed. *The Oldest City, St. Augustine: Saga of Survival.* St. Augustine: St. Augustine Historical Society, 1983.

Webster's New World Dictionary of the American Language. New York: World, 1968.

Wright, J. Leitch, Jr. *British St. Augustine.* St. Augustine: Historic St. Augustine Preservation Board, Florida Department of State, 1975.

Wright, Louis B. *The Colonial Search for a Southern Eden.* Tuscaloosa: University of Alabama Press, 1953. Reprint by Haskell House, 1973.

Index

Abaco Island 168
Abbott, Capt. Henry 169
Acadia, Nova Scotia 15
Acadians 164
Adams, John 69, 162
Adams, Samuel 73
Adams-Onis Treaty 181
Adia Settlement 55
Africa 7, 32, 53
Ainslie, John 23
Alabama 16, 32
Alabama River 42
Alachua Savanna, FL 44, 86
Albermarle, Earl of 33
Albemarle Point 11
Alexander, Gen. William "Stirling" 77, 91
Alleghenies 37, 133
Allen, Lt. Col. Isaac 115, 118
alligator 109–110
Alligator 114
Alligator Creek/Bridge 108–109
Altamaha River 16, 37, 67, 106
Amelia Harbor/Narrows 108, 151, 170, 177
Amelia Island, FL 90, 102–104, 150–151, 170
American Revolution 1–2, 14, 42–43, 48, 50, 54–56, 67, 70–71, 78, 80, 83, 92–95, 98, 101, 105, 107, 121, 124–125, 127, 129–130, 134, 139–140, 142–143, 145, 152, 159, 161, 178, 180
American Southern Department 107
American Sufferers 178–179
Amerindians 18
Amherst, Jeffery 22

Anastasia Island, FL 11–12, 14, 25, 77, 82–83, 173, 181
Andre, Maj. John 146
Anglican services 23, 61
Anglo drifters 41
Anglo-Saxons 62, 140
Anglo-Spanish 11, 66, 174
Anhalt-Zerbst, Germany 79
Annapolis, MD 61, 73
Anspach-Bayreuth, Germany 79
Apalache Indians 9
Apalache/Tallahassee, FL 29, 138
Apalachicola River 16, 33, 44
Appalachian mountains 15, 33, 35, 42, 61–62, 65, 71, 74, 88
Arbuthnot, Adml. Marriott 141
Arden, FL 151
Arkansas 137
Arnold, Gen. Benedict 49, 146
Ashe, John 119
Ashley River 11, 120
Associated Press 3
Atlantic Ocean 7, 11, 14, 29, 59, 65, 69, 75, 89–90, 143
Augusta, GA 59, 62–63, 67, 85–86, 105, 118, 143
Aviles Street 57

badges of slavery 71, 156
Bahamas 10, 45, 77, 82, 157, 159–160, 165–168, 170–171, 177–181
Baird, Grenadier Capt. Sir James 116–117
Baker, Capt./Col. John 85, 101
Baker, Maj. William 101–102

Ball, Col. Elias 159
Ballindalloch, Laird of 48
Ballindalloch Castle, Scotland 48
Baltimore, MD 92
Bank of North America 161
Bartram, John 46
Bartram, William 44, 46–48, 103, 151
Baton Rouge, LA 129, 133–135
Battle of Bloody Swamp 13
Battle of Bunker Hill 75, 110
Bay of Calos 45
Bay of Tampa 43, 164
Bayou Pierre 130
Beaufort, Parris Island, SC 8, 66–67, 120–121, 159–160
Bell, Duke 25
Bella Vista 24, 68, 179
Bennington, VT 79, 106
Bermuda 31, 150
Bethune, John 151
Betsy 82–83
Bissett, Alex 58
Bissett, Capt. Robert 57–58, 83, 128
Blanca, Count Florida 163
Bloody Swamp, Battle of 13
Blue Ridge Mountains 105
Board of Trade 41, 48, 51, 57, 69
Boston Harbor 73
Boston, MA 28, 61, 69, 72–76, 92, 94–95, 101, 113, 122, 145
Boston Massacre 72
Boston Tea Party 73
Bouquet, Henry 22
Bowen, Commodore 108–109
Box, James 23
Brandywine 106, 108
Breed's Hill 75
Bretigny, Marquis de 126
Briar Creek 119, 143
Bristol 90
Bristol, England 4, 36
British Highlanders 116
British Honduras, West Indies 33
British Parliament 72–74, 134, 178, 180
British Southern District 36, 80, 82, 98, 112, 154, 157, 168
British Stamp Act 41
Broad River 104
Broclair Bluff 156
Brown, John 97, 99, 102, 106, 108
Brown, Thomas "Burnfoot" 84, 158, 166, 168

Brown, William 170–171, 173
"Brown Bess" 81
Browne, Gov. Montfort 41–42, 77, 130
Brunswick, Duke of 55, 79
Brunswick, GA 107
Brunswick, Germany 79
Bryan, Jonathan 58
Bunker Hill, Battle of 75, 110
Bute, Earl of 34

Cabbage Swamp 108
Cahokia/St. Louis 40
Caldwell, Lt. William 100
Callahan, FL 108
Cambridge, MA 75
Camden/Pine Tree, SC 63, 122–124, 143, 157
Cameron, Ann 127
Camino Real 44
Campbell, Lt. Col. Archibald 115–116, 118–119
Campbell, Gen. John 116–117, 129, 131–132, 135–137
Campbell, Gov. William 88–89, 105
Campbelltown, FL 41–42
Campo/Camps, Father Pietro/Pedro 32, 52, 177
Canada 15–16, 22, 70, 75, 94, 143, 152, 157, 164–165, 168
Cape Breton 15
Cape Canaveral, FL 8, 14, 128
Cape Fear River 89
Cape Henry 142
Cape of Good Hope 41
Cargill, Daniel 169, 174
Caribbean Sea 7, 12, 16, 113
Carleton, Gen. Guy 78, 144–145, 152, 154, 157–158, 160, 165–166, 168
Carolina/Carolinas 4, 11, 24, 53, 63, 65, 77, 88, 95, 106, 113, 122, 124–125, 139–140, 171, 174
Carolina King's Rangers 155, 168
Carpenter's Hall 74
Casanovas, Fr. 52
Cassels, Col. James 159
Castillo de San Marcos photo 11, 12, 19, 77
Castle of Saint Mark 23
Catawba Indian tribe 88
Catherwood, Dr. Robert 28, 57
Census 1783 159
Champneys, John 167

Chapel of Our Lady 20
Chapman, John 150
Chapman, William 103–104
Charles IX, King 7
Charleston/Charles Town, SC 1, 11, 18, 22–25, 28, 45–46, 51, 54–55, 59, 61, 67, 69, 73, 78, 84, 86–90, 112–113, 117, 119–120, 122–123, 125, 138, 141, 145, 150, 152, 154–155, 157, 160, 171–172, 180
Charleston Harbor 89–90, 122
Charlotte/Wachovia, NC 63
Cherokee Indians 22–23, 28, 65, 105, 112, 138, 158, 166
Chesapeake Bay 76–77, 141
Chester, Gov. Peter 43, 129, 131, 137
Chichester Plantation 179
Chickasaw Indians 39, 138, 158
Choctaw Indians 28, 33, 37, 39–40, 112, 130, 132, 136, 138, 155
Church of England 20, 164
"Cider Royal" 63
City Gate 12, 19, 26
Clarke, Brig. Gen. Alured 172
Clarke, Col. Elijah 109
Clinton, Gen. Henry 78, 89, 91, 110, 113, 116, 122, 125, 129, 134, 136, 141–142, 144
Cockspur Island, GA 153
Colonel's Island 115, 118
Colonial Wars 78
Columbia, SC 86
Columbus, Christopher 3
Combahee Ferry, SC 145
Commerce 82–83
Commissioners for Trade and Plantations 42, 78, 147
Committees of Correspondence 83
Common Sense 79
Concord, NH 74–75, 87
Confederation of Indian Tribes 158
Congaree River 22
Congregationalist 114
Connecticut 74, 101, 107
Continental Army, Navy, and Marines 75–77, 84, 89, 91, 95, 116, 120, 122–124, 130, 140–141
Continental Line 91, 101
Conway, Gen. Henry Seymour 143–144
Cooper River 143
coquina 12
Cork, Ireland 89

Cornwallis, Gen. Charles 89–92, 121, 123–124, 140–143, 145, 157
Council of East Florida 30
Council of Safety 100
Council of the Indies 9
Court of Common Law 57
Court of Sessions 54, 112
Court of Vice Admiralty 28, 30
Cowdriver 166
Cowford 26, 58, 85, 99–102, 108–109, 151
Cowkeeper, Chief 86
Cowpens, SC 140
Crackers 18, 27, 42, 56–57, 59, 62, 84, 86, 152, 171, 176
Craig, Maj. James H. 141
Creek Indians 18, 33, 39–41, 44, 86, 88, 99, 101–102, 112–113, 132, 136–138, 155, 158, 166, 181
Cruden, John 174
Cubo defense line 19, 77
Cumberland, Duke of 36
Cumberland Island 115
Cuming, Sir Alexander 65
Cunningham, Gen. Robert 85
Cunningham, Maj. William 174
Cusac, William 148
Cyrus 177

Dalling, Gen. John 124, 132, 135–136
Dauphin Island 42, 135
Dauphine 92
Daza, Don Ignacio 11
Declaration of Independence 76, 79, 81, 86, 97
Delaware 123
Delaware Indians 158
Delaware River 1, 91–92
de Soto, Hernando *see* Soto, Hernando de
d'Estaing, Count *see* Estaing, Count d'
Detouches, Adml. Charles-René-Dominique Sochet 141
Detroit Indians 157
Deveaux, Maj. Andrew 159–160
Dickson, Col. Alexander 135
Digby, Rear Adml. Robert 164, 169
Doctors Lake 154
Dodd, Maj. Benjamin 83, 90
Dolly, Quamino 117
Dominica, island of 171–172, 177
Dorchester Heights 76

Douglas, Lt. Col. John 154, 158–159
Drake, Sir Francis 9
Drayton, Chief Justice William 25, 31, 68
Duncan, Sir William 50, 55
Dunkirk, Holland 180
Dunmore, John Murray 75–77, 80
Durnford, Elias 41, 44, 135

Earle, John 51, 55
East Florida Claims Office 179
East-Florida Gazette 160, 178
East Florida Rangers 84–86, 90, 97–99, 101–102, 106–111, 114–115, 118, 121, 127, 156, 167
East Florida Society 16
East India Company 73
Echoe, NC 22–23
Eden 4
Edmont, Lord 103
Edwards, Peter 170, 174
Egan, Stephen 103
Egmont, Lady 151
84th Regiment 172
82nd Regiment 141
Elbert, Col. Samuel 101–104, 106–107, 116–117, 151
Elizabeth, Queen 4
Elliot, John 43
Elliot, William 148
Elphinstone, Capt. Keith 152
English Channel 132
Erving, George 180
El Escribano 2
Estaing, Count d' 121
Ethiopians 76
Eutaw Springs, SC 141
Evangeline 164

Fairlamb, Capt. John 58
Farmar, Maj. Robert 35, 39–41
Fatio, Francis Philip 174–175
Feliu, Melchor 17
Fernandina, FL 103, 108
Ferry Settlement 55
Few, Capt. Ignatius 102
55th Foot 180
fire engine 57, 177
First Continental Congress 69, 72, 74, 77, 79, 81, 87, 126
Fish, Furman 181
Fish, Jesse 17–20, 25, 31, 57, 81, 149, 181
Fish, Jesse, Jr. 181

Fish, Phoebe 181
Flanders 143
Florida 5, 7–9, 15–16, 20, 24–26, 43, 74, 91, 109, 118, 163–164, 166–167
Florida Keys 43
Florida militia 83
Florida National Guard 8
Forbes, Dorothy 30
Forbes, John 22
Forbes, the Rev. John 30–31, 59
Forbes, Thomas 138–139
Fort Barrington 67, 106
Fort Bute 37
Fort Charlotte 35, 135–136
Fort Conde 35
Fort Defiance 118
Fort Duquesne 22
Fort George 111, 118, 136–137
Fort Howe 99, 114
Fort Loudoun 28
Fort Matanzas 11, photo 13, 158
Fort McIntosh, FL 99
Fort McIntosh, GA 99–100, 108
Fort Montagu 77
Fort Morris 114–116, 118
Fort Mosa line 19
Fort Mose/Mozo 12–13, 26, 77
Fort Moultrie 90
Fort Natchez 37
Fort Picolata 14, 29, 44, 85, 104, 148
Fort Pupo 44
Fort St. John 75
Fort St. Marks 11, 24, 45–46
Fort Saint Marks (Castle de San Marcos) 80, 126
Fort San Diego 13
Fort San Marcos de Apalache 44
Fort San Miguel 33
Fort Tonyn 104–105, 107
Fothergill, John 47
"Founding Fathers" 80
Fountain of Youth 7
14th Regiment 31, 75, 82
4th Georgia Continentals 114
France/French 3, 7–9, 14–15, 19, 22–23, 27–28, 32–36, 39–41, 43, 67, 70–71, 88, 97–98, 103, 105–107, 113, 121, 125–127, 132–134, 138, 141–142, 144–145, 156, 158, 160–164
Franciscan 9–10, 12, 17, 100
Franco-American defensive alliance 132, 141

Franklin, Benjamin 56, 61, 162–163
Frazer, the Rev. John 30, 52
Frederica, GA 107, 151
French and Indian War 15, 17, 21–22, 28, 34, 39, 70–71
Fuser, Lt. Col. Lewis V. 99–100, 114–115, 121–122

Gadsden, Christopher 126
Gadsden's Wharf 155
Gage, Gen. Thomas 36, 69, 74–76, 78
Galatea 92
Galvez, Bernardo de 134–138, 163
"Garden of Eden" 3, 5, 33, 35, 43, 65, 179
Gaspe 72
Gates, Gen. Horatio 123, 143
Gazette, Annapolis, MD 35
Geneva, Switzerland 33
The Gentleman's Magazine 33
George II, King 66, 73
George III, King 15–16, 20, 23, 34, 144–145, 152
George Street 30
Georgia 1, 4, 8, 11–13, 17, 21, 23, 29, 37, 55, 57–59, 63, 65–66, 74, 78, 82, 84, 86–87, 90–91, 94–95, 99–101, 103–110, 112–114, 116, 118–119, 121, 127, 133, 139–140, 146–147, 149, 151, 153–155, 158–160, 166–167, 169, 171–172, 174
Georgia-Florida border 66–67, 90–91, 97, 106–107, 167, 169, 174, 181
Georgia Gazette 84
Georgia Line 91
Gerard, Conrad Alexandre 132
Germain, Lady Betty 78
Germain, George Sackville 78, 82–83
Germans 61–63, 65, 78–79, 98, 120, 136, 145
Germantown, PA 106, 108
Germany 55, 70, 143
Gettysburg, PA 63
Gibraltar 51, 129, 132–133, 163–164, 177
Gilbert, Ephraim 31, 150
Gilbert, John 31, 150
Girardeau 116
Glasgow, Scotland 55
Glazier, Lt. Col./Maj. Beamsley 112, 115, 122, 127, 157
Gordon, John 17, 19–20, 31, 181
governor's cavalry/banditti 84, 111

Graham, Lt. Gov./Maj. John 51, 54, 108, 154
Grand Banks, Newfoundland 74
Grant, Gov. James 21–29, 30, 31, 34, 45–46, 48–52, 54, 56–57, 59, 68–69, 73, 78, 85, 92, 134, 148, 156, 164, 178, 180
Grant, William 48
Grasse, Francois de 141–142, 144–145
Gray Goose 85
Grayhast, Jonathan 148
Great Abaco Island 168
Great Bridge, VA 75
Great Wagon Road 61, 63, 64, 65, 84, 88, 118, 147
Greece 50–51
Green River 105
"greencoats" 98, 102
Greene, Gen. Nathanael 141, 143
Grenada 15
Grenadier's Royal Infantry 118
Grenville, Prime Minister George 50, 55, 71
Guana River 27, 56
Guana River State Park 27
Guilford Courthouse 141
Gulf Coast 61, 130
Gulf of Mexico 16, 32–33, 137
Gum Swamp, SC 123
Gwinnett, Button 100, 114
Gwynn Island, VA 76

Haddrell's Point 122
Haldimand, Brig. Gen. Frederick 36, 77–78, 80, 82
Halifax, NC 87, 105
Halifax, Nova Scotia, Canada 157, 167
Halifax River 55, 82, 127
Hall, Dr. Lyman 114
Hamilton, Lt. Col. John 105, 118–119
Hancock, John 69
Hanging Rock 143
Hannay 41
Hanover 82
Harbor Island 159
Harries, Capt. James 45
Havana, Cuba 1, 8–11, 15–16, 18–19, 32–33, 35, 41, 43, 45, 129, 133–138, 160, 167, 173–174, 181
Henry, Patrick 73–74, 80
Herrera, Luciano de 18, 31–32, 128, 181
Hesse-Cassel, Germany 79

Hesse-Hanau, Germany 79
Hessians 79, 81, 92, 106, 120, 157, 172
Hester, William 149
Hester's Bluff 149
Hewitt, John 57
Heyward, Thomas, Jr. 126
Hillsborough, Earl of 37
Hillsborough, Lord 150
Hillsborough township 151
Hinchinbrook 92, 107
Historic St. Augustine Preservation Board 2
Holland/Dutch 113, 145, 160–162, 180
Holmes, John 23
Holy See of Rome 23
Honduras 135
Hopkins, Esek 76–77
Hornwork defense line 77
Hortalez & Cie 97
House of Commons 48, 143–144, 152
House of Stuart 23
Houstoun, Gov. William 108–109
Howe, Robert 76, 78
Howe, Gen. Robert 107–109, 116–117
Howe, Gen. Sir William 79, 92, 106
Hudson's Ferry 119
Huger, Col. Isaac 116
Huguenots 62
Hume, Chief Justice James 174–175

Iberville Bayou 129
Illinois 130, 157
Illinois Expedition 40
Indian congress 28–29, 85–86, 131
Indian Ferry 26, 35
Indian Grey Eyes Road 26
Indian presents 45–46, 86, 112, 131, 158
Indian River 55
indigo plants 53, 55–56, 88, 103, 125, 128, 147
Innes, Col. Alexander 105, 118
Ireland 23, 59, 74, 89, 129, 142
Irish fleet 89–90
Iroquois Indians 62, 158
Isle of Orleans 15
Isle of Skye, Scotland 151
Italy 50

Jacksonville, FL 58
Jamaica 10, 124, 132, 135–137, 164, 167, 169, 171–172, 176, 178
James Island 120

Jamestown, VA 8
Jasper, Sgt. William 90
Jay, John 133, 162–163
Jefferson, Thomas 73
Jekyll Island, GA 110
Jenkins, Robert 12
Jenkins Creek 26
Jesuit missionaries 8–9, 29
Jesup, GA 99
Jews 62, 65, 156, 171
John Cruden & Co. 174
Johns Island, SC 120
Johnson, William 126
Johnston, Captain 115
Johnston, Mrs. Elizabeth Lichtenstein 160
Johnstone, Capt. George 34, 39–41, 164
Jollie, Martin 103
Jones, John Paul 77
Jones, Noble Wimberly 126

Keeper of Indian Presents 45, 86, 112
Keowee, SC 105
King's Highway/Road 24, 50, 57, 59, 60, 65, 67, 99, 104, 109, 113, 147, 154
Kingston, Jamaica 172
Kinloch, Francis 25
Kirkland, Moses 113
Knox, William 103, 164

Lafayette, Marquis de 97–98, 126, 141, 143
Lake George 151
Lake Pontchartrain 16, 35, 37
Lancaster, PA 63
Lane, Major 118
Las Casas, Bartolomé de 29
Laudonniere, Rene de 7
Laurens, Henry 22, 46, 142, 145, 162
Laurens, John 94, 145
Leaver, Robert 170
Lee, Gen. Charles 90–91, 123
Leslie, Maj. Gen. Alexander 122, 152, 154–155, 157
Leslie, John 174
Leutze, Emanuel 2
Levett, Francis 169, 174
Lewis, the Rev. John 126
Lexington, MA 75, 78, 87
Liberty Boys/Sons of Liberty 72, 83–85, 87, 94

Index 199

"liberty pole" 72, 87
Library of Congress 20
lighthouse 77
Lincoln, Maj. Gen. Benjamin 117, 119–122, 124
"Little Carpenter" 28
Little Florence Cove 46
Little St. Marks River 44
Lively 92
London 4, 16, 33, 36, 41, 48, 55, 59, 69, 78, 89, 94, 131–132, 144–145, 149–150, 177–178, 180
London Gazette 34, 143
Long Island, NY 91, 110
Long Warrior 86, 112
Longfellow 164
Lords of Trade and Plantations 30, 34
Louis XVI, King 132
Louisiana 16, 32, 137
Lower Creek Indians 44
loyalty oath 94
Luna y Arellano, Tristan de, Don 32
Lupton 128

Mackenzie, Mr. 111
Madeira 23, 110
Madrid, Spain 162–163
Mahchac 129, 133–134
Maitland, Lt. Col. John 120–121
Manifest Destiny 133
Mariana, Queen 11
Marion, Francis "Swamp Fox" 22, 143, 146
Martin, Gov. Josiah 89
Martinique 15, 33, 134
Maryland 63, 123, 136, 141, 170–171
Masks Ferry 123
Masons 31, 49, 149
Massachusetts 74, 101, 171
Matanzas Bay 19, 25, 173
Matanzas Inlet 10–11, 13–14, 77, 83, 127
Matanzas River 24, 57, 68, 154
McArthur, Lt. Col. Archibald 157–158, 160, 164, 166–167, 170
McCrady, Edward 126
McDonald, John 149–150
McDonald, R. 26
McGirth, Lt. Col. Daniel 85, 99, 114, 167, 169, 174
McGirth, Capt. James 85
McIntosh, Alexander 40
McIntosh, Capt. John 91

McIntosh, Gen. Lachlan 99
McLatchie, Charles 44
Medway River 114
Menéndez de Avilés, Capt. Don Pedro 7–9, 14, 67, 157
Menéndez Marquez, Pedro 9
mercenaries 78–79, 81
Mercury 145
Mexico 3, 10–11, 16
Middleton, Arthur 126
Middleton, Thomas 22
Midway, GA 114–115, 118
Mills, Colonel 105
Milton, Lt. John 100
Mingo Indians 158
Minorca 50, 133, 144, 163, 177
Minorcan Cultural Society 54
Minorcans 32, 51–54, 112, 171, 177
Minutemen 75
Mission of Nombre de Dios 9, 184
Mission San Luis 9
missions 28, 30
Mississippi 16, 32, 131, 171
Mississippi River 15, 32, 35–36, 39, 42, 67, 70, 130, 133–134, 137
Missouri 158
Mobile, AL 30, 35–37, 39–40, 43, 45, 129–133, 135–136, 138, 164
Mobile Bay 35, 135
Moderators 88
Mohawk Indians 158
Moncrief, James 26, 57, 80, 82, 155, 180
Montgomery, Gen. Richard 75
Montreal, Canada 22, 75
Moore, Dorothy 127
Moore, James 12
Moore, Roger 167
Moravian 63
Morgan, Gen. Daniel 140
Morris, Robert 161
Morro Castle 33, 174
Mosquito Inlet 14, 32, 50, 58, 127–128, 154
Mosquito River 24, 55
Moultrie, Alexander 126, 165
Moultrie, James 23
Moultrie, John 22–24, 30–31, 50, 54, 57–59, 61, 67–69, 83, 89, 139, 164–165, 179
Moultrie, Dr. John 24
Moultrie, Thomas 165

Moultrie, Capt./Col./Gen. William 22, 24, 89–91, 119, 165
Mount Oswald Settlement 55
Mount Pleasant 148
Mount Royal 148
Mount Vernon, VA 76
Mousa Creek 181
Mowat, Charles L. 2
Mowat, John 126
Mowbray, John 170
Mulcaster, Lt. Frederick 31, 58, 68
Musgrove Mills 143
Musgrove Swamp 117

Narragansett Bay, RI 72
Narvaez, Panfilo de 32
Nassau 77, 159, 168, 170, 174
Nassau River 28, 31, 56, 58, 101–102, 108, 150
Natchez, MS 16, 42, 129–131, 133, 135, 171
Nativity of Our Lady 8
Navigation Acts 71
Negro bill 139
Negro disaster 120–121
Negro "drivers" 53
Negro slaves 5, 8–9, 12, 18, 24, 26–27, 31, 51, 53–58, 62, 76, 83, 88, 91, 94, 98, 104, 111, 115, 120, 122, 125, 127–128, 138–140, 148–150, 152–156, 159, 165–166, 168–170, 172, 174, 176, 179
Nelson's Ferry 141
Netherlands 133
New Bermuda 31, 150
New England 4, 61, 129–130
New Hampshire 101
New Jersey 92, 115, 118
New Madrid 137
New Orleans, LA 35–37, 39, 70, 124, 129–131, 133–134
New Providence Island, Bahamas 77, 159, 167–168, 170
New Smyrna, FL 26, 30, 32, 50–52, 54–55, 57–58, 77, 83, 112, 127–128, 133, 154, 171, 174, 180–181
New World 3–4, 15–16, 43, 50, 52, 57, 163
New York, NY 61, 72–73, 78, 81, 91, 94, 105, 107, 110, 117, 122, 132, 134, 136–137, 141–142, 144–145, 152, 154, 157–158, 168–171, 177
Newfoundland 15, 145

Newport, RI 141
Nicaragua 105, 107, 110, 117, 122, 135
Nicholas, Capt. Samuel 77
Nile River 50
Ninety Six, SC 105, 118
9th Regiment 19, 45
Nombre de Dios, Mission of 9, 184
Norfolk, VA 76
North, Prime Minister Lord 144, 164
North America 7, 32, 50, 70–71, 124
North Carolina 74, 89, 91, 101, 104–105, 107, 114, 121, 123, 141, 151, 158, 174
North Carolina Highlanders 155, 168
North Edisto Inlet 122
North Hillsborough River 58
North River 27, 82
Nova Scotia 78, 166, 168

Ogeechee Swamp 91, 115
Ogilvie, Maj. Francis 19
Oglethorpe, Gen. James E. 13–14, 66, 86
Ohio River 42, 70, 157–158
Ohio River Valley 130, 157
Oliver, Lt. Gov. Thomas 93
104th Foot (Douglas) 68
oranges 125, 181
Orde, Gov. J. 172
Oswald, Richard 55–56, 162
Oswald's plantation 26
Otis, James 73
Otter 128

Pablo River 56
Paine, Thomas 79, 91
Palatka, FL 148
Palmetto State 88
pamphleteers 4, 144, 147
Panhandle 16
Panton, Leslie and Company 45, 59, 137–139, 176
Panton, William 59, 137–138
Parilla, Don Diego Ortiz 33
Paris, France 56
Parker, Commodore Sir Peter 89–90, 116, 137
Payne's Corner 31, 139
Peace and Plenty 179
peace negotiations 145
Peace Treaty, 1783, England-America 162–163
Peace Treaty, 1783, England–Spain 163, 166

Pee Dee River 123
Penman, James 148, 180
Pennsylvania 22, 61, 63, 75, 84, 92, 136, 141
Penobscot, ME 78
Pensacola Congress 131
Pensacola, FL 16, 30, 32–33, 35–37, 40–43, 45, 80, 124, 129–133, 135–138
Perceval, John 151
Perseus 92
Peru 3
Petersburg 143
Philadelphia, PA 28, 46, 52, 61–63, 69, 72–74, 79, 87, 91–92, 94, 106, 113, 116, 122, 124, 142, 145, 171–172
Philip II, King 7–8
Philippines 7, 32
Phillips, Gen. William 124
Pickens, Col. Andrew 118, 143
Picolata 59, 77
Piedmont 62–63
Pinckney, Charles Cotesworth 108
Plan of Regulation 88
plantation system 56
Plymouth, England 4
Pollock, Oliver 130–132, 134
Ponce de León, Juan 7, 100
Ponce de Leon Inlet 51
Pontiac's War 78
Port Mahon 144
Port Royal Island 119–120, 137
Portsmouth, England 178
Post Office, His Majesty's 69
Potomac River 76
POW *see* prisoners of war
Powell, Lt. Gov. James Edward 177
prefabricated structures 80–81, 150, 167, 176–177
Prevost, Lt. Col. Augustine 33, 97–99, 104–105, 108, 110–113, 115–122
Prevost, James Marcus 97–98, 102, 104–105, 108–110, 113–115, 119–120, 132
Princeton, NJ 92, 97
prisoners 10, 113, 122
prisoners of war 79
prisons 80, 107
Privy Council 30
Proclamation Line 37, 38, 44, 71
Proclamation of 1763 37, 39, 131
Protestants 7, 41, 148
Puente, Josef 128
Puente, Juan Eligio de la 17–18, 31–32

Pumpkin King 86, 112
Purysburg, SC 117

Quakers 46, 61–62
quarries 12, 24, 184
Quartering Act 71
Quebec Act 75
Quebec, Canada 15, 33, 75
Queen Anne's War 132

Rall, Gen. Johann G. 92
Ramsay, David 126
Ramsey grant 55
Rattletrap 131
Rawdon, Lord 143
Rebecca 102, 107
Red Cliffs 37
refugees 1, 84, 104–105, 159–160, 166–167, 169, 171–172, 180
Regimental Lodge of the Fourteenth Regiment 31
Regulators 88, 105
Restraining Act 74
Revere, Paul 73, 75
revolutionary petition 85
Rhode Island 74, 77, 101
Ribault, Adml. Jean 14, 103
Riedesel, Baron 124
Robertson, James 119
Rochambeau, Comte de 141
Rochon and Company 35
Rockingham, Marquis of 152
Rodney, Adml. George B. 145
Rolfe's sawmill 101–102
Rolle, Denys 147–149, 178–179
Rollestown 148–149
Roman Catholics 7, 10, 12, 16–17, 20, 32–33, 52, 54, 62, 75, 174–175, 177
Rosario defense line 77
Rose, Dr. Hugh 149
Rose Island 37
Royal African Company 5
Royal Americans 33, 98
Royal Artillery 82, 169
Royal Bahama Gazette 178
Royal Council 57
Royal Foresters 159
Royal Government of Georgia 119
Royal Military Academy 26
Royal Navy 77, 82, 90, 92
Royal North Carolina Regiment 105, 118, 143, 155

Rozetta Plantation 24
Rutledge, Edward 126
Rutledge, Hugh 126
Rutledge, Gov. John 120

St. Clair, Gen. Arthur 141
St. Francis Barracks 25, 80–81
St. John 90, 92
St. Johns Bluff 7, 14, 102, 127, 139, 149–150, 154, 173, 176
St. Johns River 7, 13–14, 26, 28–29, 44–47, 56, 58–59, 77, 83, 85, 90, 98–99, 102, 104–105, 111, 115, 148–151, 153–154, 159, 166–167, 174, 176, 181
St. Kitts 144
St. Lawrence 85–86
St. Lawrence River 15, 32
St. Louis/Cahokia 137
St. Lucia 134, 155
St. Marks/St. Marks River 44–45, 148, 174, 176
St. Marys, GA 26, 151
St. Marys River 28, 31, 37, 56, 58, 67, 82, 90–91, 99–103, 105, 108, 110, 115, 150–151, 167, 170–171, 173–174, 176–177
St. Peter's Church 30
St. Simon's Island, GA 13, 44, 151
Saints Passage, West Indies 145
Salem 73
Salisbury, NC 63, 105
Saluda River 85, 104
San Mateo, Cumberland Island, GA 8
San Sebastian Creek 26
San Sebastian River 19, 26
Sanchez, Francis Xavier 18
Sanchez, Pontio 111
Sandwich 125
Sandy Hook, PA 116
Santa Elena 8–9, 11
Santee River 22, 141, 143
Sapello River 114
Satilla River 99, 108
Sauchope, Fifeshire, Scotland 26
Savannah, GA 1, 16, 25, 31, 58–59, 63, 65–67, 69, 84, 86–87, 91, 101, 103, 105, 110, 113–114, 116, 118, 121–122, 138, 141, 145, 152–153, 155, 157–159, 172
Savannah River 63, 117–119
Savannah/Yamacraw Bluff, GA 66
Sawpit Bluff 101
Schoepf, Johann David 170

Scophol, Col. 105
Scopholites 105
Scotland/Scot 21, 26, 28, 31, 33–34, 48, 50–52, 55, 57, 59, 62–63, 65, 127, 151–152, 180
Screven, Gen. James 108, 114
sea cow 43–44
Searle, Capt. Robert (alias John Davis) 10
Second Continental Congress 79, 81, 91, 94, 97, 106, 130, 132, 145, 160
Second Spanish Period 181
Seminole Indians 44, 47, 85–86, 113, 127, 138, 151, 158, 181
Seneca Indians 158
Senegal 53
Serle, Ambrose 79
Seven Years' War 15, 41, 76
71st Regiment 117, 157, 172
77th (Montgomery) Highlanders 21–22
Sewall, Jonathan 168
Shawnee Indians 158
Sheffield, Lord 144
Shelburne, Lord William P.F. 39, 41, 163–164
Shenandoah Valley 63
shirt-men 75
Siebert, Wilbur Henry 2
Sierra Leone 53
Simsbury, CT 107
16th Foot 136
16th Regiment 82
6th (Inniskilling) Dragoons 68
60th Regiment (Royal American) 33, 98, 111, 114, 121–122, 127, 135–136, 157
64th Regiment 172
63rd Regiment 172
Skinner, Alexander 25, 27, 45, 86, 112
Slater, William 167
Smith, Capt. J.C. 116
Smith, Josiah 126
Smyrna, Greece 50
Society for the Propagation of the Gospel 30
Solona, Manuel 18
Sons of Liberty/Liberty Boys 72, 83–85, 87, 94
Soto, Hernando de 32, 67
South America 7, 32
South Carolina 1, 12, 17, 21–23, 28–29, 57, 59, 65, 74, 83–90, 94, 101, 104–106, 109, 112–113, 119–122,

124–126, 133, 146–147, 149–150, 153, 157–159, 166, 169, 172, 174
South Carolina Continentals 109, 116
South Carolina Gazette and Country Journal 76
South Carolina Medical Society 180
South Carolina Royalist 104, 108, 114, 142, 155, 168
Southern Indians 8–12, 15, 19, 25–26, 28–29, 33, 37, 39, 41, 43–45, 47, 52, 58, 62, 71, 82, 84–85, 88, 90, 100, 102, 105–106, 112, 114, 125, 131, 134, 138, 155, 157–158, 166–167, 171, 176
Spalding, James 44, 148, 151
Spalding and Company 151
Spalding and Kensall 151
Spanish Armada 4, 10
Spanish Highway 44
Spanish Hospital 57
Spitfire 114
Springer, Benjamin 150
Springfield, NJ 79
Stamp Act 71–72, 83, 87
Staten Island, NY 90, 129
Stevens, Gen. Edward 123
Stevenstone, Devon, England 147
Stewart, Lt. Col. Alexander 141, 169
Stirling Castle 180
Stokes, Chief Justice Anthony 153
Stono Ferry, SC 120
Strachey, Henry 162
Stuart, John 28–29, 40, 45, 112, 131
Sugar Revenue Act 71
Sullivan, Gen. John 91
Sullivan's Island, SC 89–90
Sumter, Thomas "The Carolina Gamecock" 143, 146
Sunbury, GA 31, 91, 101–103, 110, 113–118
Surrency, GA 65
Swamp Settlement 55
Swiss 78, 148

Talahasochte 44–45
Tallack, George 149–150
Tallahassee/Apalache, FL 9
Tanchipaho 37
Tarleton, Col./Gen. Banastre 125, 140
Tattnall, Col. Josiah 159
Taylor, Captain 99
Tea Act 73
Te Deum laudamus 8
Tennessee River 23, 42

Test Laws of Confiscation 170
37th Regiment 169–170
Thomas, Col. 105
Thomas Swamp 102
Thompson, Lt. Col. William 116
Thunderer 114
Tidewater 62
Timothy, Peter 126
Timouka Plantation 26, 55
Timucua Indians 9
"Tobacco Road" 63
Tombigbee River 42
Tomoka River 24, 55, 57, 82
Tonyn, Charles William 68
Tonyn, Jane Lydia 68, 180
Tonyn, Gov. Patrick 30, 54, 68–70, 73–74, 77–78, 82–87, 90, 92, 95, 97–101, 103–107, 109–112, 122, 125–128, 131, 133, 137–140, 143, 147, 149, 151–152, 155–159, 164, 166–167, 169, 173–180
Tory 70, 72, 74, 76, 91, 93, 105, 118, 124, 147
Tower of London 142, 145, 162
Townshend, Charles 72–73
Traders Hill 151
trading posts 28
Travels in Georgia and Florida, 1773-1774 47
Treaty of Augusta 88
Treaty of 1763, Treaty of Paris 1, 4, 15–16, 32, 55, 67, 70
Trenton, NJ 79, 92
Trout Creek 46, 90, 102, 109
Tuckaseegee Valley 23
Turnbull, Andrew Dr. 25–26, 32, 50–52, 54–55, 57, 61, 68, 112, 171, 180
Tuscarora Indians 158
Two Sisters 177
Tybee Island, GA 116, 153

Union Jack 61
"United Loyalist" 174
United States of America 106, 144, 153, 162, 169, 181
Utopia 4

Valley Forge, PA 92, 106
Veracruz, Mexico 33, 42, 135
Vernon, Adml. Edward 13
Vespucci, Amerigo 3
Vicksburg/Walnut Hills, MS 130

"Victory or death" 92
Virginia 22, 56, 63, 75–76, 80, 91, 101, 123, 141, 158, 171

Wace, Master 182
Wachovia/Charlotte, NC 63
Wakulla River 44
Waldeck, Germany 79, 136
Waldseemüeller, Martin 3
Waldseemüeller Gores 3
Walnut Hills/Vicksburg, MS 130
Walton, Col. George 116–117
War of Jenkins's Ear 12, 14, 66
Ward, Lieutenant 103
Warrior's Path 62
Washington, George 22, 75–77, 91–92, 94, 97, 101, 106–108, 123, 130, 133, 141–142
"Washington Crossing the Delaware," by Emanuel Leutze 2
watchtower/lookout tower/tower 10, 12, 14, 25, 77, 127
Watson, William 51, 128
Waycross, GA 99
Weeks, Joshua 178
Wells, John 178
Wells, Dr. William Charles 160
West Florida 1, 15–16, 21, 30, 32–36, 67, 74, 86, 95, 98, 124, 128–131, 133–137, 148, 164
West Indies 15, 35, 66, 71, 74, 77, 94, 121–122, 129, 132–134, 139, 141, 145, 155, 164–166, 169, 180
Westminster 143
Whig 70
White, Col. John 114
White, Stephen 149–150

White House 143
White Plains, NY 91
White Springs, FL 65
Whitehall 78
Williamsburg, VA 61, 75
Williamson, Gen. Andrew 109, 119
Williamson, Thomas 149, 176
Willing, Capt. Thomas 130–131, 134
Wilmington, NC 141
Wilson, Lt. John 168
Winchester, VA 63
Windward Islands 170
Winn, Capt. Richard 99
Winniett, John 154, 159
Wiregrass Trail, GA 65
Wolfe, Gen. James 33
Woodcutters' Creek 24
Woodford, Colonel 75
Woodpecker Trail 65
Wright, Charles 58
Wright, Gov. Sir James 58, 69, 74, 87, 116, 119
Wright, Jermyn 58, 91

Yallowly, Joshua 58
Yamacraw Bluff/Savannah, GA 66
Yamasee Indians 33
"Yankee Doodle" 126
Yeats, David 176
York, Duke of 36, 180
York, PA 106
Yorktown 141–143, 145, 157
Young, Col. William 169, 174

Zespedes, Vizente Manuel de 173–175, 177, 181

www.ingramcontent.com/pod-product-compliance
Ingram Content Group UK Ltd.
Pitfield, Milton Keynes, MK11 3LW, UK
UKHW042006140426
5217IPUK00015B/1007